MICROSOFT® OFFICE POWERPOINT® 2010

QuickSteps

About the Author

Carole Boggs Matthews has been connected to computers for over 35 years. During that time, she has been a programmer; systems analyst; technical consultant; and founder, co-owner, and vice-president of a software company. She has been on all sides of computer software products, from designer and builder to an accomplished user of software in her business. She has authored or co-authored more than 50 books, including *Microsoft Office PowerPoint 2007 QuickSteps, Photoshop CS4 QuickSteps, Microsoft Office 2010 QuickSteps,* and *QuickSteps to Winning Business Presentations.*

Carole lives on an island with her husband, Marty, and very old cat, Tortoise. They have a son, Michael.

MICROSOFT® OFFICE POWERPOINT® 2010

QuickSteps

CAROLE MATTHEWS

New York Chicago San Francisco
Lisbon London Madrid Mexico City
Milan New Delhi San Juan
Seoul Singapore Sydney Toronto

The McGraw·Hill Companies

Library of Congress Cataloging-in-Publication Data

Matthews, Carole Boggs.
  Microsoft® Office PowerPoint® 2010 quicksteps / Carole Matthews.
     p. cm.
  ISBN 978-0-07-163491-5 (alk. paper)
   1. Presentation graphics software. 2. Microsoft PowerPoint
(Computer file) I. Title.
  T385.M377343 2010
  005.5'8—dc22
                                                    2010010432

1234567890   WDQ WDQ   109876543210

ISBN   978-0-07-163491-5
MHID   0-07-163491-6

SPONSORING EDITOR / Roger Stewart

EDITORIAL SUPERVISOR / Jody McKenzie

PROJECT MANAGER / Madhu Bhardwaj, Glyph International

ACQUISITIONS COORDINATOR / Joya Anthony

TECHNICAL EDITOR / John Cronan

COPY EDITOR / Lisa McCoy

PROOFREADER / Paul Tyler

INDEXER / Valerie Haynes Perry

PRODUCTION SUPERVISOR / George Anderson

COMPOSITION / Glyph International

ILLUSTRATION / Glyph International

ART DIRECTOR, COVER / Jeff Weeks

COVER DESIGNER / Pattie Lee

SERIES CREATORS / Marty and Carole Matthews

SERIES DESIGN / Bailey Cunningham

To Marty, with love and admiration for my remarkable partner

Contents at a Glance

Contents

3   Chapter 3   **Working with Slides** 41

4   Chapter 4   **Working with Notes, Masters, and Slide Text** 61

5

6

7

Chapter 8 Using Special Effects and Drawing Shapes ... 143

Chapter 9 Working with Multimedia and the Internet ... 169

10

Acknowledgments

Many thanks to my technical editor extraordinaire, John Cronan, for keeping text accurate and providing reliable and astute observations in his pursuit of the truth!

Also thanks to my copy editor, Lisa McCoy, who did wonderful things to my writing, making it more readable and easier to understand. And to Paul Tyler, whose proofing ensured all text was as it should be.

Thanks also to Valerie Perry, who excellently indexed this book to make it more accessible.

Thanks also to the McGraw-Hill team, to Jody McKenzie, project editor; to Madhu Bhardwaj, project manager; and many others unknown to me who helped to produce this book. And a special thanks to Roger Stewart, sponsoring editor, who continues to have faith in our writing.

Thanks to all of you!

Introduction

QuickSteps books are recipe books for computer users. They answer the question "how do I…" by providing quick sets of steps to accomplish the most common tasks with a particular program. The sets of steps are the central focus of the book. QuickSteps sidebars show you how to quickly do many small functions or tasks that support the primary functions. Notes, Tips, and Cautions augment the steps, yet they are presented in such a manner as to not interrupt the flow of the steps. The brief introductions are minimal rather than narrative, and numerous illustrations and figures, many with callouts, support the steps.

QuickSteps books are organized by function and the tasks needed to perform that function. Each function is a chapter. Each task, or "How To," contains the steps needed for its accomplishment along with the relevant Notes, Tips, Cautions, and screenshots. Tasks will be easy to find through:

- The table of contents, which lists the functional areas (chapters) and tasks in the order they are presented

- A How To list of tasks on the opening page of each chapter

- The index with its alphabetical list of terms used in describing the functions and tasks

- Color-coded tabs for each chapter or functional area with an index to the tabs just before the table of contents

Conventions Used in this Book

Microsoft Office PowerPoint 2010 QuickSteps uses several conventions designed to make the book easier for you to follow. Among these are:

- A 🌀 or 🖊 in the table of contents or the How To list in each chapter references a QuickSteps or QuickFacts sidebar, respectively, that you'll find in a chapter.

- **Bold type** is used for words on the screen that you are to do something with, such as click **Save As, Open**, or **File**.

- *Italic type* is used for a word or phrase that is being defined or otherwise deserves special emphasis.

- Underlined type is used for text that you are to type from the keyboard.

- SMALL CAPITAL LETTERS are used for keys on the keyboard, such as **ENTER** and **SHIFT**.

- When you are expected to enter a command from the keyboard, you are told to press the key(s). If you are to enter text or numbers, you are told to type them.

- When you are to click the mouse to initiate an action or command, you will be told to "click" the appropriate command, tab, or menu item, such as **Click the File tab**, or **Click Save**.

- When you are to open a contextual menu or submenu, you will be told to "right-click" the object, such as right click the selected word.

2
3
4
5
6
7
8
9
10

Chapter 1
Stepping into PowerPoint

PowerPoint 2010 is Microsoft Office's slide show offering. While maintaining the core features and functionality of PowerPoint from years past, this version adds many features to support anyone, from the casual user who wants to set up a simple slide show to the high-end user who wants to create a sophisticated Web-oriented presentation. This version of PowerPoint continues the evolution of the *ribbon* and other user interface items (those collections of screen elements that allow you to use and navigate the program), and improves on many functional features, such as the new *File view*, which provides a single location for essential information about your document.

Chapter 1 explains how to open and close PowerPoint, interpret the ribbon and new user interface, and configure

QUICKSTEPS

STARTING POWERPOINT

In addition to using the Start menu to start PowerPoint, you can use the keyboard and shortcuts on your desktop and taskbar or Start menu.

START POWERPOINT FROM THE KEYBOARD

1. Press the Windows flag key on your keyboard to open the Start menu, or press **CTRL+ESC**.

2. Press **ENTER** to select **All Programs**, and then scroll until you find Microsoft Office. Press **ENTER** and select **Microsoft PowerPoint 2010**; press **ENTER** to start it.

CREATE A SHORTCUT ON THE DESKTOP

Another way to start PowerPoint is from a shortcut icon you place on your desktop.

1. Click **Start**, click **All Programs**, and click **Microsoft Office**.

2. Right-click **Microsoft PowerPoint 2010**, click **Send To**, and click **Desktop (Create Shortcut)**.

START POWERPOINT FROM THE SHORTCUT

Double-click the shortcut icon on your desktop.

PIN POWERPOINT TO THE START MENU OR TASKBAR

Pin PowerPoint to the Start menu or the taskbar in this way:

1. Click **Start**, click **All Programs**, and click **Microsoft Office.**

2. Right-click **Microsoft PowerPoint 2010**, and click **Pin To Start Menu** or **Pin To Taskbar**.

them according to your personal needs. You will learn how to get help from Microsoft's Office online Help, and learn how to manage and customize your task panes and the ribbon.

Start and Exit PowerPoint

Assuming that you already know how to turn on the computer and load Windows, and that PowerPoint has been installed on your computer, you may start it as you would any other program. The quickest way may be to simply double-click the PowerPoint icon on your desktop (see the "Starting PowerPoint" QuickSteps). However, the most common way is to use the Start menu.

Use the Start Menu

To load PowerPoint using the Start menu on the Windows taskbar:

1. Start your computer and log on to Windows, if necessary.

2. Click **Start**. The Start menu opens.

3. Click **All Programs**, click **Microsoft Office**, and click **Microsoft PowerPoint 2010**. The PowerPoint window will open, as shown in Figure 1-1.

Exit PowerPoint

- To exit PowerPoint, click **File** in the upper-left corner of the PowerPoint window, and click **Exit**.

    –Or–

- Click **Close** in the upper-right corner of the PowerPoint window.

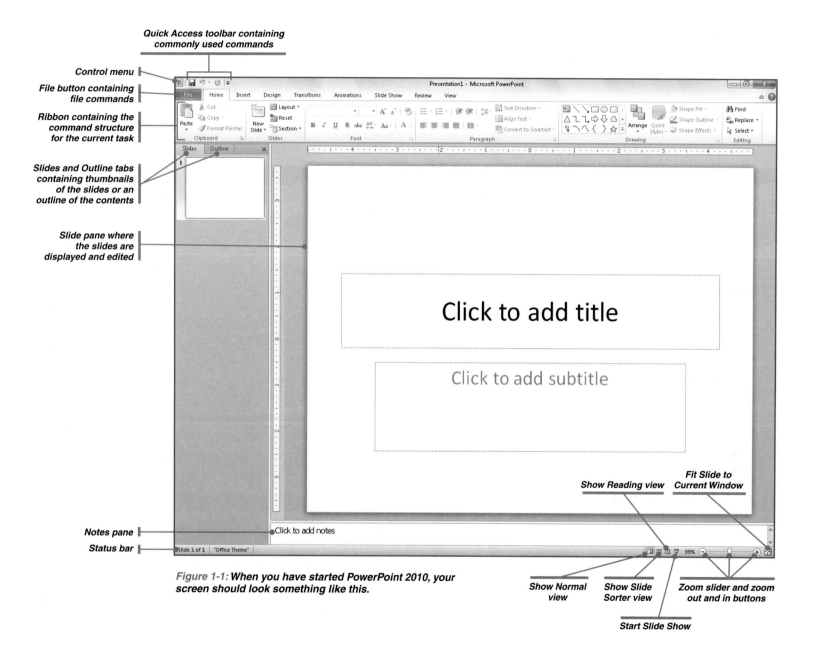

Quick Access toolbar containing commonly used commands

Control menu

File button containing file commands

Ribbon containing the command structure for the current task

Slides and Outline tabs containing thumbnails of the slides or an outline of the contents

Slide pane where the slides are displayed and edited

Fit Slide to Current Window

Show Reading view

Notes pane

Status bar

Figure 1-1: *When you have started PowerPoint 2010, your screen should look something like this.*

Show Normal view

Show Slide Sorter view

Zoom slider and zoom out and in buttons

Start Slide Show

Explore the PowerPoint Window

The PowerPoint window offers many features to aid you in creating and editing presentations.

Get an Overview of the PowerPoint Window

Here are the main components of the window, as shown in Figure 1-1:

- The *Slide pane* is the container for PowerPoint slides. It is where you create a layout and design; type headings and text; and insert graphs, diagrams, and other design or informational elements to make your presentation look exactly how you want it.

- The *File* button is in the upper-left area, and contains the file commands and PowerPoint options for manipulating the presentation document. It provides access to the File view, described in "Find the File View."

- The *Quick Access toolbar*, to the right of the Control menu button, is where the most commonly used commands are displayed. By default, these are Save, Undo, and Repeat, but you can customize this toolbar by right-clicking it to add or remove commands.

- The *ribbon*, located beneath the Quick Access toolbar, contains the commands and tools for working with the presentation (see "Become Familiar with the Ribbon"). The rest of this book explores and explains how to use the ribbon commands.

- The *Slides* and *Outline tabs* pane, to the left of the Slide pane, contains either thumbnails of the slides or the text of the presentation shown in outline format, respectively. You click either **Slides** or **Outline** to select the view you want (the Slides tab is shown in Figure 1-1).

- The *Notes pane*, located beneath the Slide pane, is where you can type notes that will be invisible to the viewer but are available to the presenter.

- The *Status bar*, located at the bottom of the window, contains the status of the active slide, as well as some additional tools.

- The *View toolbar*, located on the right of the status bar, contains commands to vary the view from Normal view (seen in Figure 1-1) to Slide Sorter view to Slide Show view to Reading view. See "Show Views" later in this chapter to see the other views.

- The *Zoom slider* allows you to zoom in and out using a slider or using the plus and minus (+ and –) buttons on either side of the slider.

- The *Fit Slide To Current Window* button resizes the PowerPoint panes to fit the size of the PowerPoint window.

QUICK**FACTS**

LEARNING ABOUT VERSIONS OF OFFICE 2010 *(Continued)*

- **Office Professional 2010** is available to be installed from a DVD or via Click-To-Run over the Internet, contains all the features of Office Home & Business, and adds Microsoft Access and Microsoft Publisher.

There are also two enterprise editions available only through a volume license. Office Standard adds Publisher to Office Home & Business, and Office Professional Plus adds SharePoint Workspace and InfoPath to Office Professional.

This book, which covers the full version of PowerPoint 2010, applies to all of the editions with a full version of PowerPoint and, to a limited extent, those features that are included in Office Starter and Office Web Apps.

Become Familiar with the Ribbon

So where are the familiar menus from previous versions of PowerPoint? The original menu structure used in earlier Office products (File, Edit, Format, Window, Help, and other menus) was designed to accommodate fewer tasks and features. That menu structure has simply outgrown its usefulness. Microsoft's solution to the increased number of feature enhancements is the *ribbon*, the container at the top of Office program windows that holds the tools and features you are most likely to use (see Figure 1-2). The ribbon collects tools for a given function into *groups*—for instance, the Font group provides the tools to work with text. Groups are then organized into *tabs* for working on likely tasks. For example, the Insert tab contains groups for adding components, such as tables, links, and charts, to your slide (or spreadsheet or document). Each Office program has a default set of tabs with additional *contextual* tabs that appear as the context of your work changes. For instance, when you select a placeholder (or objects within it—such as text or a graphic), a Format tab containing shapes and drawing tools that you can use with the particular object appears beneath the defining tools tab (such as the Drawing Tools tab); when the object is unselected, the Format tab disappears. The ribbon contains

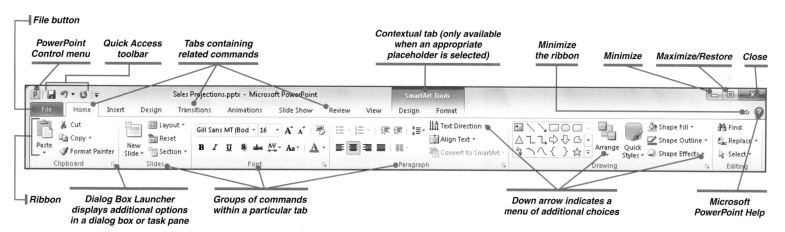

Figure 1-2: The File button, the Quick Access toolbar, and the ribbon containing groups of commands and tools are the means to create and modify a presentation. Your ribbon will look different if your window is minimized.

To see the shortcut keyboard commands for accessing the ribbon, press either **ALT** or **F10** to toggle the commands on or off. Small squares showing letters and numbers will appear. When you press **ALT** (or **F10**) and press the appropriate letter or number key, you will be executing the command. Once you begin a letter/number command using this mode, subsequent screens for that command or tool will continue to display the letter/number commands.

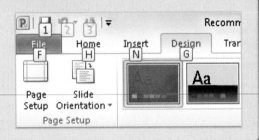

labeled buttons you can click to use a given command or tool. Depending on the tool, you are then presented with additional options in the form of a list of commands, a dialog box or task pane, or galleries of choices that reflect what you'll see in your work. Groups that contain several more tools than can be displayed in the ribbon include a *Dialog Box Launcher* icon, usually named "More," that takes you directly to these other choices. The ribbon also takes advantage of Office features, including a live preview of many potential changes (for example, you can select text and see it change color as you point to various colors in the Font Color gallery). See the accompanying sections and figures for more information on the ribbon and other elements of the PowerPoint window.

Use Tabs and Menus

As seen in Figure 1-2, tabs, displayed on the top of the ribbon or in a dialog box, contain related commands for a function, such as Insert or Design. Menus, displayed when you click a down arrow on a button, a dialog box, or a toolbar, contain commands related to a particular command or effect, such as Text Direction or Shape Effects.

Find the File View

Co-located with the ribbon are the File button and the Quick Access toolbar. The File button provides access to the File view (also known as the Backstage view), which lets you work *with* your document (such as saving it), as opposed to the ribbon, which centers on working *in* your document (such as editing and formatting). Figure 1-3 shows the File view. It offers these options:

- Use **Save**, **Save As**, **Open**, and **Close** to perform standard document functions.
- **Info** displays document properties of the presentation on the right pane, and in the center allows you to perform certain document functions: mark the final version; protect the presentation with encryption and passwords, add a digital signature; check for hidden metadata or non accessible components; check for compatibility issues before distribution; and manage multiple versions of a presentation.

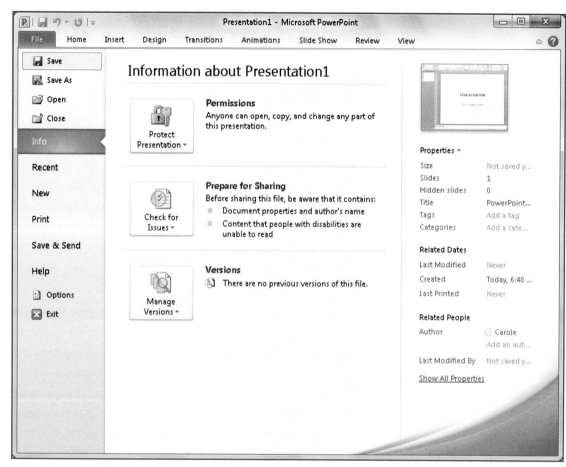

Figure 1-3: *The File view is where you handle the file-related functions of PowerPoint, such as opening, saving, printing, and closing your files.*

- **Recent** allows you to quickly retrieve recently used presentations.

- **New** displays options for creating new presentations.

- **Print** displays the view for printing all or part of a presentation, with options for sending or working with the files.

- **Save & Send** allows you to collaborate on the creation or editing of a presentation. You can save to SharePoint, publish your slides, or package them on a CD here.

- **Help** displays support and tools for working with Office; It displays a view of licensing information, Microsoft contact data, how to get updates, and other product-related information. It identifies the current version of Microsoft now installed.
- **Options** is where you set options for the application as a whole.
- **Exit** closes PowerPoint.

Click **File** again to exit the view, or click any other tab. The File commands are described in more detail in other parts of the book.

Open a Presentation

The initial PowerPoint window, shown in Figure 1-1, gives you a blank slide with the Home tab displayed. From here, you can open an existing presentation, begin creating a new one from scratch, create a presentation from one you want to modify, or create one from a template.

CREATE A NEW PRESENTATION

Although you can begin to create a new presentation by just typing in the title and subtitle placeholder boxes of the blank slide, shown in Figure 1-1, and then creating a presentation from scratch, you have more options available to you with the File button.

1. Click **File** and click **New**. The New Presentation dialog box appears, as shown in Figure 1-4.

2. Under New, select the type of presentation you want:
   - **Blank** allows you to create a slide show from scratch.
   - **Recent Templates** allows you to create a slide show from a recently used presentation.
   - **Sample Templates** presents a list of preset templates that come with PowerPoint and can be used to create a similar slide show, such as Classic Photo Album templates.
   - **Themes** provides many standard themes from which to choose, allowing you to create your own slide design, with coordinated color, fonts, and design elements.
   - **My Templates** displays a New Presentation dialog box that allows you to find an existing template that you have created. Once you have found and opened the template, you can use it as is (for a standard company look, for example) or modify it to suit your purposes.

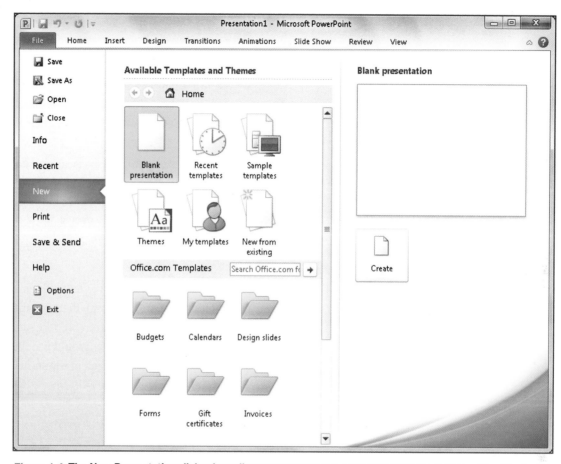

*Figure 1-4: **The New Presentation dialog box allows you to create a new presentation starting with a blank slide, from a template, or from another existing presentation.***

- **New From Existing** displays a New From Existing Presentation dialog box that allows you to find an existing presentation. Once you have found and opened the presentation, you can modify it to suit your purposes.

- **Office.com Templates** displays a list of template options. When you click one, you can download a template created by Microsoft for specific documents, such as budgets, award certificates, calendars, etc.

3. Select the option you want, and follow the prompts. Chapter 2 explains how to create a presentation.

OPEN AN EXISTING PRESENTATION

Once you have created a presentation, you will have to find it and reopen it to make changes, print, or display it in the future. To open an existing presentation:

1. Click **Office** and click **Open.**

2. If you are opening a recently opened document, click **Recent** and double-click the name of the presentation.

    –Or–

3. In the Open dialog box, find the location of the PowerPoint presentation you want. Use the techniques in Windows Explorer or Windows 7 that you normally use to find files.

4. When you have located and opened the folder containing the presentation, double-click the presentation itself to open it. You should see the presentation appear, as shown in Figure 1-5.

Show Views

In addition to the Slide Show view (which activates the display of the current presentation you are building), there are three primary views in PowerPoint: Normal view, Slide Sorter view, and Reading view used in building and managing slides. You usually would use the View toolbar to access these views, located on the lower-right area of the status bar, as shown here:

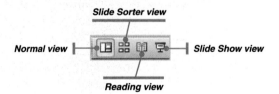

Slide Sorter view

Normal view | *Slide Show view*

Reading view

OPEN NORMAL VIEW

The Normal view displays a larger view of the slide show, with a side pane containing the Slides and Outline tabs, as seen earlier in Figure 1-5. Either:

- Click the **Normal** icon on the View toolbar, located on the lower-right area of the status bar.

    –Or–

- Click the **View** tab, and in the Presentation Views group, click **Normal**.

> **NOTE**
>
> To get back to the Normal view from another view, you can either click the Normal view button on the View toolbar or select Normal from the Presentation Views group in the View tab.

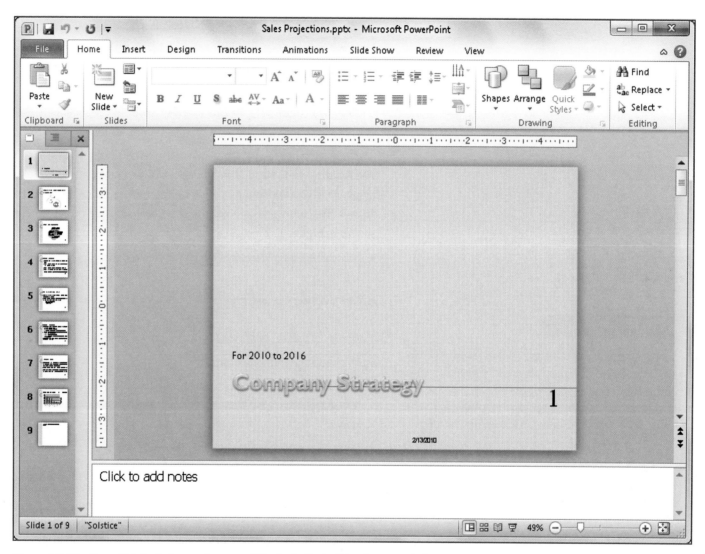

Figure 1-5: **The PowerPoint window and panes will look similar to this when an existing presentation is displayed.**

OPEN SLIDE SORTER VIEW

The Slide Sorter view displays thumbnails of the slides in your presentation, as shown in Figure 1-6, and allows you to rearrange them. Either:

- Click the **Slide Sorter** icon on the View toolbar.

  –Or–

- Click the **View** tab, and, in the Presentation Views group, click **Slide Sorter**.

OPEN READING VIEW

The Reading view starts the slide show, but then allows you to manually display each component of a slide in order as you click the Next and Previous arrows. This allows you to edit line by line each slide of your presentation, as shown in Figure 1-7.

- Click the **Reading View** icon on the View toolbar.

  –Or–

- Click the **View** tab, and, in the Presentation Views group, click **Reading View**.

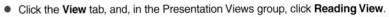

TIP

While you are in Slide Show mode, you may need to click the display of the current slide to advance the presentation to the next slide. To close the slide show and return to the previous view, press **ESC** on your keyboard.

NOTE

You can start a slide show using Windows Explorer without starting PowerPoint. Find the file in Windows Explorer, right-click the presentation's file name, and click **Show** from the context menu.

Start a Slide Show

Start a slide show in one of three ways:

- In the current view, click the **Slide Show** icon on the View toolbar, located on the right of the status bar. The slide show will start with the selected slide.

  –Or–

- Press **F5** to start the slide show from the beginning.

  –Or–

- In the Slide Show tab, Start Slide Show group, click **From Beginning** to play the slide show from the first slide, click **From Current Slide** to play the slide show from the currently selected slide, click **Broadcast Slide Show** to display it on a browser, or click **Custom Slide Show** to create a new slide show from selected slides.

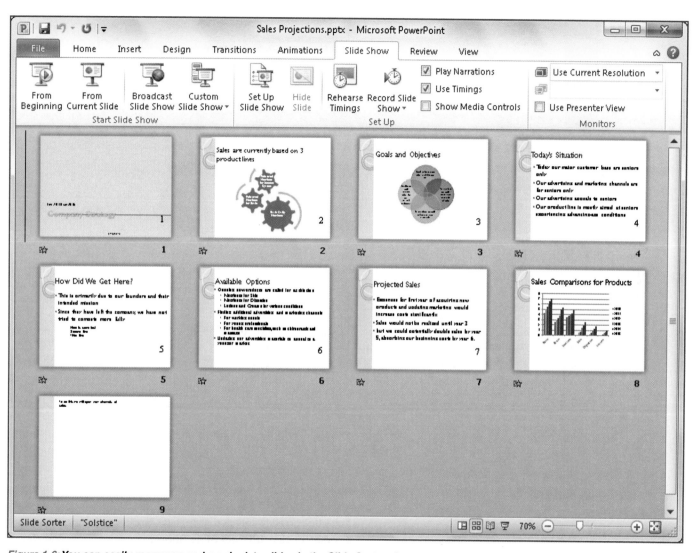

Figure 1-6: *You can easily rearrange and manipulate slides in the Slide Sorter view.*

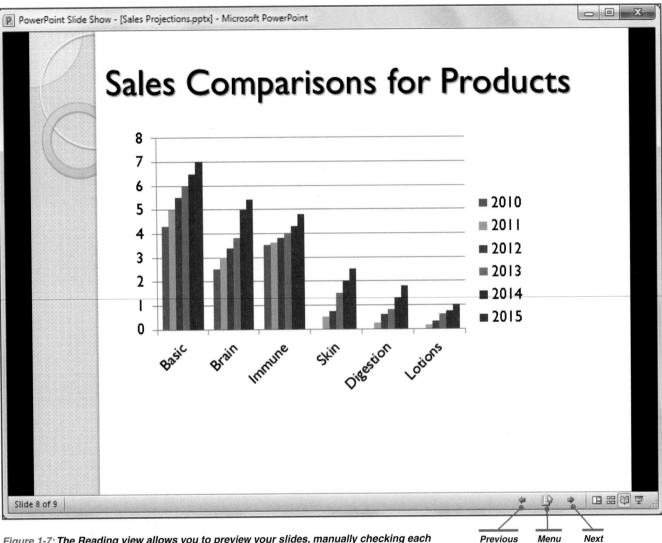

Figure 1-7: *The Reading view allows you to preview your slides, manually checking each component for timing and accuracy.*

Previous   Menu   Next

NOTE

To change the size of any pane (such as the Slides or Outline tabs pane), simply drag its borders. Point at the border until you see a two-headed arrow separated by parallel lines, and then drag the border to increase or decrease the pane size.

NOTE

You can add a command to the Quick Access toolbar from the ribbon by right-clicking the command and choosing **Add To Quick Access Toolbar**.

> Add to Quick Access Toolbar
>
> Customize Quick Access Toolbar...
>
> Show Quick Access Toolbar Below the Ribbon

Personalize PowerPoint

You can personalize PowerPoint by changing the default PowerPoint settings and by customizing the Quick Access toolbar.

Work with the Quick Access Toolbar

The Quick Access toolbar can become a "best friend" if you modify it so that it fits your way of working.

ADD TO THE QUICK ACCESS TOOLBAR

The Quick Access toolbar contains the commands most commonly used in a given program. You can add other commands to it that you regularly use.

1. Click **File** and click **Options**.
2. Click the **Quick Access Toolbar** option, and you will see the dialog box shown in Figure 1-8.
3. Above the list box on the right, click the **Customize Quick Access Toolbar** down arrow and choose whether to change the Quick Access toolbar for all documents or for just the document currently open.
4. In the list box on the left, click the **Choose Commands From** down arrow, and select the type of command you want from the listed options.
5. Then click **Add** to move its name to the list box on the right. Repeat this for all the commands you want on the toolbar.
6. Click **Reset** if you need to restore the original settings.
7. Click **OK** when you are finished.

MOVE THE QUICK ACCESS TOOLBAR

To move the Quick Access toolbar beneath the ribbon, right-click the Quick Access toolbar, and choose **Show Quick Access Toolbar Below The Ribbon**, or click **File**, click **Options**, click **Quick Access Toolbar**, and select the check box of the same name beneath the Customize The Quick Access Toolbar command list box.

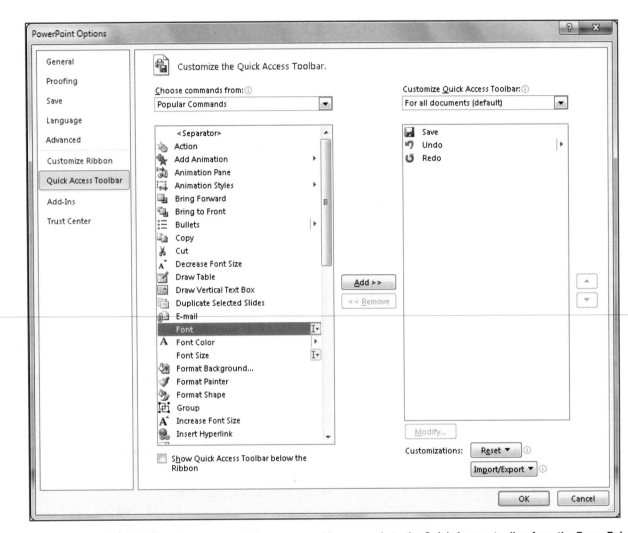

Figure 1-8: *For immediate use for common tasks, you can add commands to the Quick Access toolbar from the PowerPoint Options dialog box.*

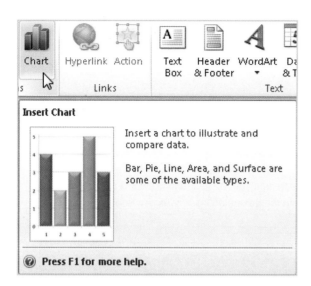

Show or Hide ScreenTips

When you hold your pointer over a command or tool, a ScreenTip is displayed. The tip may be just the name of the feature, or it may be enhanced with a small description. You can hide the tips or cause them to show feature descriptions or not.

1. Click **File** and click **Options.**

2. On the General tab, under User Interface Options, click the **ScreenTip Style** drop-down list, and choose the option you want.

ScreenTip style:	Show feature descriptions in ScreenTips ▼
	Show feature descriptions in ScreenTips
	Don't show feature descriptions in ScreenTips
	Don't show ScreenTips

3. Click **OK** to confirm your choice.

Display the Mini Toolbar

When you highlight or select text, a small mini toolbar appears with commands for working with it. Highlight the text and move the pointer over the selection until the toolbar appears. You can hide the toolbar by changing the default setting.

1. Click **File** and click **Options**.

2. Click the **General** option.

3. Click the **Show Mini Toolbar On Selection** check box to remove the check mark.

4. Click **OK** to confirm the choice.

Add Identifying Information

You can add identifying information to a presentation to make it easier to organize and to find presentations during searches, especially in a shared environment.

1. Click **File**, click **Info**, and in the right pane, click **Properties**. A menu appears for working with the document's properties.

2. Click **Show Document Panel**. A document information panel containing standard document information displays under the ribbon. An example is shown in Figure 1-9.

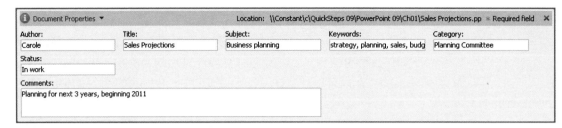

Figure 1-9: *You can more easily locate a presentation using search tools if you add identifying data.*

3. Type identifying information, such as a title, subject, and keywords (words or phrases that are associated with the presentation), a category, and the status of the presentation, and any comments.

4. To view more information about the presentation, click the **Document Properties** down arrow on the panel's title bar, and click **Advanced Properties**. Review each tab in the Properties dialog box to see the information available, and make any changes or additions.

- The **General** tab displays dates and times when the presentation was created, modified, and last accessed.

- The **Summary** tab displays information about the author, subject, company and manager, category of presentation, keywords, comments, and a hyperlink that might be included. You can include a preview picture to help identify the presentation if necessary.

- The **Statistics** tab displays data about the presentation itself, such as the number of slides, paragraphs, words, notes, etc. It reveals how many times it has been revised and the total amount of editing time.

- The **Contents** tab identifies the fonts, themes, and slide titles used in the presentation.

- The **Custom** tab allows you to add new information about the presentation. You select a name for the new information, identify the type of data it is (text versus dates, for example), add a value, and identify the properties of the new information.

5. Close the Properties dialog box when finished by clicking **OK**.

6. When finished with the document information panel, click the **Close** button (the "X") at the rightmost end of the panel's title bar to close it.

NOTE

You can change the order in which document properties are displayed by clicking **File**, clicking **Info**, clicking the **Properties** down arrow, and choosing **Advanced Properties**. Then, in the dialog box, Custom tab, click the items you wish to include in the Properties display. Click **OK** to close the dialog box.

Get Help

Help can be accessed from online Microsoft servers. A different kind of help, which provides the Thesaurus and Research features, is also available.

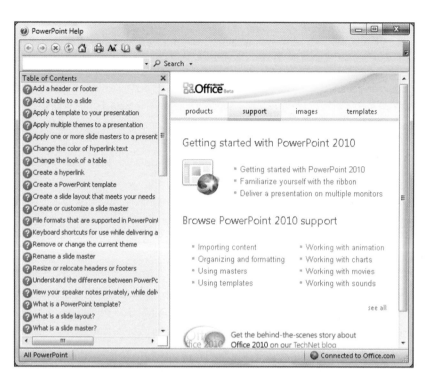

Figure 1-10: *When you click the Help icon, you will see the PowerPoint Help dialog box, where you can click the topic you want or search for more specific words.*

Open Help

The PowerPoint Help system is easily accessed. It is automatically connected to the Microsoft Office Online Help system. You can tell whether you are online or offline by checking the status bar of the PowerPoint Help dialog box.

1. Click the **Help** icon ⊚ , and the PowerPoint Help window will open, shown in Figure 1-10. You have these options:

   ● Find the topic you want, and click it.

   ● Click the **Search** down arrow, and choose the source and type of help you want.

   ● Type keywords in the Search text box, and click **Search**.

Conduct Research

You can conduct research on the Internet using PowerPoint's Research command. This displays a Research task pane, shown in Figure 1-11, that allows you to enter your search criteria and specify references to search.

2. Click the **Review** tab, and in the Proofing group, click **Research**. The Research task pane will appear to the right of the Slide and Notes panes.

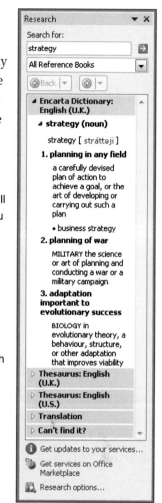

Figure 1-11: *You can use the Research pane to search many online references, define words, translate words or sentences, and more.*

> **NOTE**
>
> If you are not connected to the Internet, Help is also available offline.

ACCESSING MICROSOFT RESOURCES

Within the Help system, Microsoft maintains an online tools and resource center that you can easily access. This center allows you to communicate with Microsoft about Office and PowerPoint subjects.

1. Click **File** and click **Help**. The Microsoft Support view is displayed. You have these options:

   - **Microsoft Office Help** connects you to the Help system.

   - **Getting Started** shows you what has changed or what is new in PowerPoint so that you can start as an informed user.

   - **Contact Us** lets you send a message to Microsoft experts. You may be seeking advice for a problem or making suggestions for improvements to the product.

   - **Options** opens the PowerPoint Options window, which was discussed in several places in this chapter.

   - **Check For Updates** finds out if updates are available for Microsoft Office and, if so, allows you to download them.

   - **Additional Version And Copyright Information** (a link beneath the Office pane) displays information about your version of PowerPoint and the copyright agreement that is in effect with activated programs.

Continued . . .

3. Enter your search criteria in the **Search For** text box. Click the green arrow.

4. Beneath the text box is the reference source. To change the default source, click the down arrow to open the drop-down list, and click the reference you want to search.

5. Once your results are displayed, you may have other drop-down lists that further refine your results, depending on the reference sources you have chosen. For example:

   - **Thesaurus: English (U.K.)** displays the synonyms for the selected word according to United Kingdom English.

   - **Thesaurus: English (U.S.)** displays synonyms for the selected word according to United States usage.

   - **Translation** allows you to translate the selection into another language.

   - **Can't Find It?** displays links for other sources of information.

Save Your PowerPoint Presentation

When you have finished working on your presentation, you need to save it and exit PowerPoint. One way to make this more efficient is to have PowerPoint save the presentation automatically while you work.

Change Automatic Save Options

It is important to periodically save a presentation as you work. Having PowerPoint save it automatically will reduce the chance of losing data in case of a power failure or other interruption. To change the timing of automatic file saves:

1. Click **File** and click **Options**.

2. Click the **Save** option on the left.

3. By default, the **Save AutoRecover Information Every** check box is selected. Click it to clear the check mark if you don't want an automatic save.

4. By default, PowerPoint saves the presentation every 10 minutes. Type a time or use the spinner to set a different time for how often PowerPoint is to save your presentation.

5. Click **OK** to close the dialog box.

NOTE

In the PowerPoint Options dialog box, the Save option (which is displayed by clicking **File** and clicking **Options**) lets you set a default location where your presentation files will be saved.

TIP

If this is your first time saving the file, the Save As dialog box will appear. Enter the name of your presentation, and navigate to the location where you would like to store the file.

Save a Presentation Manually

You can save a presentation manually or create a copy of it under a different file name.

SAVE A PRESENTATION

To save a file:

- Click **File** and click **Save.**

  –Or–

- Click the **Save** button 💾 on the Quick Access toolbar.

  –Or–

- Press **CTRL+S**.

SAVE A COPY OF YOUR PRESENTATION

When you save a presentation under a different file name, you create a copy of it. Both the original presentation and the newly named one will remain. To create a copy with a new name:

1. Click **File** and click **Save As**. You will see one of two views, one a shortened view shown in Figure 1-12, and the other, a more expanded view, shown in Figure 1-13. You can toggle between the two by clicking the **Hide Folders/Browse Folders** button in the lower-left corner of the dialog box.

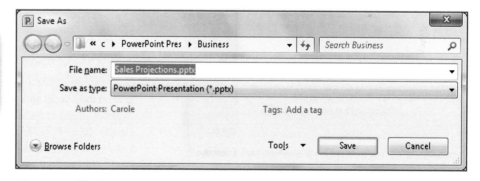

Figure 1-12: **The Save As command is a way to make a copy of your presentation so that you can modify it to meet new requirements without changing the original.**

UNDERSTANDING POWERPOINT XML FILE FORMATS

XML (eXtensible Markup Language), initially introduced into Office in 2003, is now the default file type produced by PowerPoint and other Office programs.

XML does to data what HTML (Hypertext Markup Language) has done to the formatting of Web pages—it interprets or translates data, thereby making it known to other programs. By providing a consistent set of *tags* (or identifiers) to data, along with a road map of how that data is structured (a *schema*), and a file that *transforms* the data from one use to another, documents can easily exchange information with Web services, programs, and other documents.

A key feature of these newer file formats (identified by the "x" in the file extension, such as .pptx) is how a file is now organized. Prior to PowerPoint 2003, a presentation was a single binary file, such as *filename*.ppt. Office 2010 XML files are actually a collection of several files and folders that all appear as a single file, such as the presentation, *filename*.pptx, or the template, *filename* .potx. XML provides several key advantages over binary files in addition to data parsing. XML files are:

- **Smaller**—They use ZIP compression to gain up to a 75-percent file size reduction.

- **More secure**—Executable code, such as VBA (Visual Basic for Applications), used in macros and ActiveX controls, is segregated into more secure file packages, such as macro-enabled commands.

- **More easily recovered**—Individual XML files can be opened in text readers such as Notepad, so it's not an all-or-nothing proposition when opening a corrupted file.

Continued . . .

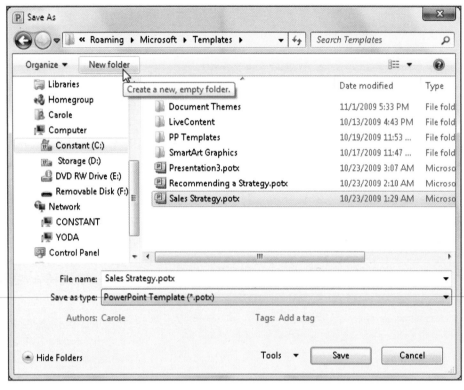

Figure 1-13: *You can create a new folder to store your presentation in while you are saving it.*

2. In the Save As dialog box, shown in Figure 1-12, type the file name.

3. You'll want to be careful to select the correct file type by clicking the **Save As Type** down arrow.

4. To find the path to the folder you want, you can either click the down arrow beneath the title bar, or if your dialog box is minimized, you can click **Browse Folders** in the lower-left area of the dialog box. If you do this, you will have available a Folders list and Favorites links list that will facilitate finding the path to the folder, shown in Figure 1-13.

5. Click **Save**.

UNDERSTANDING POWERPOINT XML FILE FORMATS *(Continued)*

So what does all this have to do with you if you simply want to create a presentation to report your monthly status? Fortunately, very little. All this XML tagging and multiple file organizing is done behind the scenes. As far as you're concerned, you have one file per presentation to save, copy, delete, or perform any standard file-maintenance actions upon.

TIP

You can also create a folder using Windows Explorer.

SAVE A PRESENTATION AS A TEMPLATE

To save a newly created presentation as a template from which to create new presentations:

1. Click **File** and click **Save As**.

2. Type a file name for your template, and locate the path to the folder under which it will be saved.

3. Click the **Save As Type** down arrow, and click **PowerPoint Template**.

4. Click **Save**.

Create a PowerPoint Folder

You can prepare a folder to store your presentation in so that you won't have to search for it every time you need it. You may have a special need that requires storing your presentations in a unique location (for example, if you have a project or task folder where you want the presentation to be stored). Or you may want to create a folder within the common Folder list or Favorites links list available in the Save As dialog box. You can direct PowerPoint to save your presentations by default to a given location.

SAVE TO A NEW FOLDER

1. When you save the presentation file for the first time, click **File** and click **Save As.**

2. In the Save As dialog box, find the folder under which you want to create a new folder. (In Figure 1-13, the folder is named "Templates.")

3. If necessary, click the **Browse Folders** down arrow to display the whole dialog box. Click the **New Folder** button as shown in Figures 1-13. A new folder with "New Folder" as the name will be inserted into the folder selected in step 2.

4. Type the name of the new folder, such as a project name or some other identifying name.

5. Type the file name, verify the type of file you are saving, and click **Save**.

CHANGE THE DEFAULT SAVE FOLDER

To store all your PowerPoint presentation files in one place, direct PowerPoint to save your files in a default folder.

1. Click **File** and click **Options**.

2. Click the **Save** option, and under Save Presentations, in the Default File Location text box, type the path to the folder where all presentations will be saved.

Default file location:	C:\Users\PowerPoint Pres\

3. Click **OK** when finished.

Close a Presentation Session

When you have completed your work for the day, you must "officially" close your presentation and then exit PowerPoint.

Closing a presentation removes it from the PowerPoint window, and exiting PowerPoint stops the program from using your computer's memory (see "Exit PowerPoint" earlier in the chapter). If the presentation has been saved, nothing will be lost. However, if you have not saved the file, you could lose all the work you have produced since the last time a save was performed, either automatically or manually (see "Save a Presentation Manually").

How to...

Chapter 2
Creating the Presentation

This chapter describes how to create a presentation. You'll find that PowerPoint provides many methods for quickly and easily creating dramatic and effective presentations. Sometimes, you'll find what you need in the prepackaged designs and templates that are already designed with specific presentation types in mind (for instance, an academic or business presentation, or one for healthcare professionals). These may be available from the online gallery. Sometimes, you'll find what you need in previous presentations you've created, so you can simply borrow slides or design elements from past successful efforts. And other times, nothing you have in your presentation library or that is offered by PowerPoint can fill your particular requirements. In this case, you can create your own template from scratch or use Office-wide themes and

QUICK**FACTS**

DEFINING THEMES, LAYOUTS, AND MASTER SLIDES

Themes in PowerPoint lend presentations color and design coordination. Around 40 theme templates are available in a ribbon gallery in PowerPoint and are available throughout most of Office. Or, you can download additional choices from Microsoft's online templates. Chapter 3 explains how themes can be changed and customized to give you almost unlimited variations in how your presentation looks.

Layouts define where the objects of a slide (such as the text, spreadsheets or diagrams, pictures, or headings and footers) will be placed and formatted. Objects are positioned on a slide using *placeholders* that identify the specific object being inserted (a text placeholder versus a chart placeholder, for instance). PowerPoint has defined several standard layout templates that you can choose when you insert a new slide. When you insert a new slide into a given theme, the slide takes on the colors and design elements of the theme, with the chosen layout attributes and placeholder positioning.

When you want to create your own themes and layouts to use in a future presentation, you create your own templates by saving them with a special file extension: .potx. Figure 2-1 depicts some of the components of layouts and themes that you may have on a slide.

You can make your templates be *master slides*—see Chapter 4 for additional information. Master slides, another type of template, define the parts of a slide that you want to be the same for a whole presentation or group of contiguous slides. (You can have multiple master slides in a presentation.) In addition to any color and design elements (such as fonts) found in themes, master slides might include unique graphics (such as a logo), a specific header or footer, and options for inserting placeholders for text and other objects while you are creating a presentation.

the styling assistance of PowerPoint. This chapter also looks at how to organize and manage your slides by creating and working with a presentation outline. Finally, you will see how to protect your presentations with passwords.

Create a Presentation

There are three ways to begin creating your presentation: using an existing presentation and then modifying it, using a preset theme and standard layouts that define the design and layout of a slide, and starting from scratch—creating your own template in the process.

Create a Presentation from Another Presentation

The easiest and most direct way to create a new presentation is to start with an existing one. To copy a presentation, rename it, and then modify it according to your needs:

1. Click **File** and then click **New**.

2. On the Available Templates And Themes pane, click **New From Existing**.

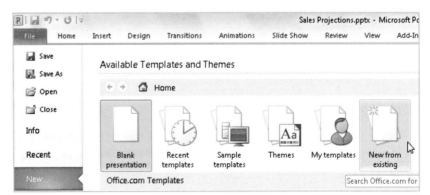

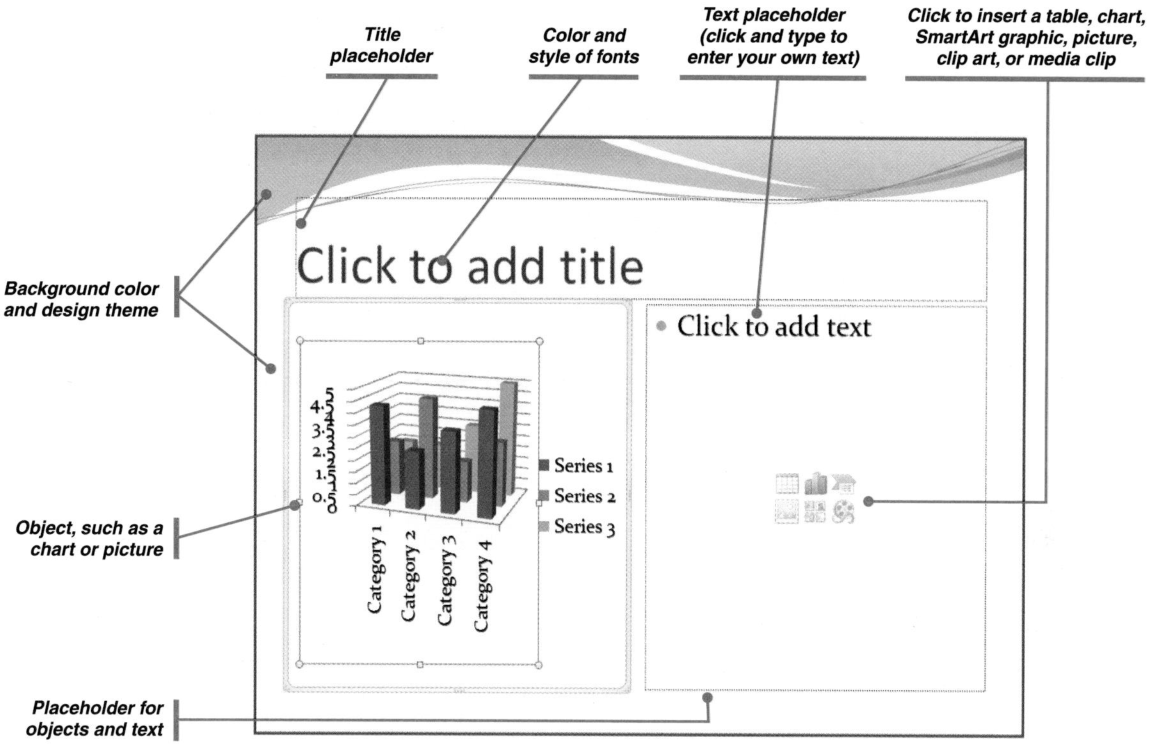
Title placeholder
Color and style of fonts
Text placeholder (click and type to enter your own text)
Click to insert a table, chart, SmartArt graphic, picture, clip art, or media clip
Background color and design theme
Object, such as a chart or picture
Placeholder for objects and text
Click to add title
Click to add text
Series 1
Series 2
Series 3
Category 1
Category 2
Category 3
Category 4

Figure 2-1: ***These components make up the theme and layout of a slide and can be saved as a template.***

3. Find and select the presentation or template you want to use, and click **Create New**, as displayed in Figure 2-2.
4. Modify the presentation by replacing the theme; highlighting text and replacing it with your own; deleting unnecessary slides; inserting new slides; inserting your own graphics, charts, and art; and rearranging the slides according to your needs (subsequent chapters in this book describe how to do these actions in detail).
5. Click **File** and click **Save As**. Enter a different name for the presentation, click the **Save As Type** down arrow, identify the file type, and click **Save**.

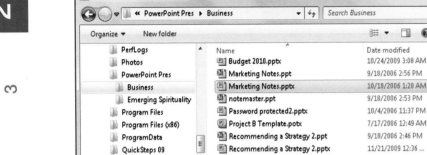

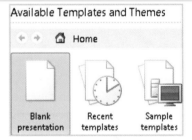

Create a Presentation Using a Standard Theme

Themes are used to give your presentation a unified and professional look. They provide background color and design, predefined fonts, and other elements that hold a presentation together. Once you have defined the overall theme, it is a simple task to add slides with the appropriate layout for the data you wish to present. You select a theme from a predefined gallery available on the ribbon. See the "Defining Themes, Layouts, and Master Slides" QuickFacts. To use one of PowerPoint's standard themes:

1. Click **File** and then click **New**. The File view appears.

2. Double-click **Blank Presentation**, and a standard blank slide will open.

Figure 2-2: In this window, you find the presentation you want to use as a model and create a new one.

3. Click the **Design** tab. You'll see in the Themes group a gallery of thumbnails, with the one on the left selected. This is the default assigned to all new blank presentations.

4. In the right end of the Themes group, click the **More** down arrow to see all the standard thumbnails of color and design themes. Again, you'll see the current theme identified under This Presentation.

5. Hold your mouse pointer over the other theme thumbnails to see their effects on the slide, as shown in Figure 2-3. When you find the theme you want to use, click its thumbnail.

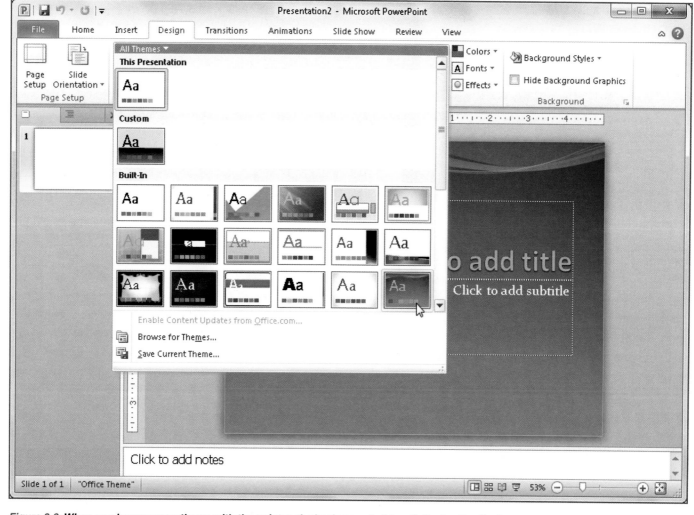

Figure 2-3: *When you hover over a theme with the pointer, the background slide will display its effect.*

WORKING WITH THEMES

You can search Office Online resources to find other templates, apply a theme to selected slides or all slides in a presentation, or set a theme to be the default for all future presentations, for a consistent business look, for example.

FIND OTHER MICROSOFT THEMES AND TEMPLATES

1. Click the **Design** tab, and in the Themes group, click the **More** down arrow.

2. Scroll beneath the last thumbnail of the Built In list, and click **Enable Content Update From Office.com**.

APPLY THEMES TO SLIDES

The quickest way to apply a theme to all slides in a presentation is to click a theme thumbnail. You can also use the context menu on a theme thumbnail to select how to apply the themes.

1. In the Slide pane of the Normal view or in the Slide Sorter view, click the slide or slides you want the theme applied to. To select non-contiguous slides, press **CTRL** while you click to select the slides. If you want the theme applied to all themes, any slide will do.

2. On the Design tab, click the **More** down arrow on the Themes group, and right-click the theme thumbnail to be applied.

Continued . . .

NOTE

Unless you change the folder location, the template will be saved in the default template folder where PowerPoint design templates are stored. You will be able to see it in File view in the My Templates folder.

6. At this point, you can either begin to add content to an actual presentation (see the "Adding Content to a Slide" QuickSteps) or you can create a template for a presentation (see "Create a Template").

Create a Template

A template contains one or more slides with attributes of the colors, themes, and standard layouts you want to have available. First, you create the slide with the desired themes and layouts. Then you save it as a template so that it can be used when formatting and adding your own colors and design theme to new presentations. Template files have .potx extensions. When you create a new template, it will be displayed in the New Presentations dialog box under My Templates in the File view. To create a new presentation:

1. Click **File** and click **New**. Double-click **Blank Presentation** to see the basic slide layout.

2. To prepare your slide:

   • Click the **Design** tab, and in the Themes group, click the **More** down arrow to select themes for the template.

   • Click the **Home** tab, in the Slides group, click the **New Slide** down arrow to list possible layouts, and then click the layout you want. Repeat this step to add one slide for each layout you want in the presentation.

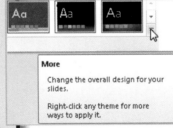

3. When you have a template with the attributes you want the presentation to have, click **File** and click **Save As**.

4. In the File Name box, type a name for the new template.

5. In the Save As Type drop-down list box, click **PowerPoint Template (.potx)**, as seen in Figure 2-4.

QUICKSTEPS

WORKING WITH THEMES (Continued)

3. On the context menu, you have these options:

- Click **Apply To All Slides** to have the theme applied to all slides in the presentation.

- Click **Apply To Selected Slides** to have the themes applied just to the slides currently selected.

SET A DEFAULT THEME FOR ALL FUTURE PRESENTATIONS

1. Under the Themes group in the Design tab, click the **More** down arrow, and right-click the thumbnail you want.

2. Click **Set As Default Theme**.

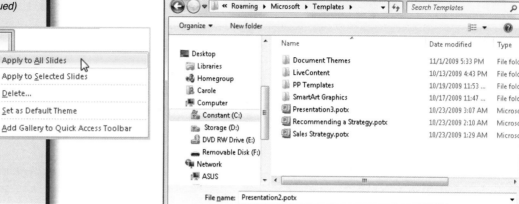

Figure 2-4: *You can save a file containing themes and layouts as a template for future presentations.*

NOTE

In order to see the file extensions in the Save As Type list, you must choose that option in Windows Explorer. In the Windows Explorer window, click **Organize**, click **Folder And Search Options**, click the **View** tab, and click **Hide Extensions For Known File Types** to remove the check mark. By default, file extensions will not be displayed.

NOTE

A theme can be further modified by changing its constituent components, color, font, and graphic effects. Chapter 3 describes how to work with themes in more detail.

6. Click **Save**. The template is now available under My Templates in the New Presentations dialog box.

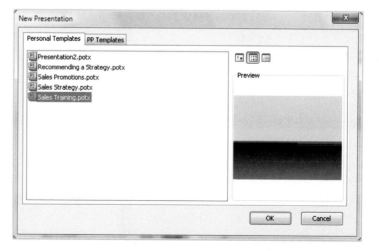

ADDING CONTENT TO A SLIDE

The following elements are available to help you present the points you are making in the slide show. This section provides an overview of the procedures. Each element is covered in depth in later chapters of this book.

WORK WITH TEXT

Text can be added to placeholders, text boxes, and some shapes; or existing text can be changed easily. Chapter 4 deals with text in detail. To add text, you click inside of a text box, some shapes, or placeholder and then begin to type.

1. To modify text attributes, highlight the text by dragging the pointer over it. A mini toolbar will appear that you can use for simple changes, such as font, font color, font size, boldface, italics, and other text attributes.

2. Click the **Home** tab, and click any of the Font group buttons. On this same tab are the paragraph setting options. (See Chapter 4 for additional information on using text.)

ADD OR CHANGE COLOR SCHEMES

Ask yourself what color schemes you might want to use. Are there company colors that you want to use or colors you want to stay away from?

1. To set your design and color foundation for the presentation, select a theme for your presentation, as described in the "Working with Themes" QuickSteps.

2. To change the color grouping for a theme, click the **Colors** button, and move the pointer over the color combinations to see the effects in the selected slide. When you're satisfied, click the color group you want. (See Chapter 3 for more information.)

Continued . . .

Create a Presentation from Scratch

When you create a presentation from scratch, you'll begin with blank slides and add layouts, color schemes, fonts, graphics and charts, other design elements, and text.

1. Click **File** and click **New**. The File view will appear.

2. Click **Create** under Blank Presentation in the right pane. A blank title page slide will be displayed.

3. On the Design tab, select a theme for the background color and design for your presentation.

4. On the slide, click in the **Click To Add Title** box, and type the title of your presentation. If you want to add a subtitle, click in the **Click To Add Subtitle** box and type your subtitle.

5. When you are satisfied with that slide, click **New Slide** in the Slides group on the Home tab to insert another blank slide with the layout you want.

   - Click the **New Slide** button itself to see a slide using the last layout.
   - Click the **New Slide** down arrow to see a menu of layout choices.

6. Click the **Insert** tab, and click the relevant buttons to add text and other content to your slides. (See the "Adding Content to a Slide" QuickSteps.)

7. Repeat steps 5 and 6 for as many slides as you have in your presentation.

8. Save the presentation. Click **File** and click **Save As**. Enter a file name, and click **Save**.

Select a Layout

As mentioned earlier, you can add a slide and select a layout by clicking the **New Slide** button on the Home tab. However, there is another way. To add a slide and select a layout:

QUICKSTEPS

ADDING CONTENT TO A SLIDE *(Continued)*

3. To change color and shading, keeping the design for slides, change the background style (see Chapter 3). In the Background group, click **Background Styles** and click an option.

SELECT AN ANIMATION SCHEME

To display animated text or objects on your slide, select your text or object and then click the **Animations** tab. In the Animation group, point to the various animation themes until you find the one you want. Click to set it. (See Chapter 8 for more information.)

SET SLIDE TRANSITIONS

To animate the transition from one slide to another, click the **Transitions** tab and point to the various choices in the Transitions group. Click the transition you like. (See Chapter 8 for more information.)

INSERT ART AND GRAPHICS

1. Click in the slide where you want the object placed.

2. Click the **Insert** tab, and in the Tables, Illustrations, or Images groups, click the button for the table, picture, clip art, screenshot, shape, SmartArt, or chart object you want to insert. Depending on what you click, you will see either a dialog box of how to find it or a menu of choices from which to select an object.

3. Find or choose the object you want, and it will be inserted on your slide where your insertion point is placed.

4. Drag the object where you want it on the slide, and resize it as needed.

   –Or–

   Create and insert your own drawing. (See Chapters 5, 6, 7, and 8 for additional information for working with objects, such as tables, clip art and images, charts and shapes.)

1. In the Slides tab, right-click the slide immediately preceding the one you want to insert.

2. Click **New Slide**.

3. Right-click the new slide in the Slides tab, and on the context menu, click **Layout**. A submenu containing layout possibilities will be displayed, as shown in Figure 2-5.

4. Click the layout thumbnail you want.

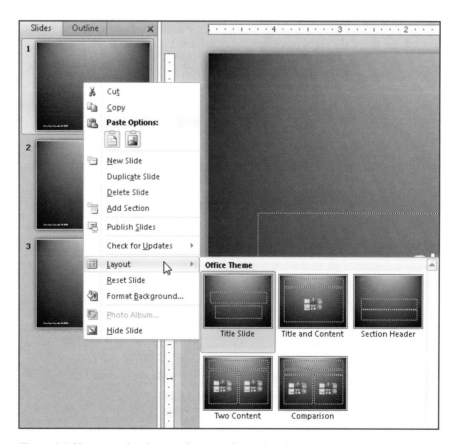

*Figure 2-5: **You can select layouts from a gallery of choices.***

Outline a Presentation

Outlining a presentation is easy in PowerPoint. You simply display the Outline tab and begin typing. The following sections explain how to create, manipulate, modify, and print an outline.

Create an Outline

The outline is created, modified, and viewed using the Outline tab, shown in Figure 2-6. An outline is created from scratch or by inserting text from other sources. You create an outline by indenting subtopics under main topics. When you create a subtopic, or indent it under the one above it, you *demote* the point, or make it a lower level than the previous topic. The demoted point is contained within the higher level. When you remove an indent, you *promote* the point, making it a new topic. The promoted point becomes a higher level, which may contain its own subtopics.

CREATE AN OUTLINE FROM SCRATCH

To create an outline from scratch, type your text on the Outline tab.

1. To open a blank presentation, click **File** and click **New**. Double-click the type of presentation you want: Blank Presentation, from My Templates, or New From Existing. Depending on what you choose, a dialog box may appear, from which you'll choose the template. The initial slide or slides are displayed.

2. Click **View** and click **Normal** in the View tab Presentation Views group. (You can also click the **Normal** view button on the View toolbar.)

3. Click the **Outline** tab so that the Outline view is available, as shown in Figure 2-6.

4. Click to the right of the Outline slide icon to place the insertion point.

5. Type the title (the title of your first slide is typically the title of your presentation). Press **ENTER** to insert a new slide.

6. Type your next title, typically the first topic or main point. Press **ENTER** when you are done. Another new slide will be inserted.

   - To add points to the slide rather than to insert a new one, click the **Home** tab, and click **Increase List Level** in the Paragraph group to move the topic to the right. It will become a subtopic under the previous slide.

Outline tab, where you create, edit, and rearrange the slides

Presentation pane, where you create the look and feel of your presentation with color, fonts, text, and design elements

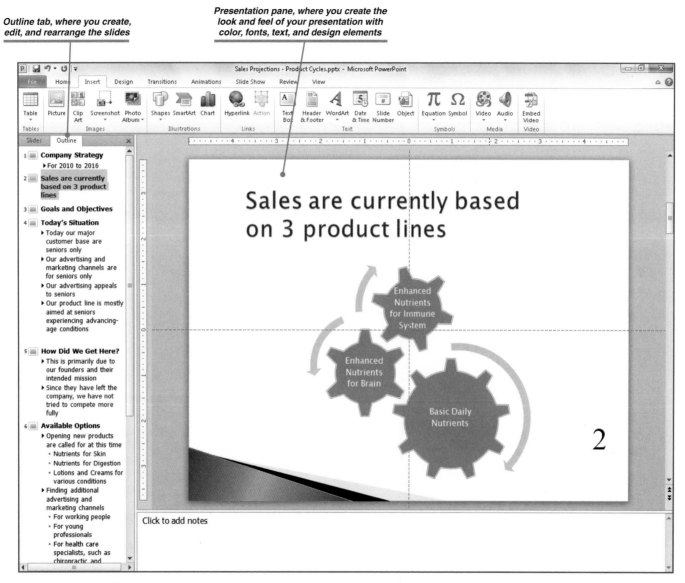

Figure 2-6: *The Outline tab is an alternative way to work with your slides to organize, create, and modify your presentations.*

TIP

The name on the Outline and Slides tabs changes to an icon when the pane is too narrow for the words to appear.

COMPANY STRATEGY
For 2010 to 2016

QUICKSTEPS

INDENTING WITH THE KEYBOARD

If you are interested in working with the keyboard rather than using the mouse, you can use key combinations to work with the outlining feature.

INCREASE INDENTS (DEMOTE)

- Press **TAB**.

  –Or–

- Press **ALT+SHIFT+RIGHT ARROW**.

DECREASE INDENTS (PROMOTE)

- Press **SHIFT+TAB**.

  –Or–

- Press **ALT+SHIFT+LEFT ARROW**.

MOVE UP A LINE/SLIDE

- Press **ALT+SHIFT+UP ARROW**.

MOVE DOWN A LINE/SLIDE

- Press **ALT+SHIFT+DOWN ARROW**.

- To move points to the left, making them a higher level, click **Decrease List Level** on the Home tab Paragraph group to move the topic to the left. It will become either a higher-level point or a new slide, depending on the original level.

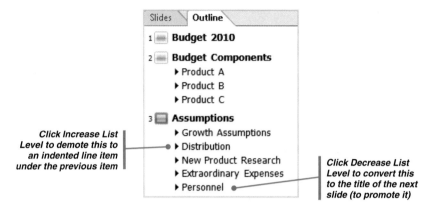

Click Increase List Level to demote this to an indented line item under the previous item

Click Decrease List Level to convert this to the title of the next slide (to promote it)

7. Continue typing and pressing **ENTER** and clicking **Increase List Level** or **Decrease List Level** to move the text into headings and bulleted points until the presentation is outlined.

Insert an Outline from Other Sources

You can create slides from an outline you have previously created in another document. Depending on the format of the text, the formatting retained and used by PowerPoint will differ. Here are some considerations to keep in mind when inserting an outline from another source:

- A **Microsoft Word (.doc)** or **Rich Text Format (.rtf)** outline will use paragraph breaks to mark the start of a new slide. Each paragraph will become a slide title. However, if the document is formatted with headings, Heading 1 will become the title of the slide, Heading 2 will be the second level, Heading 3 the third level, and so on (see Figure 2-7).

- An **HTML** outline will retain its formatting; however, the text will appear in a text box on the slide and can only be edited in the Presentation pane, not in the Outline tab. In addition, you must create a separate Hypertext Markup Language (HTML) file for each slide. (To see the HTML file in the Insert Outline dialog box, you may have to select .htm as the file type.)

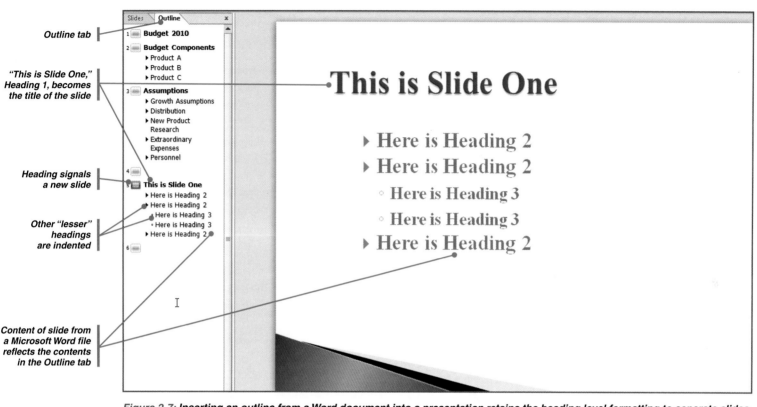

Outline tab

**"This is Slide One,"
Heading 1, becomes
the title of the slide**

**Heading signals
a new slide**

**Other "lesser"
headings
are indented**

**Content of slide from
a Microsoft Word file
reflects the contents
in the Outline tab**

Figure 2-7: Inserting an outline from a Word document into a presentation retains the heading level formatting to separate slides and bulleted items.

NOTE

Instead of using the Increase List Level and Decrease List Level buttons, you can also press **ENTER** to create a new bulleted line. Pressing **CTRL+ENTER** will create a new slide or the first subtopic line. Other options for working with outlines include specific key combinations (see the "Indenting with the Keyboard" QuickSteps) and the right-click context menu (see the "Using the Outlining Commands" QuickSteps).

- A **Plain Text (.txt)** outline will adopt the styles of the current presentation. PowerPoint will use paragraph separations to start a new slide.

To insert an outline from another source:

1. On the Home tab, in the Slides group, click the **New Slide** down arrow. On the bottom of the menu, click **Slides From Outline**.

2. In the Insert Outline dialog box, first specify the correct file type. Then find and select the document that contains the outline you want to use, and click **Insert**.

QUICKSTEPS

USING THE OUTLINING COMMANDS

Although some of the buttons available on the ribbon work well with the outlining function, you can display commands specifically for use with the Outline tab.

DISPLAY THE OUTLINING COMMANDS

1. Select the slide or line of text in the Outline tab.

2. Right-click and select one of the commands discussed in the following sections.

PROMOTE OR DEMOTE OUTLINE TEXT

- Click **Promote** to move the selected text in a slide up one level.

- Click **Demote** to move the selected text in a slide down one level.

MOVE OUTLINE TEXT UP OR DOWN

- Click **Move Up** to move the selected text of a slide up one line or item.

- Click **Move Down** to move the selected text of a slide down one line or item.

COLLAPSE OR EXPAND A SLIDE

- Click **Collapse** and from the menu, click **Collapse** to hide the detail beneath the title of a selected slide; or click **Collapse All** to hide all the detail lines in the outline.

- Click **Expand** and from the menu, click **Expand** to show the detail beneath a title of a selected slide; or click **Expand All** to show all the detail lines in the outline.

SHOW FORMATTING

Click **Show Text Formatting** to toggle between showing and not showing the formatting in the outline text.

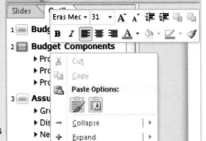

Preview and Print the Outline

To preview an outline and then print it:

1. Click **File** and click **Print.**

2. Under Settings, click the second drop-down menu, and click **Outline**, as seen in Figure 2-8.

3. Click **Print** to print the outline.

Protect Your Presentation

You can set two levels of passwords restricting access to your presentation: You can deny access to even look at a presentation, and you can permit looking but deny modifying it. You can also strip personal information from the presentation—information that is automatically stored by PowerPoint, such as your name and certain file information.

SET PASSWORDS FOR A PRESENTATION

1. Open the presentation to be password-protected.

2. Click **File** and click **Save As**.

3. Click the **Tools** button, and then click **General Options**. The General Options dialog box will appear.

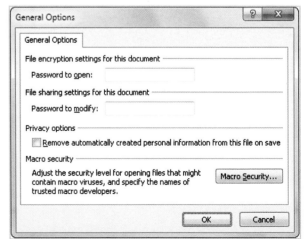

Click to print ⎯

Select "outline" to be printed ⎯

Your selected view will be previewed automatically ⎯

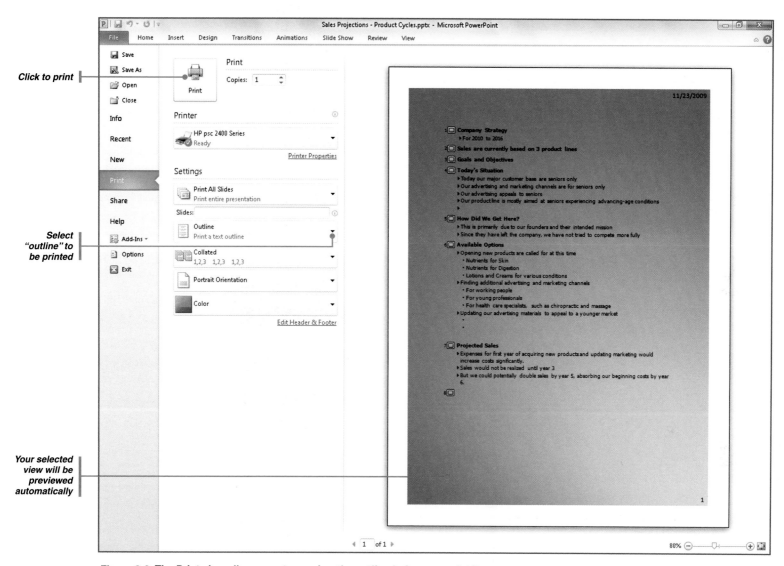

Figure 2-8: **The Print view allows you to preview the outline before you print it.**

- To restrict anyone without a password from opening and looking at the presentation, type a password in the Password To Open text box.

- To restrict anyone from modifying the presentation, type a password in the Password To Modify text box.

4. Click **OK**.

5. In the Confirm Password dialog box, reenter the password and click **OK**.

6. Click **Save** to save the file.

When anyone tries to open or modify a protected file, they will see a message.

REMOVE PASSWORD RESTRICTIONS

1. Click **File** and click **Save As**.

2. Click **Tools** on the bottom of the dialog box, and click **General Options**.

3. Clear any passwords in the Password To Open or Password To Modify text box.

4. Click **OK**.

5. Click **Save** and, if saving an existing file, confirm that you want to replace the existing file. You may be asked to save the file under another name.

STRIP FILE INFORMATION FROM THE PRESENTATION

When you set PowerPoint to strip personal information from a presentation, this is done when you save the file. Once you set the option to strip personal information from a presentation, PowerPoint will continue to do this until you change the option.

1. Click **File** and click **Save As**.

2. Click the **Tools** button, and then click **General Options**.

3. Under Privacy Options, click the **Remove Automatically Created Personal Information From This File On Save** check box.

4. Click **OK**.

5. Click **Save** and, if saving an existing file, confirm that you want to replace it.

Chapter 3
Working with Slides

Getting around in a presentation and being able to manipulate slides easily is a critical skill in becoming a capable PowerPoint user. In this chapter you will learn how to work with presentations at the slide level. In addition to navigating through the slides in various views of PowerPoint, you will learn to insert, delete, rearrange, and copy slides, as well as to change a presentation's basic components of themes, fonts, and colors.

Navigate and Manipulate Slides

Working with slides enables you to find your way around PowerPoint and to manipulate the slides, both individually and globally. This section addresses how to insert and delete slides, display slides in a variety of ways, and move and duplicate slides.

Navigate from Slide to Slide

You can use the Slide pane, the Outline tab, or the Slides tab to select and move to the slide you want.

- On the Slides tab, click the thumbnail of the slide you want.
- On the Outline tab, click the icon of the slide you want.
- On the Slide pane or Slides and Outline tabs, click the vertical scroll bar **below or above the scroll box** to move to the next or previous slide.
- On the Slide Sorter view, click the vertical scroll bar below the scroll box to move to the next screen of thumbnails. Click the down arrow or up arrow on the scroll bar to move more slowly in increments. Click each slide to select it.

Insert a Slide

You can insert new slides in various ways in several places in PowerPoint. You can also insert slides from other presentations.

INSERT A NEW SLIDE

You can insert a new blank slide from several places in PowerPoint. The most common ways are as follows:

- In the Home tab Slides group, click **New Slide** in the Slides group.
- In the Outline tab, when entering bulleted text, press **CTRL+ENTER**.
- In either the Slides or Outline tab, right-click the slide before the one you want to insert, and click **New Slide**.

–Or–

I03-01.tif - Windows Photo Viewer

NOTE

There is a trick to using **ALT+TAB**. It provides a way to cycle through the windows available on your computer at the moment. So if you are viewing a slide show, pressing **ALT+TAB** will immediately return you to the Normal view. However, if you continue to press **ALT** while you click **TAB**, the selection box will cycle through the windows now open on your computer. When you release the **ALT** button, you'll end up in the selected window.

TIP

Before closing the Reuse Slides task pane, you can browse for other files and insert slides without closing the task pane.

TIP

To delete a slide from the Slide Sorter view, the Outline tab, or the Slides tab, click the thumbnail of the slide to select it, and press **DELETE**. You can also right-click the thumbnail slide and click **Delete Slide** from the context menu. (In the Outline tab, you must click the icon to select it, but right-click on the text.)

● In the Slides or Outline tab, click the slide before the one you want to insert (in the Outline tab, place your insertion point at the end of the slide text), and then press **ENTER**.

● In the Slide Sorter view, right-click the slide preceding the new one, and click **New Slide** or press **CTRL+M**.

INSERT A SLIDE FROM ANOTHER FILE

To insert a slide copied from another presentation into the displayed presentation, you must display the slides from the source presentation and then select the slide or slides that you want to copy to your destination presentation.

1. Open your destination presentation, and click the slide in the Slides tab immediately before the one to be inserted.

2. Click the **Home** tab, and in the Slides group, click the **New Slide** down arrow. From the drop-down menu, click **Reuse Slides** (at the bottom of the menu). The Reuse Slides task pane will be displayed.

3. Click the **Insert Slide From** down arrow, click the name of the source presentation containing the slide to be copied, and then click the right arrow. If your presentation is not on the list, click **Browse** to find the source file. Choose **Browse File** from the menu. Find and select the file you want, and click **Open**. The Reuse Slides task pane, illustrated in Figure 3-1, will contain thumbnails of the presentation.

4. To insert the slides into the presentation, you must work back and forth between the Slides tab (the destination) and the Reuse Slides task pane (the source).

● Scroll to the thumbnail of the image in the Reuse Slides task pane, and click the one you want to insert. It will be inserted when you click it.

● To insert all the slides in the Reuse Slides task pane, right-click a thumbnail and click **Insert All Slides** from the context menu.

● To apply the formatting of the source slides to those in the destination Slides tab, right-click and click **Apply Theme To All Slides** to copy the formatting to all of them, or click **Apply Theme To Selected Slides** to copy the format only to selected destination slides.

● To retain the formatting of the source slides as you copy them, click the **Keep Source Formatting** check box at the bottom of the task pane.

☑ Keep source formatting

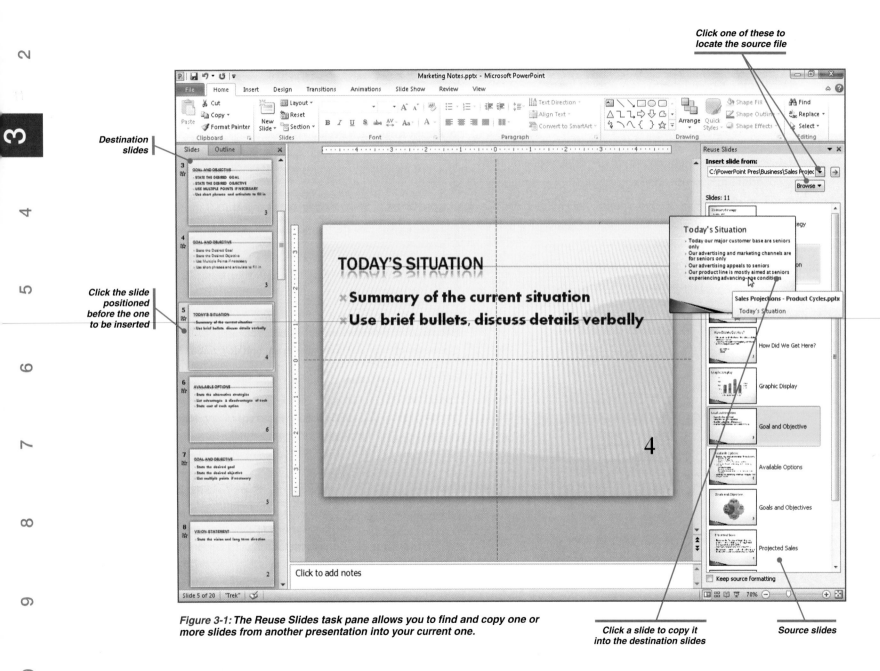

Click one of these to
locate the source file

Destination
slides

Click the slide
positioned
before the one
to be inserted

Click a slide to copy it
into the destination slides

Source slides

Figure 3-1: The Reuse Slides task pane allows you to find and copy one or
more slides from another presentation into your current one.

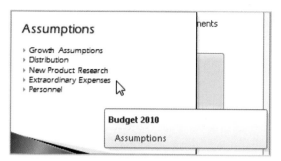

TIP

On the Slide Sorter view, you can click the **Zoom** slider or drag the indicator in the status bar to view more or fewer slides by increasing or decreasing the size of each thumbnail.

TIP

To enlarge one of the presentations so that it occupies the whole window again, click its **Maximize** button.

TIP

Another way to increase or decrease the size of a pane, for example, the Notes pane, is to place the pointer over the border between the Slide pane and the Notes pane, and drag the two-headed arrow icon up or down to increase or decrease a pane, respectively.

- To view a larger image of a slide in the Reuse Slides task pane, place the pointer over the slide thumbnail image but do not click.

5. When you have inserted all the slides you want, click **Close** on the Reuse Slides pane.

Display Multiple Presentations at Once

Opening and displaying two or more presentations offers many possibilities for dragging a slide from one presentation to another, copying color or formatting from one slide or presentation to another, and comparing the presentations or slides side by side.

1. Open multiple presentations by clicking **File** and clicking **Open**, and complete the sequence of locating and opening the presentations.

2. Click the **View** tab, and from the Window group, choose one of the following views:

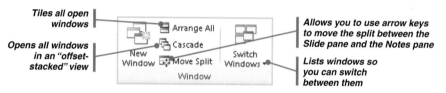

- Click the **Arrange All** button to display a smaller view of each presentation window, such as seen side-by-side in Figure 3-2.

    –Or–

- Click the Cascade button to see the windows stacked on top of each other, as seen in Figure 3-3.

- Click **Move Split** and then press the **UP ARROW** or **DOWN ARROW** key to move the split between the Slide pane and the Notes pane. You can also move the split between the Slides/Outline tabs and the Notes pane by pressing the **RIGHT ARROW** and **LEFT ARROW**. Press **ENTER** or **ESC** to exit the Move Split mode, or just click the slide.

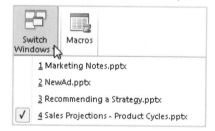

- Click **Switch Windows** to go back and forth between two or more presentations.

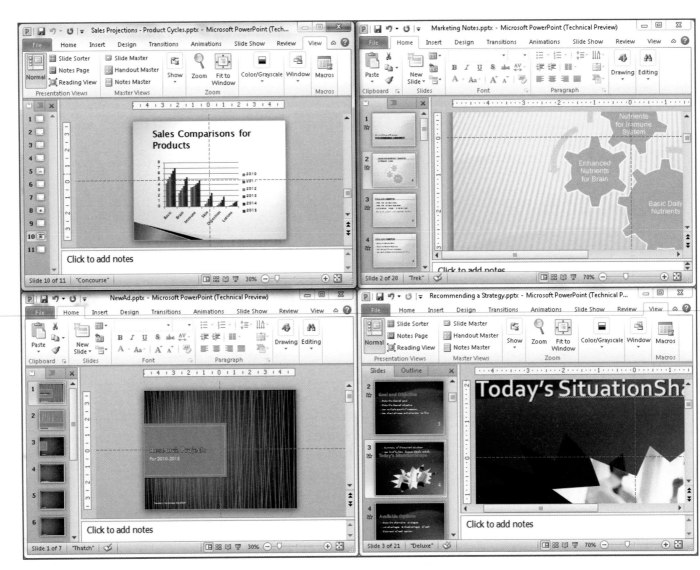

Figure 3-2: You can see each individual window by using the Arrange All command.

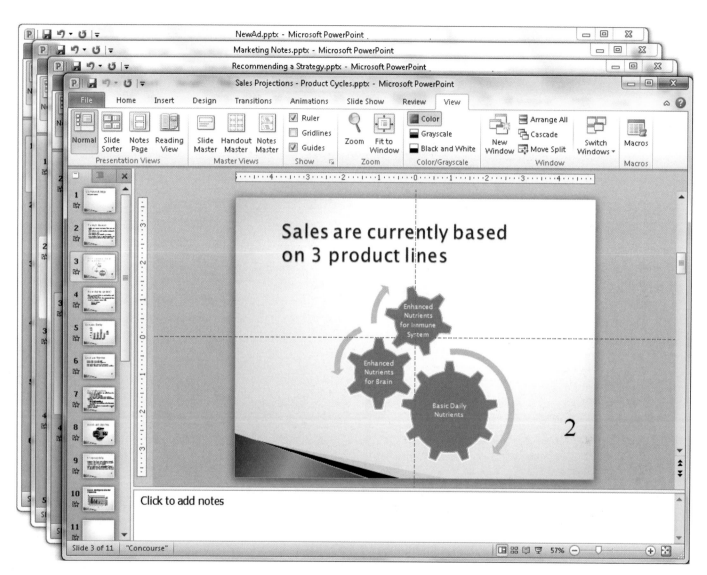

Figure 3-3: Using the Cascade command, you can arrange the presentations in a stacked sequence.

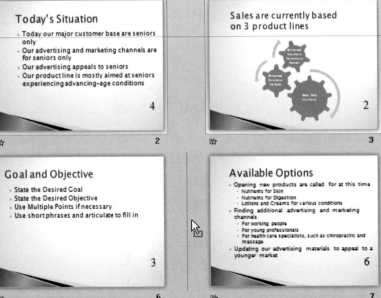

QUICKSTEPS

MOVING OR COPYING SLIDES IN A PRESENTATION

You can move or copy slides most easily from the Outline tab, the Slides tab, or the Slide Sorter view.

- To copy a slide, right-click the slide to be copied, and click **Copy** on the context menu. Right-click the slide preceding where you want the new slide to go, and click **Paste** and then click **Keep Source Formatting** on the context menu.

- To move a slide, click the slide icon or thumbnail to be moved, and drag it to the new location. The insertion point will indicate where the slide will be inserted.

- You can select and drag multiple slides at the same time. To select more than one slide at a time on the Slides tab or the Slide Sorter view, press **SHIFT** if they are contiguous and click the first and last slides. If they are noncontiguous, press **CTRL** and click the thumbnails you want copied. Then, in either case, drag the slides while pressing **CTRL**.

Copy Slides Between Presentations

To copy attributes, such as formatting, color, alignment, fonts, and so on, from one presentation to another, you must first display both presentations in the Slide pane.

1. Open the PowerPoint presentation in Normal view. Click **File** and click **Open**. Choose the source presentation to be opened. Then repeat for the destination presentation.

2. In the View tab Window group, click **Arrange All**. The two presentations will be displayed side-by-side. In the Presentations View group, click **Normal** for both displayed presentations.

3. Select the slide you want to copy. Then right-click and select **Copy** from the context menu.

4. Select the slide before the one to be inserted. Right-click and click **Paste** and then click **Use Destination Theme** to copy just the slide content without the formatting, or click **Paste** and click **Keep Source Format** to copy all the formatting.

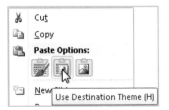

Duplicate a Slide

An alternate way to copy or duplicate a slide uses the Duplicate Slides command. A duplicated slide is an exact copy placed directly after the original slide. You can then drag the slide to where you need it.

- In the Slides tab, select the slide you want to duplicate. Right-click the slide, and click **Duplicate Slide** from the context menu.

- To duplicate multiple selected slides in the Slide Sorter view, the Outline tab, or the Slides tab, select the slides (press **CTRL** while you click the slides to select them; for contiguous slides, you can press **SHIFT** and click the first and last slide in the range), click the **New Slide** down arrow (on the Home tab), and click **Duplicate Selected Slides**.

Copy a Design Using Browse

To copy just the design (and not the content) of a presentation, use the Browse command of the Design Themes feature.

1. In Normal view, open the presentation to which you will apply the design of another presentation.

2. Click the **Design** tab, click the **More** down arrow for the Themes group, and click **Browse For Themes**.

3. In the Choose Theme Or Themed Document dialog box, find the document or presentation containing the theme you want to copy, and click it.

4. Click **Apply**, and the theme will be copied to the original presentation.

Use Zoom

You can zoom in or out of a slide, which enables you to work at a detailed level or back off to see the total slide, respectively.

NOTE

If you have more than one design theme applied to a presentation, the first one will be copied, and if you haven't opened the presentation recently, you will be asked if you want the remaining themes to be made available.

NOTE

To copy rather than move while dragging, on the Slides tab and Slide Sorter view, using the thumbnails, right-click and drag the selected slides to the new location. When you release the pointer, click **Copy** on the context menu that appears.

QUICKSTEPS

WORKING WITH SLIDES USING A KEYBOARD

If you are more comfortable using the keyboard rather than the mouse, several commands are available to you for working with slides. Some of them use a combination of mouse actions and keyboard commands, such as Copy.

START A NEW PRESENTATION

Press **CTRL+N**.

INSERT A NEW SLIDE

Press **ALT**, press **H**, press **I**, and then use the arrow keys to select a layout from the menu. Press **ENTER** when finished.

REMOVE A SLIDE

Press **DELETE** or press **CTRL+X**.

COPY A SLIDE

1. Use the **UP ARROW** and **DOWN ARROW** keys to select the slide to be copied.

2. Press **CTRL+C**.

3. Using the arrow keys on the keyboard, move to the slide positioned immediately before where you want the copied slide to be. Press **CTRL+V**.

CAUTION

When you are inserting a new slide, you need to be careful where you place the insertion point. That will determine where the new slide will be positioned. It's possible to insert a slide into the middle of another one, splitting its contents unintentionally. Make certain you place the insertion point precisely where you want the new slide to go.

- To control the zoom with a specific percentage, click the **View** tab, and click the **Zoom** button in the Zoom group. When the Zoom dialog box appears, click the percentage you want displayed, or use the Percent spinner. A smaller percentage will reduce the image; a larger percentage will increase it. Click **OK** when finished.

- If you have changed the size of the window using Zoom, you can restore its size. Click the **View** tab, and then click the **Fit To Window** button in the Zoom group. The image will be reduced or increased in size to fit in the Slide pane. If you are not in the View tab, a quicker way to do this is to click the **Fit Slide To Current Window** button, located on the right of the status bar.

- To increase or decrease the zoom effect with a slider, drag the **Zoom** slider on the right of the status bar, or click the **Zoom In** or **Zoom Out** button on either side of the slider to zoom in or out in smaller increments. The percentage of the zoom will be shown to the left of the slider.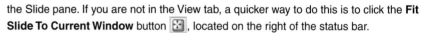

Change the Look and Feel of Slides

At some point, you will likely want to change the look and feel of slides in a presentation. The slides may have been created from another presentation, and you want this one to be unique. You may need to just tweak a few components of the presentation. You can change the theme, color, fonts, and special effects.

Change a Theme

As you learned in Chapter 2, you can select a built-in (or PowerPoint-standard) theme for your slides. These themes themselves can be changed to fit your own presentation requirements. The theme can be changed for a single slide or for the whole presentation by altering the fonts, color, and design elements.

CHANGE THE COLOR OF A THEME

Each theme consists of a set of four colors for text and background, six colors for accents, and two colors for hyperlinks. You can change any single color element

or all of them. When you change the colors, the font styles and design elements remain the same.

1. With your presentation open, click the **Design** tab.

2. If you want to change the theme colors on only some of the slides, select those slides. Hold down **CTRL** and select the noncontiguous slides you want, or hold down **SHIFT** and select the starting and ending contiguous slides you want.

3. In the Themes group, click **Colors**. The menu of color combinations will be displayed, as seen in Figure 3-4.

4. Run the pointer over the rows of color combinations to see which ones appeal to you.

5. When you find the one you want, right-click the row and click **Apply To All Slides** to change the colors throughout the whole presentation, or click **Apply To Selected Slides** to change the colors on selected slides.

CHANGE THEME FONTS

Each theme includes two fonts: The *body* font is used for general text entry, and a *heading* font is used for headings. The default font used in PowerPoint for a new presentation without a theme is Calibri for headings and body text. Once a theme is assigned to slides, the fonts may be different, according to the design of the theme; however, they can be changed.

1. In the Design tab Themes group, click **Fonts**. The drop-down list displays a list of theme fonts.

2. Point to each font combination to see how the fonts will appear in your presentation.

3. Click the font name combination you decide upon. The font will replace both the body and heading fonts in your presentation.

CREATE A NEW SET OF THEME FONTS

You may also decide that you want a unique set of fonts for your presentation. You can create a custom font set that will then be available in the list of fonts for current and future presentations.

1. In the Design tab Themes group, click **Fonts.**

2. Click **Create New Theme Fonts** at the bottom of the drop-down list.

TIP

You may have to drag your text placeholder to the right or left to see the effects of the fonts as you pass your pointer over them.

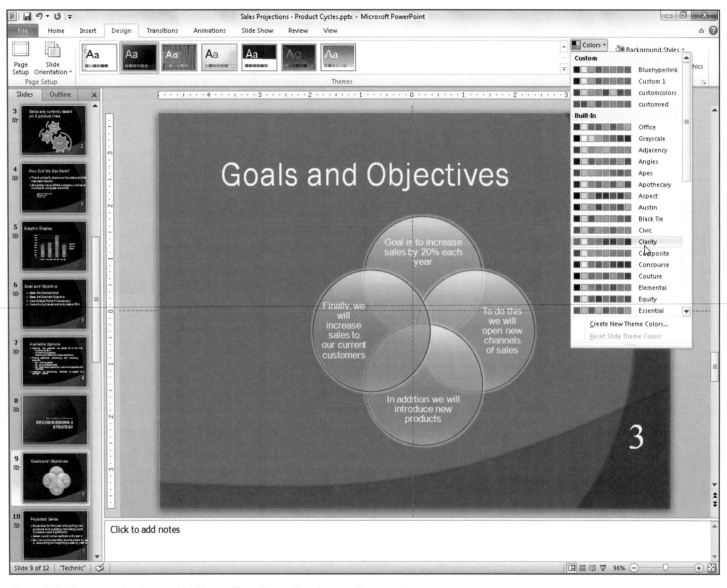

Figure 3-4: *The menu of color combinations offers alternatives for your theme colors.*

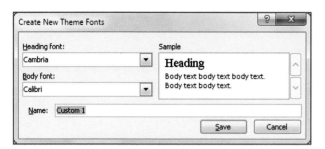

Figure 3-5: *You can choose a heading or body font from the fonts available in your Windows system.*

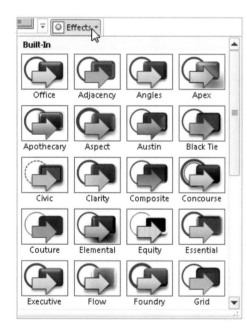

3. In the Create New Theme Fonts dialog box (see Figure 3-5), click either the **Heading Font** and **Body Font** down arrow, or both, to select a new font combination. View the new combination in the Sample area.

4. Type a new name for the font combination you've selected, and click **Save**. Custom fonts are available at the top of the theme Fonts drop-down list.

CHANGE THEMED GRAPHIC EFFECTS

Shapes, illustrations, pictures, and charts include graphic effects that are controlled by themes. Themed graphics are modulated in terms of their lines (borders), fills, and effects (such as shadowed, raised, and shaded). For example, some themes simply change an inserted rectangle's fill color, while other themes affect the color, the weight of the border, and whether it has a 3-D appearance.

1. In the Design tab Themes group, click **Effects**. The drop-down list displays a gallery of effects combinations.

2. Point to each combination to see how the effects will appear on your presentation, assuming you have a graphic or chart inserted on the slide (see Chapters 5, 6, 7, and 8 for information on inserting tables, charts, graphics, and drawings, respectively).

3. Click the effects combination you want.

Create Custom Theme Colors

You can create a new theme, save it, and use it in your presentations. You select a group of text, background, accent, and hyperlink colors and then give them a name.

1. Click the **Design** tab, and then in the Themes group, click **Colors**.

2. At the bottom of the menu of colors, click the **Create New Theme Colors** link. The Create New Theme Colors dialog box will appear; a working example is shown in Figure 3-6.

**Displays a selection of colors
for the named elements**

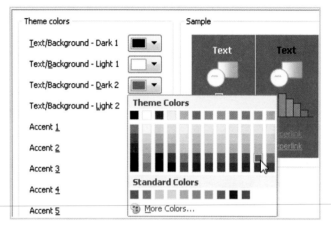

3. To select a color for one of the color groups, click the down arrow for the text/
background, accent, and/or hyperlink group, and then click the color you want
to test. It will be displayed in the Sample area. Notice that in the Theme Colors
gallery, the 12 theme colors are across the first row and there are 5 shades of
each underneath them.

4. Go through each set of colors that you want to change.

5. When you find a group of colors that you like, type a name in the Name text box,
and click **Save**.

USE CUSTOM COLORS

Using a similar technique, you can create your own unique color mix for
text, background colors, accents, and hyperlinks.

**Click to reset the colors
to the original selections**   **Type a name and click Save
to create the custom theme**   **Selected colors
are reflected here**

*Figure 3-6: The Create New Theme Colors dialog box allows
you to create new color themes for use in your presentations.*

1. Select the slides that you want to apply the new colors to.

2. Click the **Design** tab, and click
Colors. At the bottom of the rows
of color combinations, click **Create
New Theme Colors**. The Create New
Theme Colors dialog box will appear.

3. Click the theme color group that you
want to work with. The Theme Colors
submenu will be displayed. Click **More
Colors**.

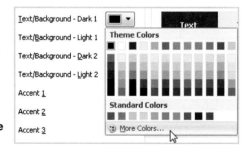

TIP

Click **Reset** to restore the original colors in the Create
New Theme Colors dialog box Sample area and start over.

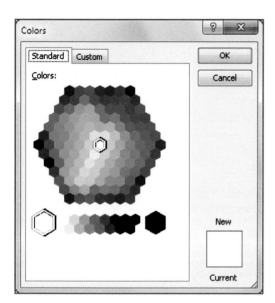

Figure 3-7: *You can precisely change the color by clicking the specific color shade you want.*

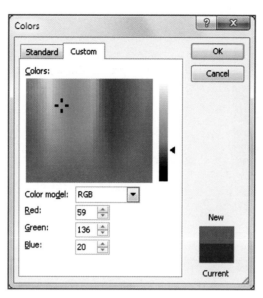

Figure 3-8: *You can create unique colors by "mixing" the combination of red, green, and blue.*

4. In the Colors dialog box, you have two options:

   ● Click the **Standard** tab to see the dialog box shown in Figure 3-7. Click the color unit you want to see displayed in the New preview pane. When you find the color you want to see in the Sample pane of the Create New Theme Colors dialog box, click **OK**.

   ● Click the **Custom** tab to see the dialog box shown in Figure 3-8. Click the approximate color you want on the color rainbow. Then drag the slider to get precisely the color you want. You will see it displayed in the New preview pane. When you find the color you want to see in the Sample pane of the Create New Theme Colors dialog box, click **OK**.

   –Or–

   ● Click the **Red**, **Green**, or **Blue** up arrows or down arrows to get the precise color mix you want. Displayed is the RGB color standard (Red, Green, Blue) color, but you can also select the HSL color standard (Hue, Saturation, and Luminosity). When you are finished, click **OK**.

5. When you have the colors you want, type a name in the Name text box, and click **Save**.

CHANGE THE BACKGROUND STYLE

You can change the slide background on one or all slides in a presentation. When you change the background style after you have a theme already assigned to the slides in your presentation, the design elements from the theme will remain—only the background color or shading changes.

1. If you want only some of the slides changed, select the ones to which you want to apply a new background style.

You may find you want to change something in a custom theme after you've been using it for a while. To edit a custom theme in Normal view, click the **Colors** button in the Design tab Themes group, and right-click the custom theme you want to edit. From the context menu, click **Edit**. The Edit Theme Colors dialog box, similar to that shown in Figure 3-6, will be displayed.

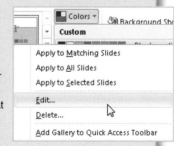

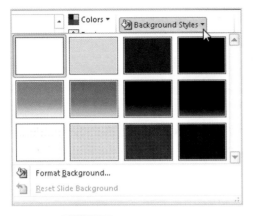

2. Click the **Design** tab, and in the Background group, click **Background Styles**. A menu of styles is displayed.

3. Run your pointer over the thumbnails to see which ones appeal to you. As you do this, the slide in the Slide pane will reflect the selection.

4. When you find the style you want, click it to change all the slides. Or right-click the thumbnail, and click **Apply To Selected Slides** to change only the selected slides. The menu will close, and the slides in the presentation will be changed.

Save a Custom Theme

If you have worked on a presentation, customizing it to meet your own needs, you can save it as a custom theme, preserving the theme elements and making it available to you in the Themes group gallery.

1. With your custom theme open, click the **Design** tab.

2. Click the **More** button for the Themes group, and click **Save Current Theme.**

3. In the Save Current Theme dialog box, type the name you want for the theme, and click **Save**.

NOTE

See Chapter 8 for information on how to create gradient backgrounds, insert patterns or textures, or insert a picture into the background using fill effects.

QUICKSTEPS

USING FOOTERS ON SLIDES

To work with any aspect of footers, you need to display the Header And Footer dialog box (shown in Figure 3-9). (Headers are available for Notes and Handouts only— see Chapter 4.) To display and use this dialog box:

1. Select the slide or slides that need footers.

2. Click the **Insert** tab, and click **Header & Footer** in the Text group.

3. Click the **Slide** tab for footers.

4. When you have finished making your selections, described next, click **Apply** to apply the choices to selected slides only, or click **Apply To All** to apply the choices to all slides. *Continued . . .*

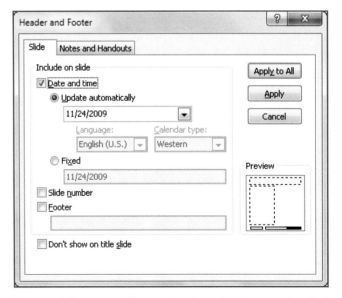

Figure 3-9: You can add footers to selected slides or to the whole presentation.

DISPLAY THE TIME OR DATE

You must first display the Header And Footer dialog box, as described in the preceding section, and then click the **Date And Time** check box.

- To apply a time or date that always reflects the actual time and date, click **Update Automatically**. From the drop-down list box, click the date only, time only, or time and date format you prefer.

- To apply a fixed time or date or other text, click **Fixed**. In the Fixed text box, type the text that will always appear in the footer.

ENTER A FOOTER

After displaying the Header And Footer dialog box:

1. Click the **Footer** check box.

2. In the Footer text box, type the text for the footer.

ENTER A SLIDE NUMBER

In the Header And Footer dialog box, click the **Slide Number** check box to place a check mark in it.

HIDE THE FOOTER ON THE TITLE PAGE

Once you have displayed the Header And Footer dialog box, click the **Don't Show On Title Slide** check box if you don't want the footer displayed on the title page.

REMOVE FOOTERS

Once you have displayed the Header And Footer dialog box:

1. Clear the **Date And Time**, **Slide Number**, and **Footer** check boxes.

2. To remove the footer for selected slides, click **Apply**; to remove the footer for all slides, click **Apply To All**.

☑ Date and time
◉ Update automatically
11/1/2009
11/1/2009
Sunday, November 01, 2009
1 November 2009
November 1, 2009
1-Nov-09
November 09
Nov-09
11/1/2009 6:39 PM
11/1/2009 6:39:59 PM
18:39
18:39:59
6:39 PM
6:39:59 PM

☑ Footer
CONFIDENTIAL

☑ Don't show on title slide

Copy Attributes with Format Painter

The Format Painter can be used to copy all attributes (such as font, alignment, bullet style, and color) from one slide to another, as well as from one presentation to another.

To copy text and graphic attributes between slides:

1. Display the source slide in the Slides tab or Slide Sorter view. Copy the object containing the attributes to be copied, such as the text or graphic.

2. Click the **Home** tab. Click **Format Painter** 〈 Format Painter 〉 in the Clipboard group once to copy the source format to one slide. If you want to use the source slide to reformat several slides, double-click **Format Painter** to turn it on until you click it again to turn it off (or press **ESC**).

3. Find the destination slide in either the same or different presentation, and select the text (drag over it) or graphic (click it) that will receive the new attributes.

4. If you are copying the source attributes to multiple slides, continue to select destination text or graphics on the slides.

5. When you are finished, click **Format Painter** to turn it off or press **ESC**.

Work with Hyperlinks

Inserting hyperlinks in a presentation allows you to link to other files or presentations, to a Web site, to an e-mail address, or to another slide within the current presentation.

INSERT A HYPERLINK

To insert a hyperlink in the presentation:

1. On your slide in the Slide pane or Outline tab, highlight the text by dragging the pointer over the characters that you want to contain the hyperlink.

2. Click the **Insert** tab, and in the Links group, click the **Hyperlink** button.

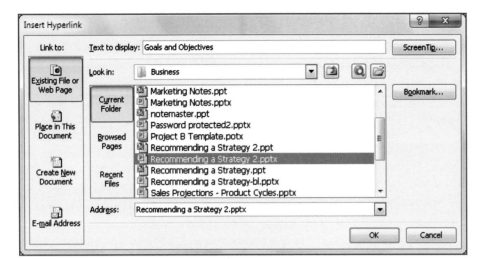

3. In the Insert Hyperlink dialog box, find the destination for the link.

- If the destination is within the presentation itself, click **Place In This Document**, and click the destination slide.

- If the destination is on an existing document or Web page, click **Existing File Or Web Page**, as seen in Figure 3-10, and follow the prompts to the destination.

- If you must create a new document for the hyperlink to point to, click **Create New Document**, and proceed as directed.

- If you want to place a hyperlink to an e-mail address, click **E-mail Address**.

4. Click **OK**.

Figure 3-10: Hyperlinks can provide a means to "jump" from one part of a presentation to another slide, presentation, Web page, or e-mail address.

REMOVE A HYPERLINK

To remove a hyperlink from text or an object in the Slide pane:

1. Right-click the text or object containing the hyperlink.

2. Click **Remove Hyperlink** from the context menu.

CHANGE A HYPERLINK COLOR

To change the color of hyperlinks in a presentation:

1. Highlight the link to be changed.

2. Click the **Design** tab, and click the **Colors** button on the Themes group.

3. At the bottom of the list of color combinations, click **Create New Theme Colors**. The Create New Theme Colors dialog box will appear with your current theme's color selected in each of the sets.

4. Click the hyperlink color you want to change to open the colors gallery (click **Hyperlink** to change the color for unused links and click **Followed Hyperlink** for links that were previously used), and click the new color.

5. Type a name for the custom theme color, and click **Save** to make the change to the hyperlinks in the presentation. Your changed color will be applied to the links in your presentation, and a custom theme color will be listed in the Theme Color list. By default, it will be named "Custom 1," unless you rename it. (Subsequent saved custom changes will be named using sequential numbers.) Click anywhere on the current slide.

TIP

To remove both the text and the hyperlink, select the text and press **DELETE**.

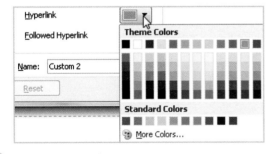

NOTE

The hyperlink only works in Slide Show view.

Compare and Merge Presentations

A new feature in PowerPoint 2010 allows you to compare two presentations, one designed to contain the merged changes. This is useful, for instance, when you have a presentation that has been reviewed by others and you want to select and merge desired edits. You compare changes slide by slide, seeing what is different between the slides and accepting those from the secondary file to be merged onto the designated presentation.

1. In PowerPoint, open the slide show containing the slides to be updated. This file will contain the merge results.

2. On the Review tab, click **Compare** in the Compare group. The Choose File To Merge With Current Presentation dialog box appears.

3. Find the presentation containing the changed slides, and click **Merge**. The Compare view will be displayed (see Figure 3-11). Also, when you have done this, more of the commands in the Compare group become available.

4. You have these options:

   - Click **Slides** on the Revisions pane to see the slide being compared.

   - Click the **Revision** icons to see the list of changes to a slide. Place a check mark next to the changes you want to retain and merge into the primary file. If you change your mind, you can clear the check box and restore the original.

   - Once you have identified those changes you want to merge, click **Accept** in the Compare group. If you want to reject them, click **Reject**.

   - Click **Previous** and **Next** in the Compare group to see the previous and next slide with changes, respectively.

   - Click **Reviewing Pane** to toggle the pane on and off.

5. When you are finished with the merge, click **End Review** and save your file. Click **Yes** to verify that you do indeed want to end the compare.

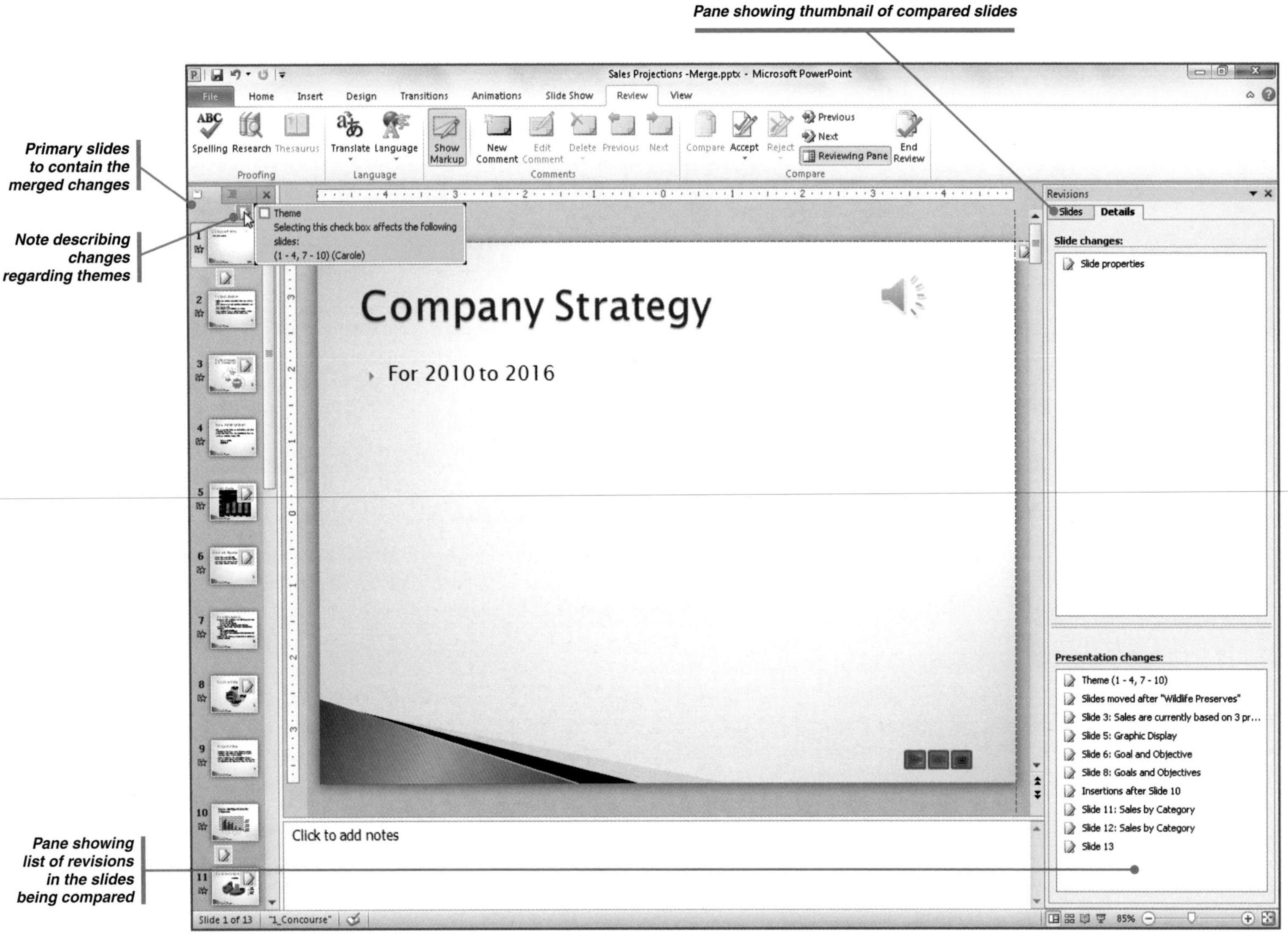
Pane showing thumbnail of compared slides
Primary slides to contain the merged changes
Note describing changes regarding themes
Pane showing list of revisions in the slides being compared
Sales Projections -Merge.pptx - Microsoft PowerPoint
File
Home
Insert
Design
Transitions
Animations
Slide Show
Review
View
Spelling
Research
Thesaurus
Translate
Language
Show Markup
New Comment
Edit Comment
Delete
Previous
Next
Compare
Accept
Reject
Previous
Next
Reviewing Pane
End Review
Proofing
Language
Comments
Compare
Theme
Selecting this check box affects the following slides:
(1 - 4, 7 - 10) (Carole)
Company Strategy
For 2010 to 2016
Click to add notes
Revisions
Slides
Details
Slide changes:
Slide properties
Presentation changes:
Theme (1 - 4, 7 - 10)
Slides moved after "Wildlife Preserves"
Slide 3: Sales are currently based on 3 pr...
Slide 5: Graphic Display
Slide 6: Goal and Objective
Slide 8: Goals and Objectives
Insertions after Slide 10
Slide 11: Sales by Category
Slide 12: Sales by Category
Slide 13
Slide 1 of 13
"1_Concourse"
85%

***Figure 3-11:** Compare allows you to compare slides from two presentations and select which changes should be merged with the primary presentation.*

Chapter 4
Working with Notes, Masters, and Slide Text

This chapter covers three important features that make a presentation more effective: notes, slide masters, and slide text. Using notes for preparing speaker and handout notes allows you to fully prepare a presentation so that you remember all you wanted to say and so that the audience remembers your important points as well. Slide masters allow you to make changes to your presentations that are reflected on each slide or on only some of them.

This chapter also addresses how to work with text, from selecting a layout or inserting a placeholder, to modifying text by editing, positioning, moving, copying, and deleting it. The Office Clipboard is covered, as is checking the spelling of standard and foreign languages. Special features, like AutoFit and AutoCorrect, are also discussed.

Work with Notes

Notes are used to create speaker notes that aid a speaker during a presentation and to create handouts given to the audience so that it can follow the presentation easily. The notes do not appear on the slides during a slide show presentation; they are only visible for the presenter's benefit.

Create a Note

To create speaker notes, which can also be used as handouts, you can either use the Notes pane in Normal view (as shown in Figure 4-1) or the Notes Page (shown in Figures 4-2 and 4-3). In both views, you can see a thumbnail of the slide with your notes pertaining to it. Each slide has its own Notes Page. You can also add charts, graphs, or pictures to the notes. To add or change attributes or text to all notes in a presentation, make changes to the notes master.

Create a Note in the Notes Page

1. To open the Notes Page, click the **View** tab, and in the Presentation Views group, click **Notes Page**. The Notes Page opens, as shown in Figure 4-2.

2. To increase the size of the notes area, click the **View** tab, and in the Zoom group, click **Zoom**.

3. Click the zoom magnification you want, and click **OK**.

4. To move to another slide, click the scroll bar.

Preview and Print Speaker Notes and Handouts

Speaker notes and handouts are printed in a similar way. However, the Notes Page prints an image of one slide plus its notes, and a printed handout contains a variable number of thumbnail slides on a page, an example of which is shown in Figure 4-3.

Zoom

Zoom to
- ⦿ Fit   Percent: 77 %
- ○ 400%
- ○ 200%
- ○ 100%
- ○ 66%
- ○ 50%
- ○ 33%

OK   Cancel

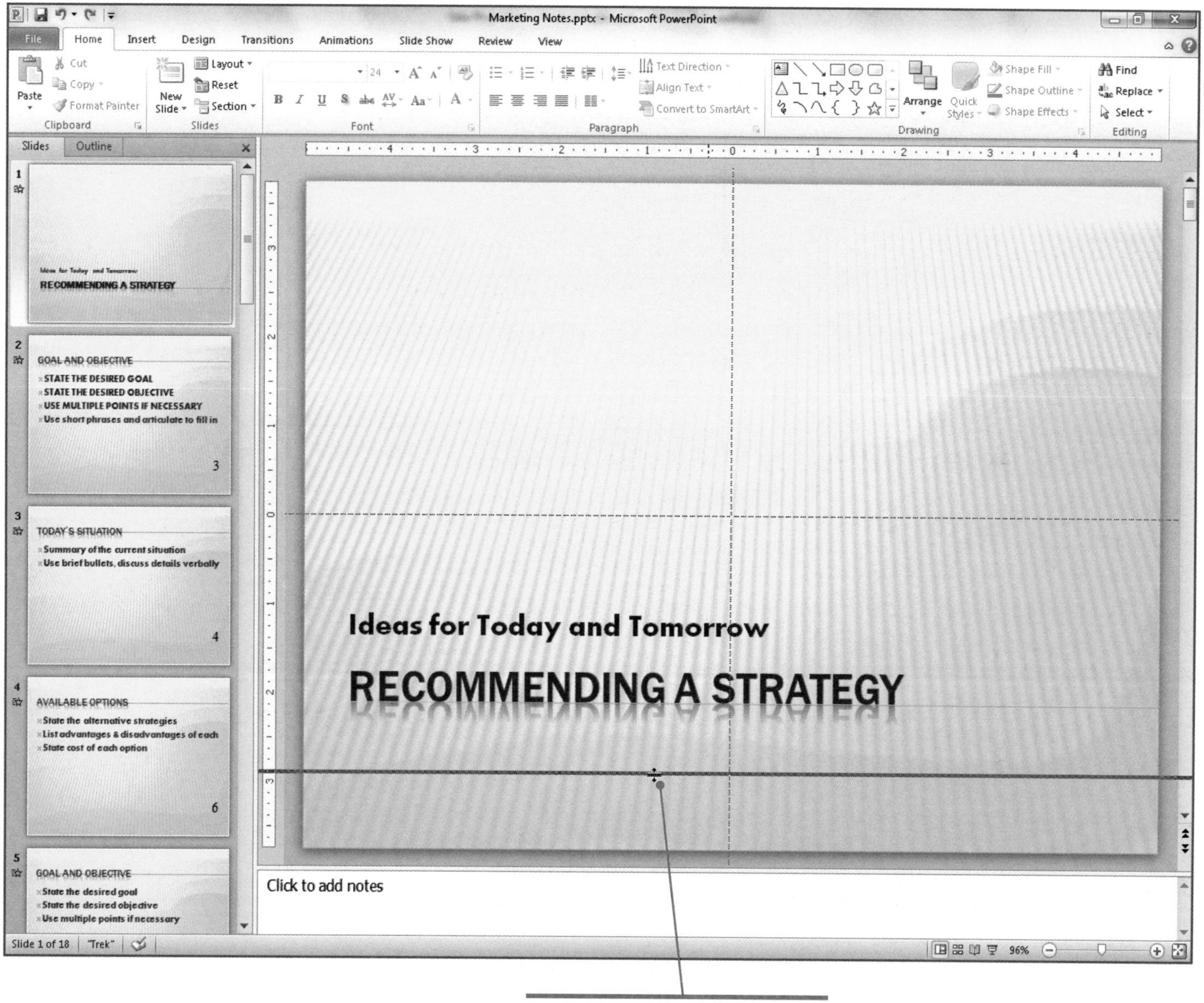

Drag the border to enlarge the Notes pane

Figure 4-1: In the Notes pane of the Normal view, you can expand the area where you add your notes by dragging the border of the Notes pane upward to increase its size.

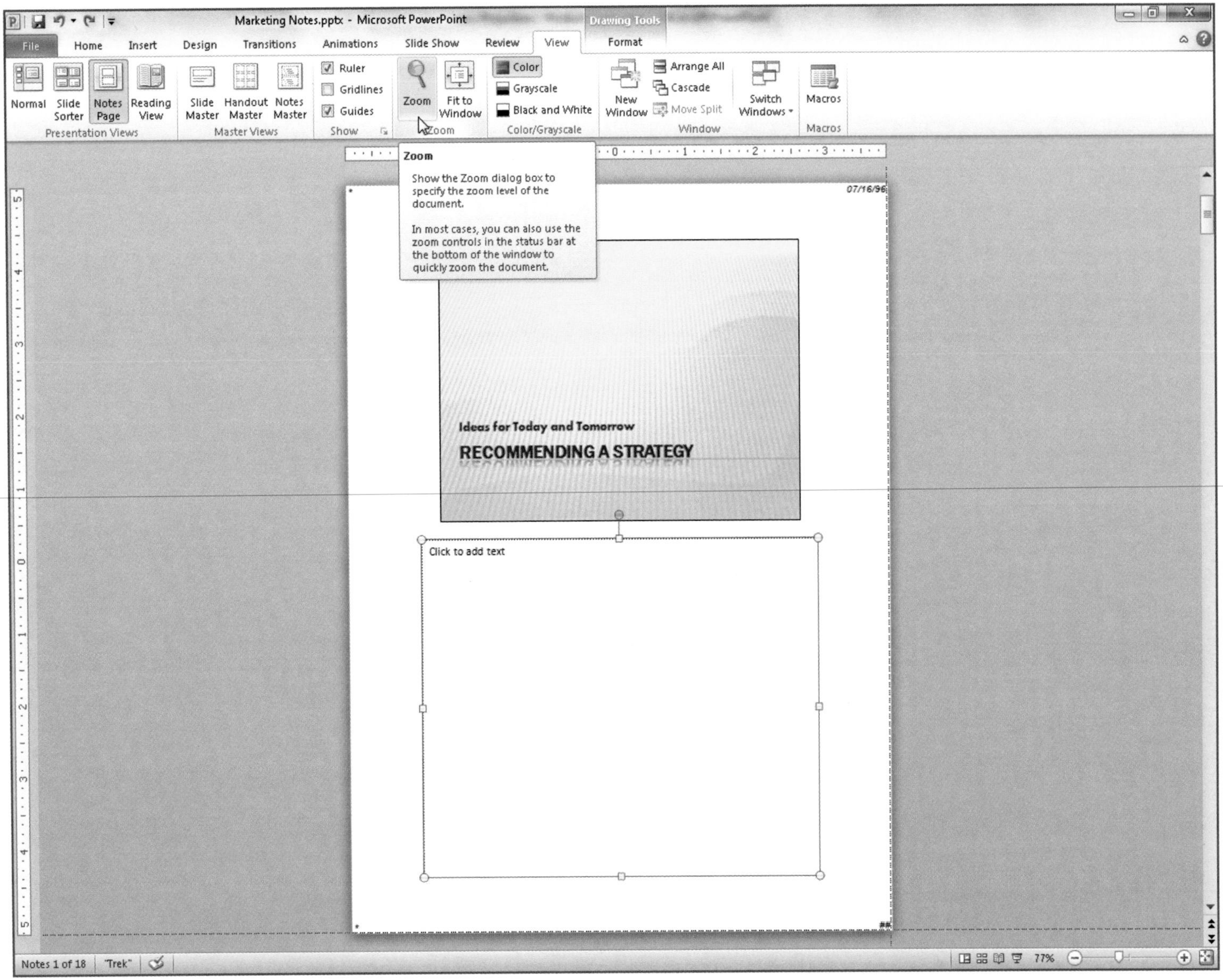

Figure 4-2: The Notes Page displays what the printout will look like before entering your notes and allows you to zoom in on the image to have more room for editing.

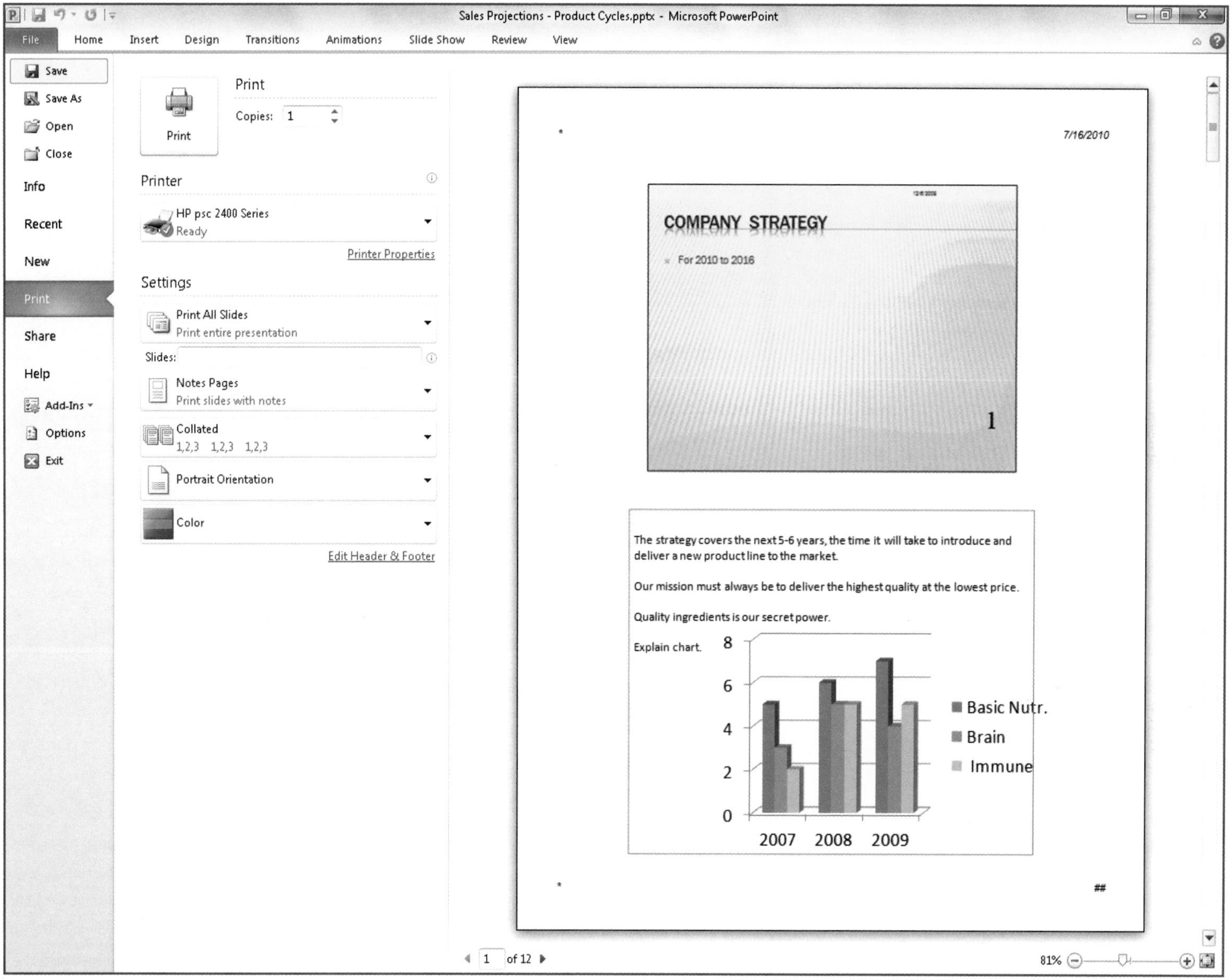

Figure 4-3: A printed handout contains thumbnails of slides and allows you to select the number of slides displayed on a page.

UICKSTEPS

USING HEADERS AND FOOTERS ON NOTES AND HANDOUTS

To put headers and footers on notes and handouts:

1. Click the **View** tab, and in the Presentation Views group, click **Notes Page**.

2. Click the **Insert** tab, and then click **Header & Footer** in the Text group.

3. Click the **Notes And Handouts** tab. The Header And Footer dialog box, shown in Figure 4-4, appears.

4. Choose any of the following items by placing a check mark next to them:

   - To include a date or time in the header, click **Date And Time**, and choose between **Update Automatically**, for a time/date that updates according to the current date, or **Fixed**, for a time/date or other text that remains the same each time it is printed.

   - Click **Header**, click in the text box, and type the header text for notes and handouts.

   - Click **Page Number** to place a page number on the note or handout page.

   - Click **Footer,** click in the text box, and type footer text.

5. Click **Apply To All**.

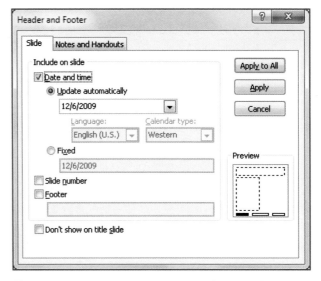

Figure 4-4: *You can create a header and footer to display on note and handout pages.*

To preview your notes:

1. Select the slides to be printed.

2. Click the **File** tab `File`, and click **Print**. The Print view appears.

3. Under Settings, set one of these options, depending on whether you're printing notes or handouts:

   - To print Notes, click the second drop-down list, as pointed to in Figure 4-4, and click **Notes Pages**. The preview pane, shown in Figure 4-5, displays the slide and notes as they will be printed.

   - To print Handouts, click the second drop-down list and select one of the options under Handouts, depending on how many slides you want to show per page. The Preview pane displays the number of slides you have selected.

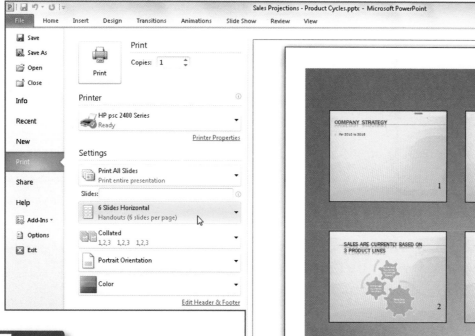

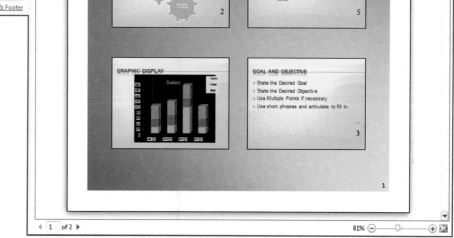

✓ Frame Slides

Figure 4-5: The Print window displays a preview of the speaker notes with the accompanying slide to view what will be printed.

QUICKSTEPS

WORKING WITH SLIDE MASTERS

You can duplicate masters, create title masters that vary from the other masters, protect your masters from being accidentally or intentionally changed, or create multiple new title and slide masters. To view the slide master, click the **View** tab, and click **Slide Master**.

DUPLICATE A SLIDE MASTER

To duplicate a slide master:

- Right-click the master slide thumbnail to be duplicated. It may be a master slide or a layout master slide. The options on the context menu will vary depending on the type of master you select.

- For a slide master, click **Duplicate Slide Master**. The slide master and all the sets of layouts it carries will be duplicated.

| Duplicate Slide Master |
| Delete Master |

- For a layout master, click **Duplicate Layout**, and just the layout master will be duplicated.

| Duplicate Layout |
| Delete Layout |

CREATE A TITLE MASTER

To make the format of your title page different from the rest of your slides, create a title master to contain its unique formatting or design elements.

1. Click the layout thumbnail immediately beneath the slide master in the Slides tab. This is normally the title layout master.

2. Click in the title placeholder, and type and format your title. Enter a subtitle if necessary.

3. Insert a logo or other graphic by clicking the **Insert** tab and clicking the type of graphic you want. Follow the prompts to find what you want.

Continued . . .

4. You have these other Settings options:

- Choose **Print All Slides**, **Print Selection**, **Print Current Slide**, or **Custom Range** to enter the slide numbers for specific slides or slide ranges.

- Choose whether you'll print one side of a page or both sides, and if both, whether the printout will flip on the top of the document or the side.

- Choose whether to collate or not collate the document.

- Choose the orientation of the document—Portrait is vertically aligned, Landscape is horizontally aligned.

- Choose **Color**, **Grayscale**, or **Pure Black And White**.

- Under Print Settings at the top of the pane, enter the number of copies.

5. Click **Print** to print the notes or handouts, and then click **File** to return to the previous page.

Work with Slide, Notes, and Handout Masters

Working with masters gives you an opportunity to change a presentation globally. This is desirable when you have a large number of slides and making changes to all the slides would be laborious and subject to error. Another good use of master slides is when you need more than one theme for a presentation. PowerPoint gives you a set of master slides for slides, notes, and handouts for each theme. In the set of masters, the slide master controls the slides of a presentation; the notes master controls the global aspects of notes; and the handout master controls the handouts. Notes and handout masters are not automatically created: they are only created if you want to use global attributes for them.

Manage Slide Appearance

A presentation has a *slide master* containing formatting and other design elements that apply to all slides in a presentation (or to a set of slides with the same "look"). Usually associated with that slide master are several *layout masters* that

WORKING WITH SLIDE MASTERS

(Continued)

RETAIN A SLIDE MASTER

To retain a set of slide masters within the presentation even if they are not being used, use the Preserve Master button.

1. Right-click the main slide master (the No.1 slide in the set) to be protected.

2. From the context menu, click **Preserve Master** to protect the selected master. You will see gray thumbtacks or pushpins beside the master thumbnail slide.

apply to other slides in a presentation. The title slide, for example, has a layout master for unique positioning of page components, formatting, headings, and design elements. The slide master may get its specific formatting from a theme template that you used, and you can change the master without changing the original template. This is one way that you can customize your presentation even after using a suggested theme to get you going. The original theme is not changed—only the theme as it is in your presentation. It becomes a custom theme.

EDIT A SLIDE MASTER OR MASTER LAYOUT

In a set of slide masters is one slide master that sets the standards for all slides in the presentation. Editing a slide master changes all the slides to which it applies. The set of associated layout masters, about 12 of them, will, by default, carry the slide master's theme and other formatting. The layout masters are specific to a type of layout that might be part of the presentation. For example, you might have one particular layout for all slides containing graphs. Another example for a specific type of layout is the title layout master. A layout master usually carries the same color, design elements, and formatting as the theme assigned to a master slide. You can change particular layouts to be different from the slide master, and then the overall theme will become a custom theme. A presentation can have more than one set of masters, each carrying specifications for different themes.

1. Click the **View** tab, and in the Master Views group, click **Slide Master**. The slide master is displayed (see Figure 4-6).

2. Add headings or subheadings and dates or slide numbers. Add graphics, another or modified theme, or background color. Add headers or footers or other elements of the master, just as you would a normal slide. Editing and formatting changes you can make include:

   • To change the overall font style, click the first thumbnail to select the slide master. Either click the placeholder for the text you want to change or highlight the actual heading or body text. Use the tools in the mini toolbar to modify your text—for example, Font for the font face. See the "Changing Font Attributes in Master Slides" QuickSteps.

   • To change the bullets for bulleted text, click the placeholder containing the bullets to select them all, or select a specific level of bullet to change that level and its child bullet levels. Click the **Home** tab, and in the Paragraph group, click the **Bullets** down arrow, and click the style of bullets you like. You can point at each

Use the slide master to set fonts for the presentation

The title layout master establishes the title, a logo (optional), and any other text you want on the title slide

Layout masters give you standards for presentation or custom layouts

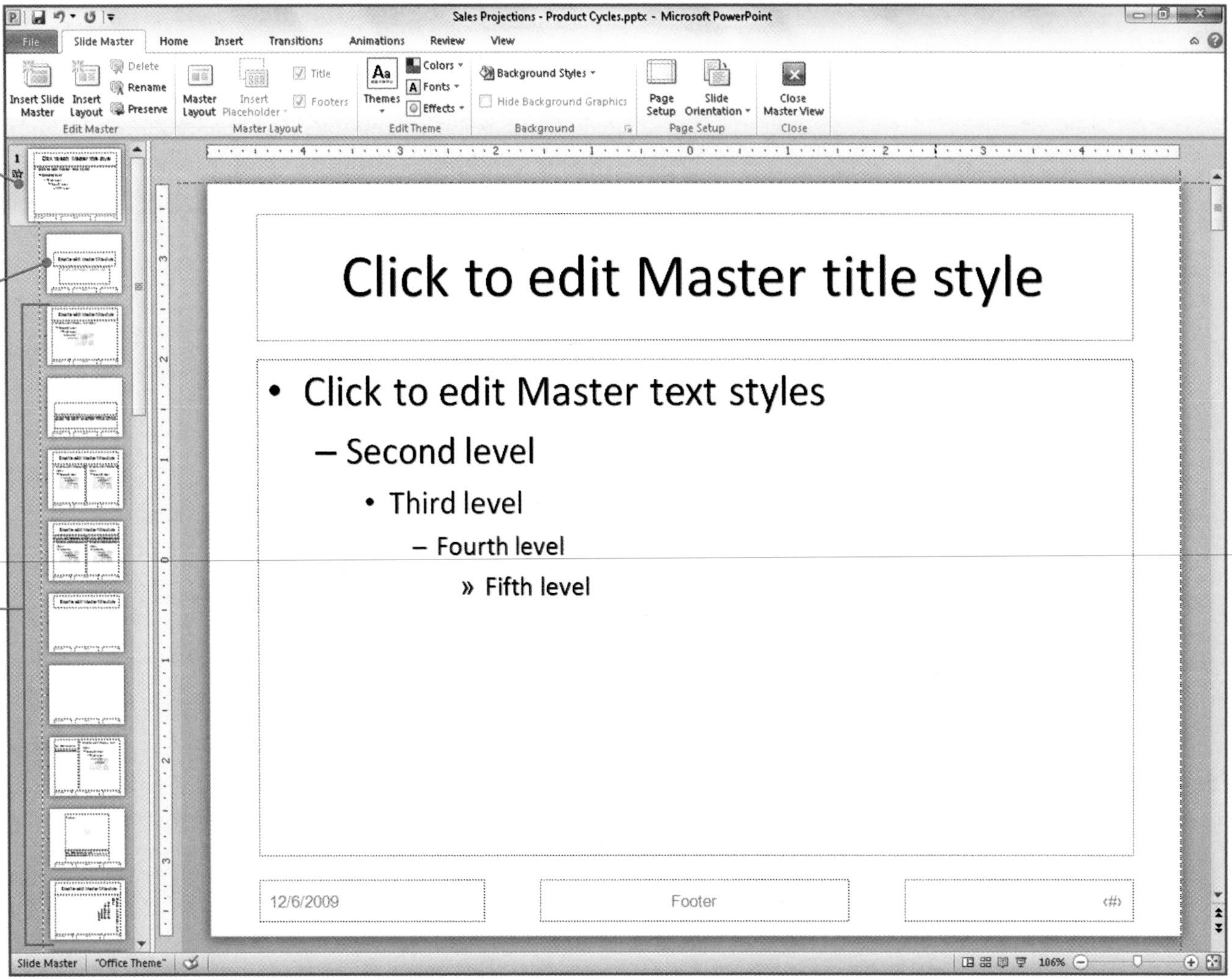

Click to edit Master title style

- Click to edit Master text styles
  - Second level
    - Third level
      - Fourth level
        » Fifth level

12/6/2009 | Footer | ‹#›

Figure 4-6: The masters for a new presentation contain a slide master (no. 1) and several layout slides, with the default "Office Theme."

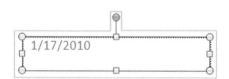

bullet type to see the results in the background master slide. See the "Using Lists" QuickSteps for additional information on how to change the appearance of bullets.

- To insert a picture as a bullet, click **Bullets And Numbering** on the bottom of the list to display a dialog box. Click the **Bulleted** tab, click **Picture**, and click the bullet picture you want. To insert a new picture, click **Import** and then find the picture you want. Click **OK** on the Picture Bullet dialog box.

- To change the appearance of numbers for numbered lists, double-click the placeholder containing the numbered lists. Click the **Numbering** down arrow in the Paragraph group, and click the style of numbers you like. You can point at each item in the list to see the results in the background master slide. To use a size or color that isn't in the menu of choices, click **Bullets And Numbering** on the bottom of the list to display a dialog box. Click the **Numbered** tab, and click the **Size** spinner to increase or decrease the size. Click **Start At** to reset the beginning number. Click the **Color** down arrow to select a new color for the set of numbers. Click **OK** to close the Bullets And Numbering dialog box.

- To change the date and time, footer, and slide number, you can either type directly into the master slide, or click the **Insert** tab and select **Header & Footer** in the Text group. To use the placeholders directly, just click in the placeholder and type the words or date format you want. To use the dialog box, where you can select the format from a menu (such as a different date format), refer to the "Using Headers and Footers on Notes and Handouts" QuickSteps earlier in this chapter. To change the font for the time or date, click a text placeholder to select it (you may have to click directly on the placeholder text to select it, such as on <date/time> in the Date Area placeholder). Then click the **Home** tab, and in the Font group, click the **Font** or **Font Size** down arrow, and select the font or size you want from the drop-down list.

CREATE MULTIPLE SLIDE AND LAYOUT MASTERS

Multiple slide masters and their associated sets of layout masters are used in a presentation to create different looks in layout or formatting for different sections of the presentation.

To create additional new slide masters:

1. Click the **View** tab, and click **Slide Master**.

2. Right-click the slide master, and click **Duplicate Slide Master**. A new set containing a slide master and its associated layout masters will be added to the master slides.

Duplicate Slide Master
Delete Master

TIP

When you apply a new theme to a presentation, slide masters are automatically created.

NOTE

When multiple themes are used to create more than one section in order to create multiple "looks" for the presentation, a set of slide masters will be automatically created for each section. You can then modify the masters as needed to create an even more unique look.

CHANGING FONT ATTRIBUTES IN MASTER SLIDES

You can change font attributes either by changing the fonts using the Home tab, Font and Paragraph group tools, explained in Chapter 2, or by applying WordArt styles to title text, explained here. WordArt adds artistic flair and professionalism to a presentation.

EDIT TEXT

When you edit text in a slide master, you use the normal editing tools.

1. First, select the text or placeholder text in the master slide to be changed. The mini toolbar, shown in Figure 4-7, will be displayed.

2. Move the pointer over the toolbar to make it clear as the image can be vague, fading into the background.

3. Click the tools you need to change your text.

You can also click the Home tab and use the Font and Paragraph tools found there.

CHANGE WORDART

You can convert text to WordArt styles. When you double-click a text or title placeholder, the Drawing Tools Format tab becomes available. On it are the WordArt styles that can be applied to selected placeholders or text.

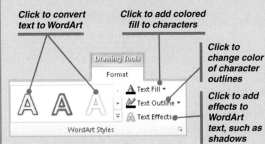

Click to convert text to WordArt

Click to add colored fill to characters

Click to change color of character outlines

Click to add effects to WordArt text, such as shadows

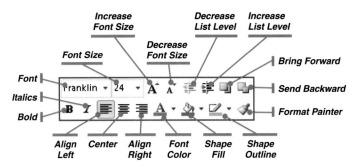

Figure 4-7: This group of text-editing commands can be found on the Home tab and Master editing mini toolbar.

3. Click the **Slide Master** tab to make any changes or incorporate different design templates to the new masters as needed. Click other tabs as needed, such as the Home tab for the formatting tools.

4. Click the **Slide Master** tab, and then click **Close Master View** in the Close group to close the Slide Master view.

Work with the Notes Master

To make global changes to all notes in a presentation, use the notes master. Here you can add a logo or other graphics, change the positioning of page components, change formats, and add headings and text design elements for all notes.

1. Click the **View** tab, and click **Notes Master**. The notes master will be displayed, as shown in Figure 4-8.

2. To adjust the zoom so that you can see the notes area better, click the **View** tab, and click **Zoom**. Choose the magnification and click **OK**. Or use the zoom controls on the bottom of the window.

3. You can change the notes master as follows:

   • Change the formatting of the text elements, such as font size or style, or change the bullets or indents.

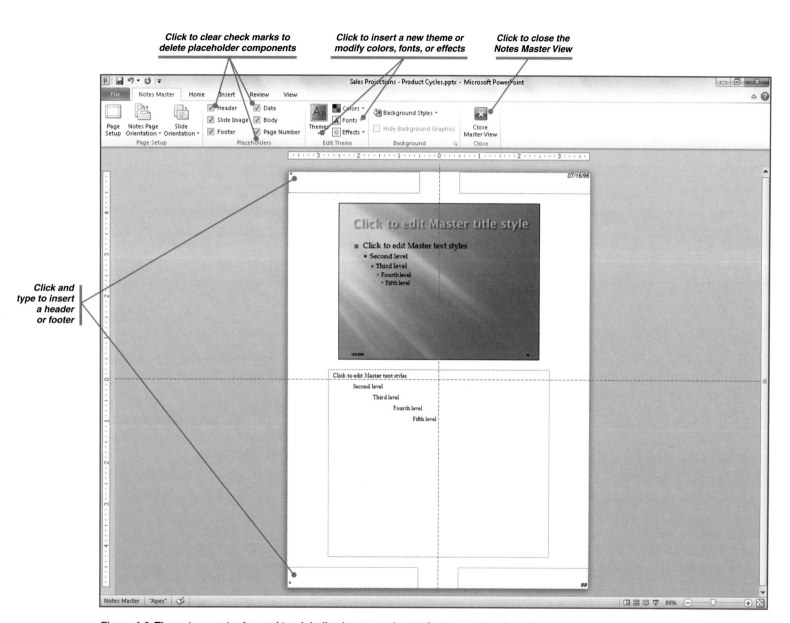

Click to clear check marks to delete placeholder components

Click to insert a new theme or modify colors, fonts, or effects

Click to close the Notes Master View

Click and type to insert a header or footer

Figure 4-8: The notes master is used to globally change such note features as headers, footers, logos, or graphics; note text formatting; and placement of note elements.

- Drag the position of the slide or note text placeholder (the dotted box) to a different location by placing the pointer over the border until you see a four-headed arrow and then dragging.

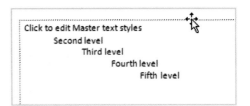

- Change the size of the slide or note text placeholder by clicking the border and then placing the pointer over a placeholder handle until you see a two-headed arrow and then dragging the border of the placeholder to resize it.

- Add a logo by clicking the **Insert** tab and clicking the **Picture**, **Shapes**, **Clip Art**, or other graphic button. Resize the graphic as needed, and drag it where you want it to appear on all notes.

- Add text that will appear on all notes, such as page number, date, or title.

4. Click the **Notes Master** tab, and then click **Close Master View** in the Close group to close the notes master.

Change the Handout Master

Handouts display thumbnails of the slides on a printed page. You can have one, two, three, four, six, or nine slides per page. To prepare your handouts for printing with titles and other formatting, use the handout master.

1. Click the **View** tab, and click **Handout Master**. The handout master will be displayed, as shown in Figure 4-9.

2. On the Handout Master tab, in the Page Setup group, click **Slides Per Page** to set the number of slides to be displayed in the handout: one, two, three, four, six, or nine, or the slide outline.

3. Make the following changes to the handout master as needed:

- Click **Page Setup** in the Page Setup group to set the slide size, initial numbering of slides, and orientation of slides and notes, handouts, and outline.

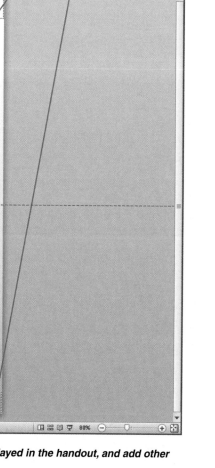

Figure 4-9: The handout master allows you to add titles for handouts, vary the number of slides displayed in the handout, and add other text or objects as needed.

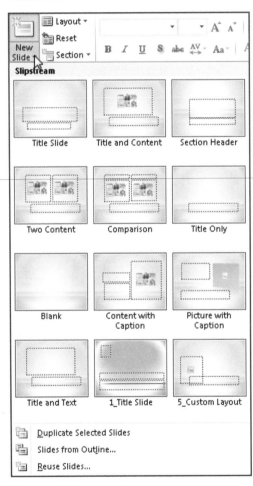

Figure 4-10: You can choose among several standard layouts containing text boxes.

- Click **Handout Orientation** in the Page Setup group to give the handout a portrait or landscape orientation.
- Click **Slide Orientation** in the Page Setup group to give the slides on the handout a portrait or landscape orientation
- Click **Header**, **Date**, **Footer**, or **Page Number** in the Placeholders group to remove the check marks if you do not want them to appear on the handouts. They are selected by default. If you choose to include them, enter the text in the text boxes for the header and footer information.
- To format the date, click in the date text box, click the **Insert** tab, and click **Date & Time**. Choose a format and click **OK**. Return to the Handout Master tab.
- To select a style for the background, click **Background Styles** in the Background group and choose one.
- If you want graphics to be hidden when printed, click the **Hide Background Graphics** check box in the Background group.

4. To close the handout master, click **Close Master View** in the Close group.

Work with Text

Entering and manipulating text is a major part of building a presentation. Text is not only titles and bulleted lists. It is also captions on a picture or a legend or labels on a chart. Text can be inside a shape or curved around it on the outside. Text communicates in a thousand ways. Here is how you work with text in PowerPoint.

Find and Use a Text Layout

PowerPoint provides standard layouts to create a consistent "look" for your presentation, for example to insert text, columns, graphics, charts, logos, and other pictures. Chapters 1 and 2 discussed layouts in more detail. You may have changed the standard layouts through editing master slides, as explained earlier in this chapter. In that case, your edited master layouts will be displayed in the menu. Here, we are concerned with text layouts.

When you create a new blank slide, you must choose whether to use an existing layout that Microsoft provides or to create your own layout (see Figure 4-10).

1. In Normal view, click the slide immediately preceding the one you want to insert.

2. Click the **Home** tab, and click the **New Slide** down arrow.

3. Look for the placement of text, titles, and content. Examples of text placeholders are shown in Figure 4-10.

4. Click the layout you want.

5. To enter the text, just click within the title or text placeholders and begin typing, (See Chapters 5 through 8 for more information on working with other content placeholders.)

Insert a New Text Box

Even when you use a predefined layout that Microsoft provides, you will find times when you want to insert a new text box.

1. Display the slide to contain a new text box.

2. Click the **Insert** tab, and click **Text Box** in the Text group. The pointer first turns into a line pointer.

3. Place the pointer where you want to locate the text box, and drag it to the width you want—it will compress down to one-line height regardless of how deep you make the text box. As you drag, the pointer will morph into a crosshair shape. Don't worry about where the box is located; you can drag it to a precise location later. When you release the pointer, the insertion point within the text box indicates that you can begin to type text.

4. Type the text you want, and when you are finished, click outside the text box.

Work with Text Boxes

You work with text and text boxes by typing text into a text box, moving or copying the text box, resizing the text box, positioning the text box, deleting it, rotating it, filling it with color, and more.

ENTER TEXT INTO A TEXT BOX

To enter text into a text box, simply click inside the text box; the insertion point will appear in the text box, indicating that you can now type text. Begin to type.

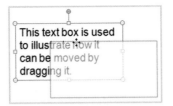

MOVE A TEXT BOX

To move a text box, you drag the border of the placeholder.

1. Click the text within a text box to display the text box outline.

2. Place the pointer over the border of the text box and between the handles. The pointer will be a four-headed arrow.

3. Drag the text box where you want.

RESIZE A PLACEHOLDER

To resize a placeholder, you drag the sizing handles of the text box.

1. Click the text to display the text box border.

2. Place the pointer on the border over the handles so that it becomes a two-headed arrow.

3. Drag any of the sizing handles in the direction you want the text box expanded or reduced. Use the corner handles to drag diagonally. As you drag, the pointer will morph into a crosshair.

DELETE A TEXT BOX

To delete a text box:

1. Click the text within the text box to display the border.

2. Click the border of the text box again to select the text box, not the text (the insertion point will disappear and the border will be solid).

3. Press **DELETE**.

COPY A TEXT BOX

To copy a text box with its contents and drag it to another part of the slide:

1. Click the text within the text box.

2. Place the pointer on the border of the text box (not over the handles), where it becomes a four-headed arrow.

3. Drag the text box while pressing **CTRL**.

ROTATE A TEXT BOX

When you first insert a text box (or click it to select it), a rotate handle allows you to rotate the box in a circle.

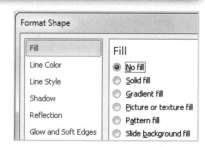

1. Place the pointer over the rotate handle.
2. Drag it in the direction it is to be rotated.
3. Click outside the text box to "set" the rotation.

POSITION A TEXT BOX PRECISELY

To set the position of a text box precisely on a slide:

1. Click the text box to select it. A Drawing Tools Format tab will appear.
2. In the Format tab, Arrange group, click **Rotate**.
3. On the Rotate menu, click **More Rotation Options**. The Format Shape dialog box will appear.
4. Click the **Position** option.
5. Click the **Horizontal** or **Vertical** spinners to enter the exact measurements in inches of the text box from an originating location. Click the **From** drop-down list boxes to select the originating location of the text box between the upper-left corner and center.
6. Click **Close**.

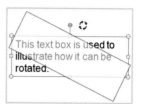

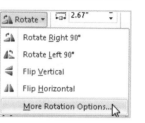

CHANGE THE FILL COLOR IN A TEXT BOX

To change the background color of a text box, you have two choices: You can use the Shape Fill tool on the Drawing Tools Format tab or the Format Shape dialog box. The Shape Fill tool is faster, but the Format Shape dialog box gives you more choices. We'll discuss the Format Shape dialog box here; the Shape Fill tool is explained in Chapter 8.

1. Right-click the text box, and click **Format Shape** from the context menu. The Format Shape dialog box appears.
2. Click **Fill** and then select the type of fill you want to see. Solid Fill will result in a uniform colored fill; Gradient Fill results in a variation between shades of one or more colors (Figure 4-11 shows an example); Picture Or Texture Fill allows you to browse for a background picture or select from a menu of preset textures; Pattern Fill displays a menu of possible patterns that you can use, or you can find your own pattern; Slide Background Fill uses the current slide background as fill. After making your choice, the options you see will vary, depending on your choice. In Figure 4-11, you can see the options for a Gradient Fill selection.

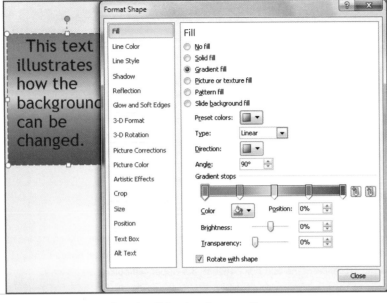

3. Click the **Preset Color** (or other color option) to select a color. Set other attributes as you wish, such as the type and direction of the gradient. If necessary, drag the dialog box to one side so that you can see the changes in the text box as you try out different shades or types of fill, as illustrated in Figure 4-11.

4. When finished, click **Close**.

SET PARAGRAPH AND TAB SETTINGS

To change the default paragraph spacing and tab settings, you can use the Paragraph dialog box, as seen in Figure 4-12.

1. Click the paragraph text in a placeholder or text box to be changed. Click the **Home** tab, and click the **Paragraph Dialog Box Launcher** on the lower-right of the Paragraph group.

–Or–

Right-click the paragraph text in a placeholder or text box to be changed, and click **Paragraph**. The Paragraph dialog box appears.

Figure 4-11: You can drag the dialog box (or sometimes the text box) to the side so that you can see the effects of settings as you work with the options.

2. Configure the following settings as required:

- Set the general positioning by clicking the **Alignment** down arrow and then clicking **Left**, **Centered**, **Right**, **Justified**, or **Distributed** (which forces even short lines to be justified to the end of the line), depending on how you want the text aligned.

- Set the indentation. Click the **Before Text** spinner to set the spacing before the text begins on a first line; click the **Special** down arrow to allow for hanging indents, an indented first line, or no indents.

- Set the spacing. Click the **Before** spinner to set spacing before the line starts (in points); click the **Line Spacing** down arrow, and click **Single**, **1.5 Lines**, **Double**, **Exactly** (where you set the exact spacing in points in the At box), or **Multiple** (where you enter the number of lines to space in the At box).

- Click the **Tabs** button to set tabs precisely in the Tabs dialog box. Click **OK** to close the Tabs dialog box.

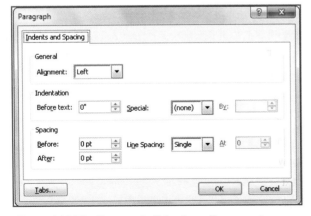

Figure 4-12: The Paragraph dialog box allows you to change paragraph and tab settings.

3. Click **OK** to close the Paragraph dialog box.

CAUTION

When you adjust the line spacing, the AutoFit feature, which is on by default, may cause the text to be resized to fit within the text box. See the "Setting Margins, Word Wrap, AutoFit, and Columns" QuickSteps to change the default.

QUICKSTEPS

SETTING MARGINS, WORD WRAP, AUTOFIT, AND COLUMNS

All of the procedures in this section make use of the Drawing Tools Format Shape dialog box. To display it, right-click the text box and select **Format Shape**. Select **Text Box** from the menu on the left, as shown in Figure 4-13.

SET MARGINS IN A TEXT BOX

To change the margins in a text box, change the Internal Margin setting to **Left**, **Right**, **Top**, or **Bottom**.

DISABLE WORD WRAP FOR TEXT

Under Internal Margin, disable (or enable) the word-wrap feature for text in a text box by clicking **Wrap Text In Shape**. A check mark in the check box indicates that word wrap is turned on.

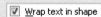

ANCHOR TEXT IN A TEXT BOX

To anchor the text layout within a text box, select how the text will be positioned in the text box horizontally and vertically. Under Text Layout, click the **Vertical Alignment** down arrow, and click the position to which you want the text anchored. Your choices are Top, Middle, Bottom, Top Centered, Middle Centered, and Bottom Centered. For example, if you choose Middle Centered, your text will be positioned in the center of the text box both horizontally and vertically.

Continued . . .

Figure 4-13: A text box can have its own margins and alignment. You can set defaults for automatic word-wrap features and establish columns.

CHANGE CAPITALIZATION

To set your capitalization standard or to correct text typed in the wrong case:

1. Select the text for which you want to change the case.
2. Click the **Home** tab, and click the **Change Case** Aa▾ button in the Font group.
3. Select one of the following options:
   - **Sentence case** capitalizes the first word in a sentence.
   - **lowercase** makes all text lowercase.
   - **UPPERCASE** makes all text uppercase.
   - **Capitalize Each Word** capitalizes all words.
   - **tOGGLE cASE** switches between uppercase and lowercase letters, for instance, when you have accidentally typed text in the wrong case.

QUICKSTEPS

SETTING MARGINS, WORD WRAP, AUTOFIT, AND COLUMNS *(Continued)*

ROTATE TEXT WITHIN A TEXT BOX

To rotate text within a text box, under Text Layout, click the **Text Direction** down arrow, and choose an option: Horizontal, Rotate All Text 90°, Rotate All Text 270°, or Stacked.

SET UP COLUMNS WITHIN A TEXT BOX

To set up columns within a text box, click the **Columns** button. The Columns dialog box appears. Click the **Number** spinner and the **Spacing** spinner to set your column attributes, and click **OK**.

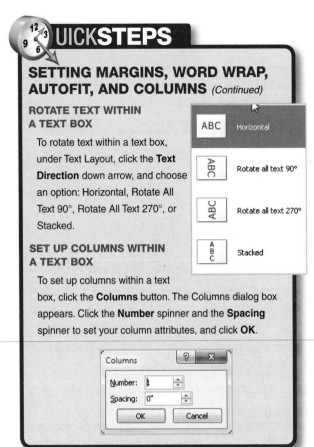

NOTE

All the cut-and-paste techniques can also be used to copy information. Just select **Copy** instead of Cut from the context or ribbon menus, or press **CTRL+C**. To copy using the drag-and-drop technique, right-drag the text (drag with the right mouse button held down), and click **Copy Here**.

Use the Font Dialog Box

To set multiple font and character attributes at once or to set the standard for a slide, it is easier to use the Font dialog box than individual buttons. (See the "Changing Font Attributes in Master Slides" QuickFacts earlier in this chapter.)

1. Select the text to be changed.

2. Click the **Home** tab, and click the **Font Dialog Box Launcher** in the lower-right area of the Font group. The Font dialog box will appear, as shown in Figure 4-14.

3. Click the **Latin Text Font** down arrow, and select the type of theme text (Heading or Body) or font name. This establishes what will be changed in the selected text.

4. Choose the options you want, and click **OK**.

Align Text

You have several ways to align text: horizontally on a line, vertically on a page, or distributed horizontally or vertically. This section describes how to use these aligning techniques.

Figure 4-14: Using the Font dialog box, you can change all occurrences of certain fonts within selected text.

QUICKSTEPS

USING LISTS

Lists are either numbered or bulleted. You can choose the shapes of bullets, change the style of numbering, and use SmartArt for your lists.

CHOOSE BULLET SHAPES

1. Select the text to be bulleted.
2. Right-click the text and point to **Bullets**. The context menu opens.

   –Or–

   On the Home tab, click the **Bullets** down arrow. A context menu will open.

3. Use the options presented, or, to display more options, click **Bullets And Numbering** at the bottom of the menu. The Bullets And Numbering dialog box appears, as shown in Figure 4-15.

4. To select the bullet appearance, click one of the options:

   - To change the size, adjust the **Size** spinner to the percentage of text you want the bullet to be.

   - To change the color, click the **Color** down arrow, and select a color.

   - To select or import a picture to use as a bullet shape, click **Picture** and select one of the menu images, or click **Import** to find your own. Then click **OK**.

   - To select a character from a variety of symbol fonts, click **Customize**. Make your selection, and then click **OK.**

5. Click **OK** to close the dialog box.

Continued . . .

Projected Sales

☐ Expenses for first year of acqu
  updating marketing would incr

☐ Sales would not be realized ur

☐ But we could potentially doub
  our beginning costs by year 6.

Figure 4-15: The Bullets And Numbering dialog box offers ways to change the appearance, size, and color of bullets or numbers in a list.

ALIGN TEXT ON A LINE

You align text by centering (placing text in the center of the horizontal margins), left or right-aligning, or justifying it (where the left and right edges of text are aligned). All four options are available on the Home tab Paragraph group.

1. Select the text to be aligned, and click the **Home** tab. (Selecting any part of a paragraph will align the entire paragraph.)
2. From the Paragraph group, choose one of these options:

ALIGN TEXT IN A PLACEHOLDER

To align text with the top, middle, or bottom of a text box or placeholder, place the cursor in the text box; then in the Home tab, Paragraph group, click the **Align Text** button, and click your choices from the menu. Click **More Options** to precisely specify measurements.

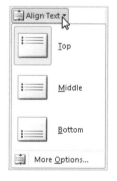

USING LISTS *(Continued)*

CHANGE NUMBERING STYLES

1. Select the text to be numbered.

2. Right-click the text and point to **Numbering**. A context menu opens.

–Or–

On the Home tab, click the **Numbering** down arrow. A context menu will open.

3. Use the options presented, or, to display more options, click **Bullets And Numbering**. The Bullets And Numbering dialog box will appear.

   - To change the size, adjust the Size spinner to the percentage of the text size you want the numbering to be.

   - To change the color, click the **Color** down arrow, and select a color.

   - To set a beginning number or letter, change **Start At**.

4. Click **OK**.

USE SMARTART FOR LISTS

To make your lists artistic and professional-looking, you can choose some of the SmartArt options offered by PowerPoint 2010. These dramatically change the look and feel of lists. See Chapter 8 for additional discussions about SmartArt.

1. Select the list.

2. On the Home tab, click the **Convert To SmartArt** down arrow in the Paragraph group.

–Or–

Continued . . .

ALIGN A TEXT PLACEHOLDER TO THE SLIDE

You can align a placeholder or text box horizontally or vertically on a slide—that is, the spacing on the top and bottom will be equal or the spacing from the left and right edges of the slide will be distributed evenly.

1. Click the placeholder or text box to select it.

2. On the Drawing Tools/SmartArt Tools Format tab, Arrange group, click the **Align** button. A menu will appear.

3. Click one of these options:

   - Click **Distribute Horizontally** to align the object centered horizontally on the slide.

   - Click **Distribute Vertically** to align the object centered vertically on the slide.

Copy Formatting with Format Painter

To copy all formatting attributes from one text segment to another, you use the Format Painter. With it, you can copy fonts, font size and style, line and paragraph spacing, color, alignment, bullet selection, and character effects.

1. Select the text containing the formatting attributes to be copied.

2. On the Home tab, click **Format Painter** in the Clipboard group.

3. Find the destination text to contain the copied attributes, and drag the paintbrush pointer over the text to be changed.

Use AutoCorrect

AutoCorrect is a feature that helps you type information correctly. For example, it corrects simple typing errors and makes certain assumptions about what you want to type. You can turn it off or change its rules.

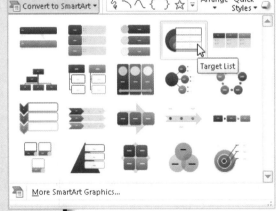

USING LISTS (Continued)

Right-click the text or text placeholder that you want to display with special effects, and point to **Convert To SmartArt**. A gallery of styles is displayed.

3. Point to an option, and you will see the SmartArt effect on the slide. Click the effect you want. There may be small left- and right-pointing arrows on the left side of the text box indicating that you may enter text into the list, such as is displayed in Figure 4-16. Click either arrow to see the text box. Drag the **Type Your Text Here** text box to a part of your work area where you can work easily with it. Type your text into the bulleted selection, and it will appear in the SmartArt object.

4. To remove the text box, simply click the arrows on the left side of the SmartArt text (you might need to separate the two text boxes to see them). They act as toggles that you can use to display and hide the text box.

5. When you are finished, close the Type Your Text Here box by clicking the **X** in the upper-right corner. Click outside the SmartArt text box to deselect it.

TIP

If you want to copy more than one text selection, double-click the **Format Painter** to turn it on for additional uses. You can copy multiple text selections, one after the other. To turn it off, click **Format Painter** again or press **ESC**.

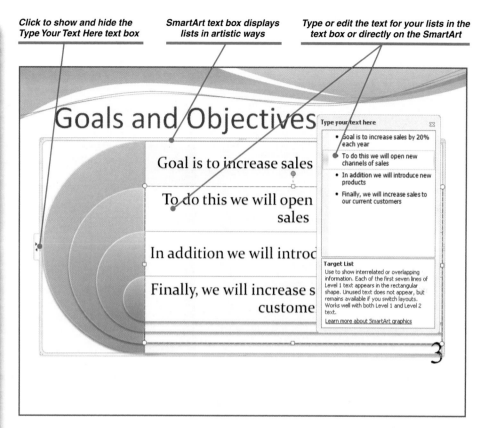

Click to show and hide the Type Your Text Here text box

SmartArt text box displays lists in artistic ways

Type or edit the text for your lists in the text box or directly on the SmartArt

Figure 4-16: SmartArt effects can make your lists dramatic and professional-looking.

TURN AUTOCORRECT OPTIONS ON OR OFF

The AutoCorrect feature assumes that you will want certain corrections always to be made while you type. Among these corrections are: change two initial capital letters to the first one only, capitalize the first letter of each sentence, capitalize the first letter of table cells and names of days, correct accidental use of the CAPS LOCK key, and replace misspelled words with the results it assumes you want. (See "Change AutoCorrect Spelling Corrections" to retain

EDITING WITH THE KEYBOARD

Working with text in PowerPoint is similar to working with text in Microsoft Word. This section presents familiar ways to move the pointer and to select, delete, and insert text.

MOVE THE POINTER WITHIN YOUR TEXT

- To move to the beginning of the line, press **HOME**.
- To move to the end of a line, press **END**.
- To skip to the next word, press **CTRL+RIGHT ARROW**.
- To skip to the previous word, press **CTRL+LEFT ARROW**.

SELECT TEXT

- To select all text contained within a text box, press **CTRL+A**.
- To select a word, double-click it.
- To select a paragraph, click within the paragraph three times.
- To select all text from where your cursor is to the end of the line, press **SHIFT+END**.
- To select all text from where your cursor is to the beginning of the line, press **SHIFT+HOME**.
- To select multiple lines, press **SHIFT+UP ARROW** or **SHIFT+DOWN ARROW**.
- To select one character at a time, press **SHIFT+LEFT ARROW** or **SHIFT+RIGHT ARROW**.

DELETE TEXT

- To delete the character to the right of the cursor, press **DELETE**.
- To delete the character to the left of the cursor, press **BACKSPACE**.
- To delete other text as needed, select text using the keyboard, highlighting it and pressing **DELETE**.

INSERT TEXT

To insert one or more characters within a text box, use **TAB** to select the text box, use the arrow keys to place the pointer where you want to type, and then type.

the correction of misspelled words but to change the correction made.) To turn off the automatic spelling corrections that PowerPoint makes:

1. Click the **File** tab, and click **Options**.

2. Click **Proofing**, and under AutoCorrect Options, click the **AutoCorrect Options** button. The dialog box shown in Figure 4-17 will appear. The AutoCorrect tab should be selected by default.

3. Find the option you want to turn off or on, and clear the relevant check box. If a check mark is in the box, the option is enabled. If it is not, the option is turned off.

Figure 4-17: The AutoCorrect dialog box is where you change the automatic corrections made to text and spelling.

CHANGE AUTOCORRECT SPELLING CORRECTIONS

PowerPoint may automatically correct spellings that are not really incorrect. You can add a new spelling correction, replace a current spelling correction with a new one, or replace the result that is now used. You do this by replacing

MOVING TEXT

There are at least four ways you can move text. You can use the cut-and-paste technique, the ribbon, right-click from a context menu, or use the drag-and-drop technique.

CUT AND PASTE TEXT WITH THE KEYBOARD

1. Select the text to be moved, and press **CTRL+X** to cut the text.

2. Click the pointer to place the insertion point, and press **CTRL+V** to paste the text in the new location.

CUT AND PASTE WITH THE RIBBON

1. Select the text to be moved.

2. Click the **Home** tab, and click **Cut** ✂ Cut in the Clipboard group.

3. Click where you want the text inserted, and click **Paste** in the Clipboard group. Note that Paste has two parts: If you click the top of the button, a paste of your text is made. If you click the down arrow in the bottom of the Paste button, a menu of formatting options is presented for retaining or discarding formatting in the source text, formatting as a picture and keeping the text only with no formatting, or performing a "special paste."

Continued . . .

NOTE

The Exceptions button in the AutoCorrect dialog box is used to provide exceptions to the capitalization rules. Clicking the button provides an opportunity to add to a list of either initially capitalized exceptions or exceptions about when to capitalize a word, such as after an abbreviation.

one word with another in the AutoCorrect dialog box. When you first open the dialog box, both the Replace and With boxes are blank. In this case, you simply add what you want. To replace an entry, you first delete an entry—one that is not a mistake you typically make—and then you replace it with a typing error you commonly make. To replace a current spelling result, you type over the current result with the correction you want.

1. Click the **File** tab, and click the **Options** button. Then click **Proofing**.

2. Click the **AutoCorrect Options** button, and the AutoCorrect dialog box appears, shown in Figure 4-17. If it is not already selected, click the **AutoCorrect** tab.

   - To add new entries when both the Replace and With boxes are blank, fill in the **Replace** and **With** boxes, and click **Add**.

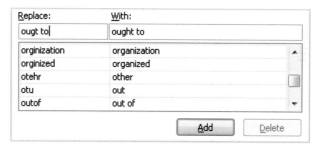

   - To add an entry using an existing one, click the existing entry to select it. Click the text in the Replace box and replace it with your new entry. Click the text in the With box and replace it too. Click **Add**. The original existing text will remain.

   - To replace entries in the Replace and With boxes, click the text in the With box, and replace it with your new entries. Click **Replace**. The "old" text will not be deleted; it is still in the list. You must use the **DELETE** button to actually get rid of an entry in the list.

   - To delete and replace an entry, click the entry to be replaced, and press **DELETE**. Then type the new spelling option. Click **Add**.

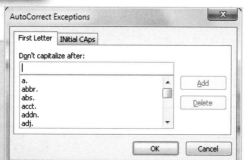

CUT AND PASTE WITH A CONTEXT MENU

1. Select the text to be moved.

2. Right-click and click **Cut**.

3. Right-click the new location, and click **Paste**. Note that Paste has two parts: If you click the top of the button, a paste of your text is made. If you click the down arrow in the bottom of the Paste button, a menu of formatting options is presented for retaining or discarding formatting in the source text, formatting as a picture and keeping the text only with no formatting, or performing a "special paste."

USE THE DRAG-AND-DROP TECHNIQUE

To use the drag-and-drop technique to move text within the same text box, to other text boxes, or to other slides (when moving to other slides, you can only use the Outline tab):

1. Select the text to be moved.

2. Using the pointer, drag the text to the new location. An insertion point shows you where the text is about to be moved.

3. Release the pointer when the insertion point is in the correct location.

TIP

To quickly use the spelling checker, right-click the misspelled word. A context menu will display several options for correct spellings. Click the correct word if it is on the list. You can also click **Ignore All** to ignore all usages of the misspelling or click **Add To Dictionary**. You can display the Spelling dialog box by clicking **Spelling** at the bottom of the context menu.

USE AUTOFIT

AutoFit is used to make text fit within a text box or AutoShape. It often resizes text to make it fit. You can turn it on or off.

1. Click the **File** tab, click **Options**, and then click **Proofing**.

2. Under AutoCorrect Options, click **AutoCorrect Options**. The AutoCorrect dialog box appears.

3. Click the **AutoFormat As You Type** tab.

4. Under the Apply As You Type section, choose these options:

   - To remove the AutoFit feature for titles, clear the **AutoFit Title Text To Placeholder** check box.

   - To remove the AutoFit feature for body text, clear the **AutoFit Body Text To Placeholder** check box.

5. Click **OK** twice.

Use the Spelling Checker

One form of the spelling checker automatically flags words that it cannot find in the dictionary as potential misspellings. It identifies these words with a red underline. However, even when the automatic function is turned off, you can still use the spelling checker by manually opening it.

CHECK THE SPELLING IN A PRESENTATION

You can direct the spelling checker to go through all text in all placeholders on a slide, looking for words that are not in the spelling dictionary. When it finds one, it displays the Spelling dialog box, seen in Figure 4-18.

1. Click in the presentation where the spelling checker should begin.

2. To display the spelling checker, press **F7**. The Spelling dialog box will appear when the spelling checker finds a word that is not in the dictionary.

3. Choose any of these options to use the spelling checker:

   - If the word is incorrect, look at the Suggestions list, and click the one you want to use. It will appear in the Change To box. Click **Change** to change the single occurrence of the word, or click **Change All** to change all occurrences of that same word.

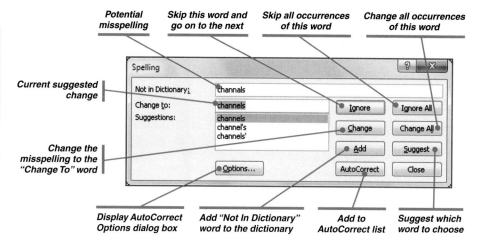

USING THE OFFICE CLIPBOARD

The Office Clipboard is shared by all Microsoft Office products. You can copy objects and text from any Office application and paste them into another. When you cut or copy text, it is automatically added to the Office Clipboard. The Clipboard contains up to 24 items. The 25th item will overwrite the first one.

OPEN THE CLIPBOARD

To display the Office Clipboard, click the **Home** tab, and then click the **Clipboard Dialog Box Launcher** in the Clipboard group. The Clipboard task pane will open.

COPY CLIPBOARD ITEMS TO A PLACEHOLDER

First click to place the insertion point in the text box or placeholder where you want the item on the Office Clipboard inserted. Then:

1. To paste one item, click the item on the Clipboard to be inserted.
2. To paste all items, click **Paste All** on the Clipboard.

DELETE ITEMS ON THE CLIPBOARD

1. To delete all items, click **Clear All** on the Clipboard task pane.
2. To delete a single item, click the arrow next to the item, and click **Delete**.

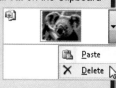

Continued . . .

Figure callouts (top):
- Potential misspelling
- Skip this word and go on to the next
- Skip all occurrences of this word
- Change all occurrences of this word
- Current suggested change
- Change the misspelling to the "Change To" word

Figure callouts (bottom):
- Display AutoCorrect Options dialog box
- Add "Not In Dictionary" word to the dictionary
- Add to AutoCorrect list
- Suggest which word to choose

Figure 4-18: Use the Spelling dialog box to look for misspellings, correct them with suggested words or your own, and add words to the dictionary.

- If the identified word is correct but not in the dictionary, you can add it to a custom dictionary by clicking **Add**, or you can skip the word by clicking **Ignore** or **Ignore All** (to skip all occurrences of the same word). The spelling checker will continue to the next misspelled word.

- Click **AutoCorrect** to add the word to the AutoCorrect list of automatic spelling changes that will be made as you type. Immediately the word will be placed in the AutoCorrect list.

- Click **Suggest** if you are unsure of the correct spelling and want PowerPoint to suggest the most likely spelling.

- Click **Options** to display the Proofing options in the PowerPoint Options dialog box.

4. Click Close to end the search for spelling errors. When the spelling checker is finished, a message will be displayed to that effect. Click OK.

QUICKSTEPS

USING THE OFFICE CLIPBOARD

(Continued)

SET CLIPBOARD OPTIONS

1. On the Clipboard task pane, click the **Options** down arrow at the bottom. A context menu is displayed.

> Show Office Clipboard Automatically
> Show Office Clipboard When Ctrl+C Pressed Twice
> Collect Without Showing Office Clipboard
> ✓ Show Office Clipboard Icon on Taskbar
> ✓ Show Status Near Taskbar When Copying
>
> Options

2. Click an option to select or deselect it:

- **Show Office Clipboard Automatically** always shows the Office Clipboard when copying.

- **Show Office Clipboard When CTRL+C Pressed Twice** shows the Office Clipboard when you press **CTRL+C** twice to make two copies (in other words, copying two items to the Clipboard will cause the Clipboard to be displayed).

- **Collect Without Showing Office Clipboard** copies items to the Clipboard without displaying it.

- **Show Office Clipboard Icon On Taskbar** displays the icon in the notification area of the taskbar when the Clipboard is being used.

- **Show Status Near Taskbar When Copying** displays a message about the items being added to the Clipboard as copies are made.

SET SPELLING DEFAULTS

Set these options to determine how the spelling checker works.

1. Click the **File** tab, click **Options**, and click **Proofing**. The spelling area is shown in Figure 4-19.

2. Select or deselect these options to best meet your needs. The defaults already have check marks in the check boxes. Click to remove them. Click to select any that have no check mark.

3. Click **OK** to accept your changes.

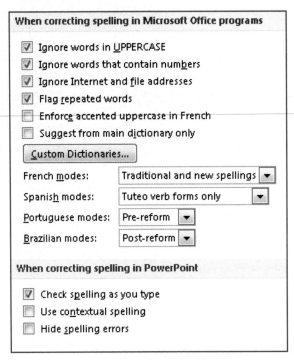

Figure 4-19: The PowerPoint Options dialog box Proofing pane sets the defaults for the changes PowerPoint will make to your text as you type.

Chapter 5
Creating Tables in Slides

This chapter addresses how to create tables in slides. This includes how to insert tables into slides, enter text into tables, select text, adjust columns and rows, and add or delete more columns and rows. It discusses how to format and align text held within tables, how to add borders, and how to work with cells, including how to shade, merge, and split them, and rotate text within the cells. You will also learn to enter formulas.

Create Tables

Creating tables is easily handled in PowerPoint. You select the Table command in the Tables group on the Insert tab and choose an option, specifying the number of rows and columns you want, and then fill in the data. That's just about all there is to it. Of course, thinking about what data will be included is a decision that PowerPoint can't do much to help you with. But once you have decided on the number of rows and columns, PowerPoint offers a wide variety of choices about how to present that data clearly and professionally.

Row **Column headings**

COMPARISON OF SALES FOR 2010
(IN MILLIONS)

	NW District	North District	West District	NE District	Total Sales
1ˢᵗ Qtr.	140	125	72	200	537
2ⁿᵈ Qtr.	340	420	427	200	1,387
3ʳᵈ Qtr.	500	525	125	250	1,400
4ᵗʰ Qtr.	550	340	222	200	1,312
Total	1,530	1,410	842	850	4,632

Row headings **Column** **Active cell**

Figure 5-1: A table is made up of columns and rows, and data is contained in each individual cell—the unique intersection between a row and a column.

NOTE

As you can see in Figure 5-3, when a table is inserted, PowerPoint adds two new contextual tabs, Design and Layout, to the Table Tools group.

Insert a Table

There are four ways to create a table on a slide. You can insert one from layout templates, directly insert a table onto a slide, draw a table, or insert one from Microsoft Word or Excel. Figure 5-1 shows an example of a typical table.

INSERT A TABLE FROM A TEMPLATE

A common way to create a table is to use one from the various templates that Microsoft provides. With this approach, you insert a table into a placeholder.

1. Click the slide immediately before the one on which the table is to be inserted.

2. On the Home tab, in the Slides group, click the **New Slide** down arrow to insert a new slide into the presentation. The slide layout menu will be displayed, as shown in Figure 5-2. Your layouts will look different from those in Figure 5-2, depending on your theme.

3. Find a layout with a content icon (such as the Title And Content layout), select it, and click the **Table** icon.

4. In the Insert Table dialog box, fill in the number of columns and rows, and click **OK**. The table will be inserted onto your slide, as shown in Figure 5-3.

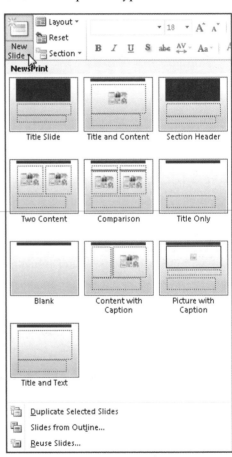

Figure 5-2: When you insert a new slide, you can select a layout that allows you to define the contents you expect on a slide, such as a table or other object.

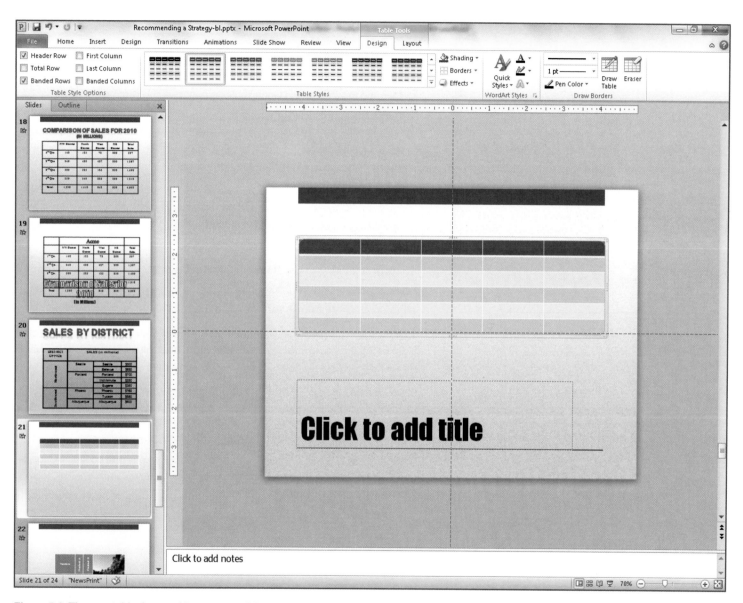

Figure 5-3: The new table, inserted into a new slide, contains the number of columns and rows that you specified, and the ribbon contains all the tools you need.

UNDERSTANDING TABLE BASICS

A PowerPoint table, similar to a worksheet in Microsoft Excel, is a matrix, or grid, with *column headings* across the top and *row headings* down the side. The first row of a typical table is used for column *headers*. Column headers represent categories of similar data. The rows beneath a column header contain data further categorized by a row header along the leftmost column or listed below the column header. In a table, columns are sometimes referred to as *fields*, and each row represents a unique *record* of data. Each intersection of a row and column is called a *cell* and contains a unique bit of information. A cell is considered *active* when it is clicked or otherwise selected as the place in which to place new data.

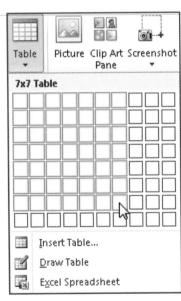

Figure 5-4: You can create a table by dragging over the squares in the menu for the number of rows and columns you want in the table.

INSERT A TABLE FROM SCRATCH

In this case, you simply insert a table onto the slide.

1. Click the slide where you want the table inserted.

2. Click the **Insert** tab, and in the Tables group, click the **Table** down arrow.

3. Drag the pointer until the number of squares selected represents the number of columns and rows you want, as shown in Figure 5-4. The table will be immediately placed on your slide. Point to a table border, and drag it to where you want it on the slide.

   –Or–

   On the Table menu, click **Insert Table**, fill in the number of columns and rows, and click OK.

DRAW A TABLE

To draw a table, you use the table drawing pen in Normal view to draw the boundaries and interior design of the table (see "Work with Borders" later in the chapter for more information on drawing a table).

1. If you need a blank slide, click the **Home** tab, and then in the Slides group, click the **New Slide** down arrow. Select the **Blank** or **Title Only** slide layout. If you want to draw the table on an existing slide, click the slide to select it.

2. To help you draw more precisely, display gridlines: On the Home tab, in the Drawing group, click the **Arrange** button to see a menu of options. Under Position Objects, click **Align**, and on the context menu, click **View Gridlines** to display a grid of lines on your slide. (See Chapter 6 for additional information on using gridlines.)

3. On the Insert tab, in the Tables group, click **Table**, and on the context menu, click the **Draw Table** option. Your pointer, when placed on the Slide pane, will turn into a drawing tool ✏ in the shape of a pencil.

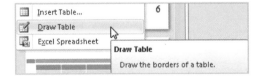

4. Drag to create the outline of the table. Drag the pointer diagonally across the slide to define the outside border of the table. When you release the pointer, a selected placeholder box will be displayed.

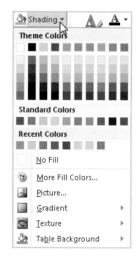

5. In the Table Tools Design tab, click **Draw Table** in the Draw Borders group to turn on the Draw Table tool.

6. Begin to draw the table you want. Draw vertical and horizontal lines. When you start a line, it will be extended in the direction you want until it reaches a border or another horizontal or vertical line. To draw diagonal lines, start the line from an intersection or corner of two lines.

- To erase a line, click the **Eraser** button on the Table Tools Design tab, Draw Borders group. The pointer will morph into an eraser, which you can use to drag over the portion of a line you want to remove.

- To insert color into the columns and rows you have drawn, select the cells to be colored (see the "Selecting Table Components" QuickSteps), and click the **Shading** down arrow in the Table Styles group. Click the color you want.

- To add a bevel, shadow, or reflection effect to the table, highlight the cells to be altered, and click **Effects** in the Table Styles group. Click the effect you want, and then choose the variation you want.

- To add text, click a cell to select it, and then type your text.

Figure 5-5 shows an example of a table drawn in PowerPoint with cell and background shading, beveled cells with shadow effects, and WordArt in the title.

COPY A TABLE FROM WORD

You can create a table in Microsoft Word, Access, or Publisher, and copy it using the Clipboard onto a PowerPoint slide.

1. In Word, create your table.

2. Select it by dragging across all the cells of the table.

3. Click the **Home** tab, and click **Copy**. The table will be placed on the Clipboard.

4. In PowerPoint, find the slide where you're going to insert the Word table.

5. Click the **Home** tab, and click the **Clipboard** group **Dialog Box Launcher**. Then click the appropriate item from the Clipboard task pane. The table will be inserted onto the slide, as shown in Figure 5-6.

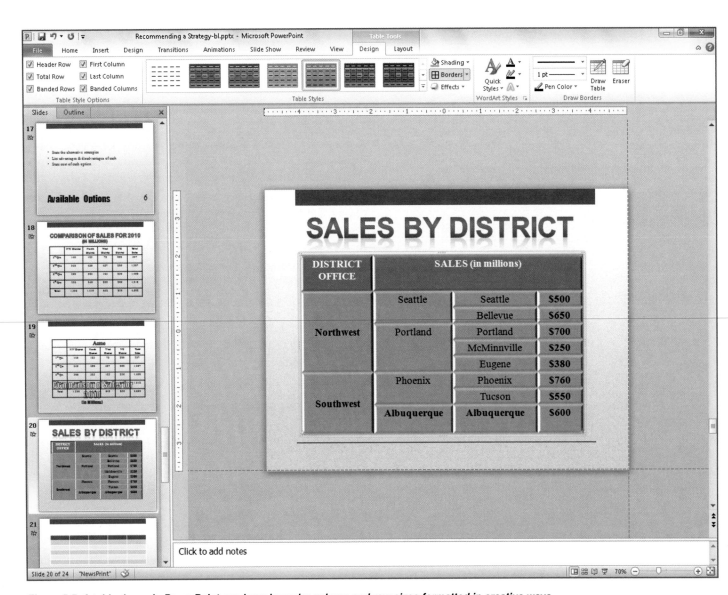

Figure 5-5: *A table drawn in PowerPoint can have irregular column and row sizes formatted in creative ways.*

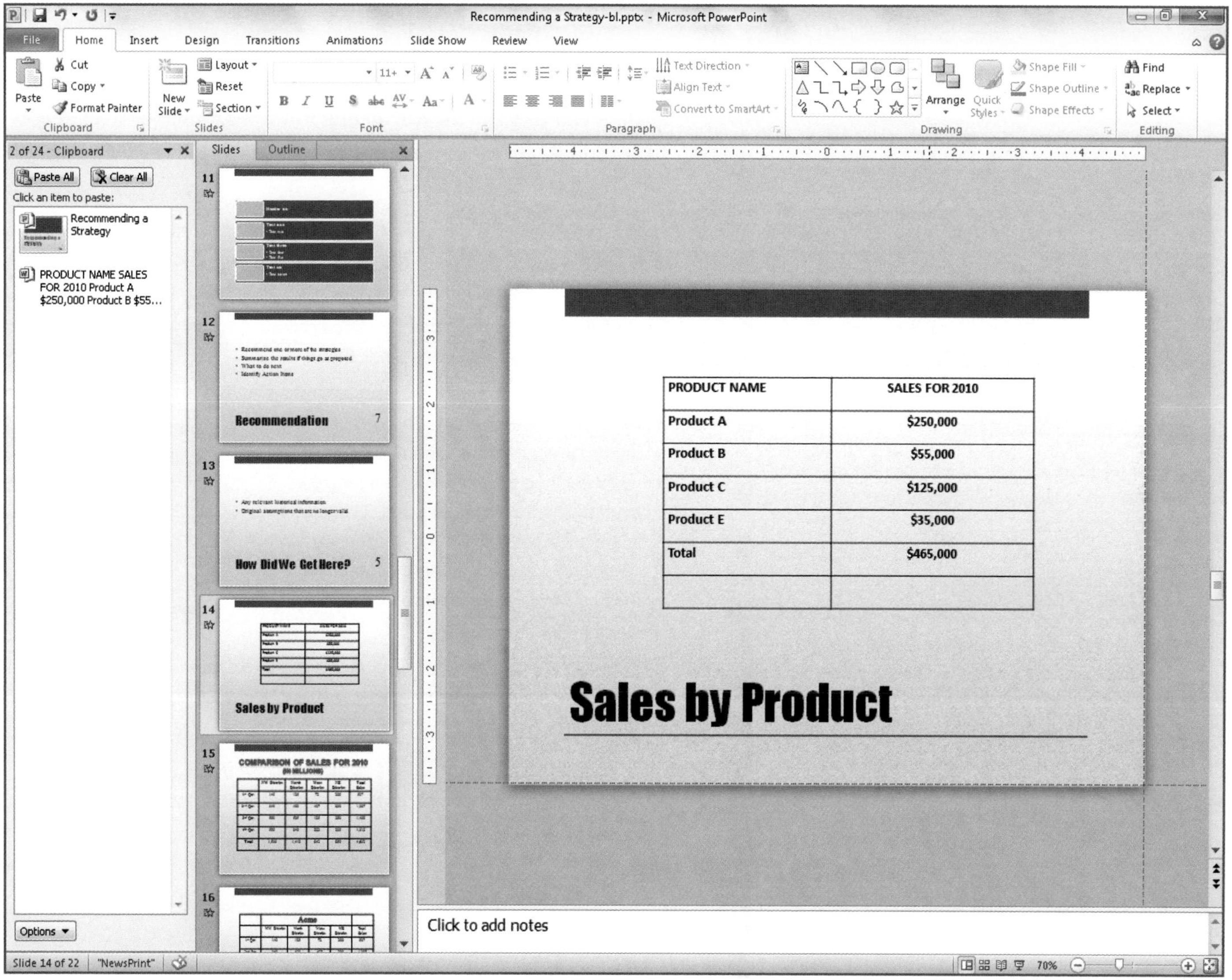

Figure 5-6: *Since the Clipboard is shared between Microsoft Office programs, it is easy to create a table in Excel or Word and then copy it into PowerPoint.*

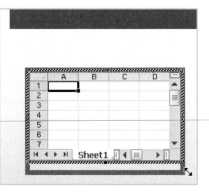

USE EXCEL TO CREATE A POWERPOINT TABLE

You can insert an empty Microsoft Excel spreadsheet within PowerPoint and still use Excel's commands and functions to enter data and create a table. This enables you to retain the calculating functions found in Excel. A PowerPoint table cannot calculate; it can only be displayed. To use Excel to create a table within PowerPoint:

1. In PowerPoint, create or select the slide that is to contain your Excel spreadsheet. On the Home tab, click **New Slide** in the Slides group, and click the **Title Only** or **Blank** layout, or select a different layout from the slide layout menu.

2. Click the **Insert** tab, and in the Tables group, click **Table**. From the menu, click **Excel Spreadsheet**.

3. An Excel spreadsheet will be inserted. Click the border and drag the spreadsheet where you want it on the slide. You can resize it by dragging the sizing handles. Then click in the cells and type your data. You will be able to use Excel ribbon and context menu commands while working with the spreadsheet.

4. When your table is ready, click outside the Excel table. The Excel commands will close, and PowerPoint commands will return.

NOTE

To access the Excel commands again, double-click the table.

TIP

For more information on using Excel commands within PowerPoint and for information on working with charts or graphs, see Chapter 7, or refer to *Microsoft Excel 2010 QuickSteps*, published by McGraw-Hill/Professional. See Chapter 7 to learn how to simply copy data to the Clipboard from an Excel worksheet and paste it onto a slide in PowerPoint.

NOTE

These instructions for adding text to cells may not work exactly the same in Microsoft Excel. For instance, in Excel tables, the text being typed continues to the right covering adjacent cells.

Work with Tables

When working with tables, you can enter and format text, add color, and add table effects.

Enter Text

When entering text into a table cell, there are several navigational tips to keep in mind:

● To add data to a table, click a cell and type. If you type to the end of the cell, your text will wrap to the next line, making the cell taller.

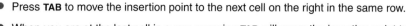

ALIGNING TEXT

Text is aligned in the upper-left corner of a cell by default. You can align text vertically and horizontally within a cell.

ALIGN TEXT HORIZONTALLY

First, click in a cell, or select a row, column, or the whole table by dragging over it or clicking the edge or border of the table. The tools for aligning text can be found in the Layout tab or on the mini toolbar that appears when you move the pointer over the selected text a bit.

ALIGN TEXT VERTICALLY

Select the cell, row, column, or the whole table by dragging over it or clicking the edge or border of the table. The tools needed to align text vertically are found in the Layout tab.

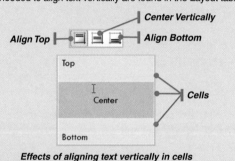

Effects of aligning text vertically in cells

- Press **TAB** to move the insertion point to the next cell on the right in the same row.
- When you are at the last cell in a row, pressing **TAB** will move the insertion point to the first cell of the next row. If you are in the last cell in a table, pressing **TAB** will insert a new row and place the insertion point in the first cell of that row.

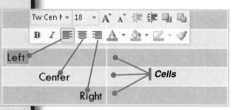

Effects of aligning text horizontally in cells

- Press **DOWN ARROW** or **UP ARROW** to move the insertion point up or down one row in the same column.
- Press **ENTER** to insert another line within a cell—that is, to make the cell taller by one line. If there are already multiple lines in a cell, pressing **ENTER** will move the insertion point down a line.

Format Text

To format text, that is, to change fonts and font style, font size, font color, and character effects (such as **Bold**, <u>Underline</u>, and *Italics*), you can use either the Font group on the Home tab or the formatting mini toolbar that appears when you select text. (Detailed information on using text formatting is described in Chapter 4.)

USE THE FONT GROUP

1. Select the text in the cells that you want to format by highlighting them.
2. Click the **Home** tab, and click one of the buttons in the Font group.

USE THE FORMATTING MINI TOOLBAR

1. Select the text in the cells by highlighting them.
2. When the toolbar appears over the selected cells, move your pointer over the selected cells to make the toolbar active.
3. Click the button you want on the formatting toolbar.

ROTATING TEXT IN CELLS

You can rotate text 90 degrees clockwise within the cells of a table. This can help you to display information in a more efficient manner.

1. In your PowerPoint table, select the cell wherein the data will be rotated.

2. Click the **Layout** tab, and click the **Text Direction** button in the Alignment group. A menu of rotating options will be displayed, as shown in Figure 5-7.

3. Click **Horizontal**, **Rotate All Text 90°**, **Rotate All Text 270°**, or **Stacked**. The text is rotated or stacked accordingly.

Vendors	Product A	Product B
Smith & Co	500	25
Darrel Mfg.	200	0

TIP

If none of the margins choices meet your needs, click **Custom Margins** on the Cell Margins context menu, as shown in Figure 5-8. Configure the settings in the Internal Margin area, and click **OK**.

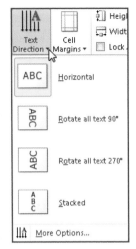

Figure 5-7: Using the Text Direction command, you can rotate or stack text in several ways to position it exactly within a table.

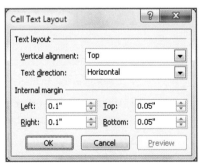

Figure 5-8: You can set the internal margins of cells using the Cell Text Layout dialog box.

Set Cell Margins

You can change the margins within a cell. The default margin setting is "Normal" and is a margin of .05 inches at the top and bottom of the cell and .1 inches on either side. You can choose No Margins, Narrow, or Wide Margins.

1. Select the cell or cells for which the margins will be changed. The Table Tools Design and Layout tabs should be showing.

2. Click the **Layout** tab, and click **Cell Margins** in the Alignment group, as shown in Figure 5-9.

3. Click the margin you want.

Delete a Table

To delete a table and its contents:

1. Click the border or edge of the table to select it.

2. Press **DELETE**.

Use the Table Design Tab

The Table Design tab is an important tool when working with tables. You display it by clicking the table you're working on. The tab provides tools to manipulate and format the table. Table 5-1 shows the functions of the tab.

Use Table Style Options

When designing your table, you can quickly specify some special formatting. This is particularly useful when you have column or row headings, total columns or rows, or want the table to be banded so that the columns or rows can be read more easily.

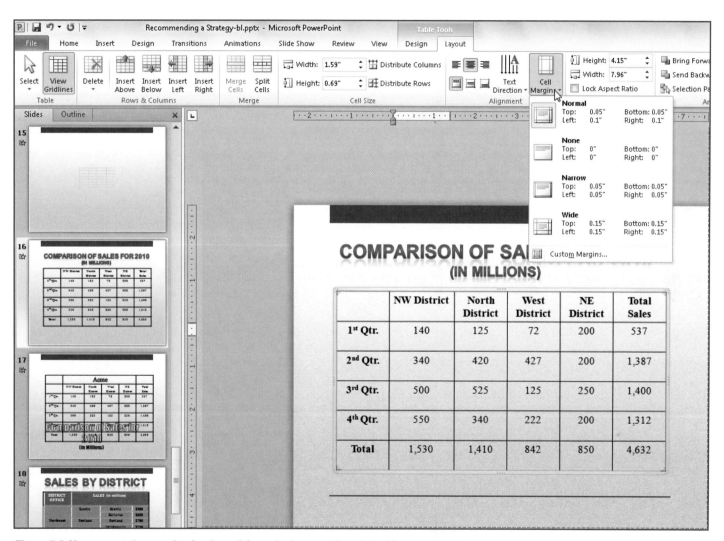

Figure 5-9: You can set the margins for the cell from the Layout tab and the Alignment group.

Highlight your table and place check marks in the pertinent check boxes on the Table Tools Design tab in the Table Style Options group to enable the features. (See Table 5-1 for explanations for each of the check boxes.)

GROUP NAME	TOOL NAME	DESCRIPTION	SEE THIS SECTION FOR MORE INFORMATION
Table Style Options			
☑ Header Row	Header Row	Identifies that special formatting exists for the header row.	"Use Table Style Options"
☑ Total Row	Total Row	Identifies a total row on the bottom of the table that is holding totals.	"Use Table Style Options"
☑ Banded Rows	Banded Rows	Indicates that rows are banded to distinguish between odd and even rows.	"Use Table Style Options"
☑ First Column	First Column	Indicates that the first column is to contain special formatting.	"Use Table Style Options"
☑ Last Column	Last Column	Indicates that the last column of the table is to have special formatting.	"Use Table Style Options"
☑ Banded Columns	Banded Columns	Indicates that columns are banded to distinguish between odd and even columns.	"Use Table Style Options"
Table Styles			
Table Styles	Table Styles	Displays a menu of color and design styles for tables.	"Enhance Tables with Preset Styles"
◇ Shading ▾	Shading	Applies the current color or displays a menu of fill colors. You can fill a table or selected cells with a selected color. You can also fill with gradient colors, patterns, textures, or a picture.	"Use Special Effects in the Table Background"
⊞ Borders ▾	Borders	Determines which lines in the table will be displayed.	"Use Special Effects in the Table Background"
▢ Effects ▾	Effects	Allows for beveling, shadowing, and reflections to be used for special effects in tables.	"Use Special Effects in the Table Background"
WordArt Styles			Chapter 8
A Quick Styles ▾	Quick Styles	Provides a menu of artistic text.	Chapter 8
A ▾	Text Fill	Clicking the down arrow displays a menu of color for selected text; clicking the icon applies the current color.	Chapter 8
A ▾	Text Outline	Clicking the down arrow displays a menu of color for outlines; clicking the icon displays a menu of color for selected text outlines.	Chapter 8
A ▾	Text Effects	Displays a menu of effects that can be applied to text: shadow, beveling, etc.	Chapter 8

Table 5-1: Tools on the Table Design Tab

GROUP NAME	TOOL NAME	DESCRIPTION	SEE THIS SECTION FOR MORE INFORMATION
Draw Borders			"Work with Borders"
	Pen Style	Displays a menu of border styles.	"Work with Borders"
1 pt ———	Pen Weight	Displays a menu of border sizes in points.	"Work with Borders"
Pen Color	Pen Color	Converts lines to a selected color when you click them.	"Work with Borders"
Draw Table	Draw Table	Use to draw a table with irregular columns and row sizes	"Draw a Table"
Eraser	Eraser	Erases lines as you click them or drag over them.	"Draw a Table"

Table 5-1: Tools on the Table Design Tab (Continued)

TIP

To remove all formatting of table styles from the Table Tools Design Table Styles menu and begin again, click the **Clear Table** button on the bottom of the menu.

Clear Table

NOTE

Chapter 8 describes how to use WordArt for text. In a table, you find WordArt features on the Table Tools Design tab in the WordArt Styles group.

Enhance Tables with Preset Styles

PowerPoint 2010 contains preset styles for quickly giving tables color and other design styles. Figure 5-10 shows the styles available to you (your colors will look different depending on the theme of your presentation). These can then be modified with further special effects. (See "Use Special Effects in the Table Background.") The original style comes from the presentation's theme.

1. To select the table, click anywhere in the table and display the Table Tools Design tab.

2. Click the **More** button on the Table Styles group. The menu of preset styles will open.

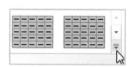

3. Move your pointer over the choices, and you will see the results of each on the table beneath the menu. (You may have to move the table to the side to see the results.) When you see a choice you'd like to try, click it. The table will be formatted with that style. You can easily change it again.

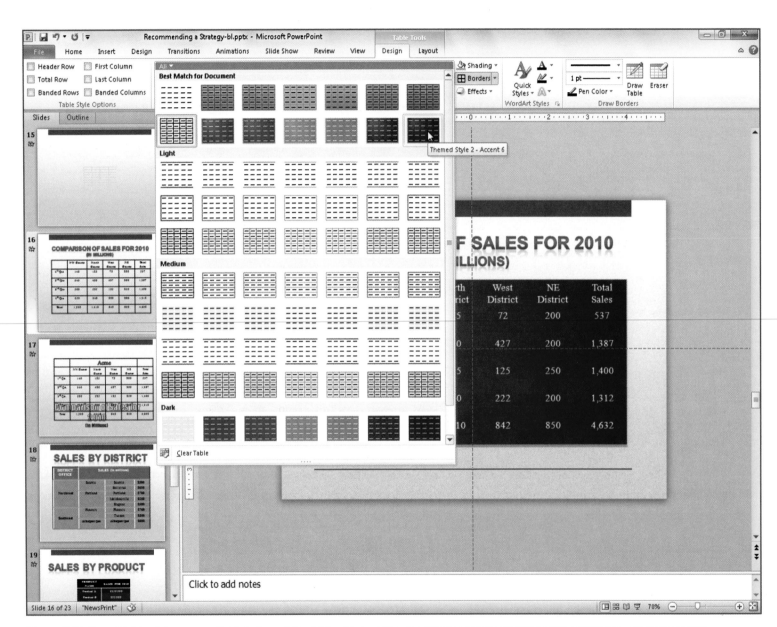

Figure 5-10: Preset table styles are available to format the table with a professional-looking and colorful design, which you can then modify.

Use Special Effects in the Table Background

You can use some special effects, such as gradient, colors, and texture, in the table background.

1. Select the cells you want to have the special effect; click the border or edge of the table to select the whole table.

2. On the Table Tools Design tab, click the **Shading** down arrow. A menu is displayed.

3. Click an option, such as **Gradient** or **Texture**. A submenu is displayed.

4. Click your choice, and the gradient effect or texture will be applied to your table.

SHADE CELLS, COLUMNS, ROWS, OR A TABLE

You can create automatic banding using PowerPoint's preset table styles, or you can do it on your own. Shading cells, columns, or rows makes them easier to read. If you shade the background of the whole table, you can add color and a refining touch. Background shading can also be used to distinguish the table from the slide itself. Figure 5-11 shows an example of a table with shaded columns and rows that make it more readable.

1. Select the row, column, or cell to be shaded. To select the whole table, click the border or edge of the table, or highlight all cells in the table.

2. On the Table Design tab, click the **Shading** down arrow, and click the shade of color to be applied to the selected area of the table. The selected area will be filled accordingly. You can point at various shades before selecting one to see the effect they will have on the table—you may have to move the table to see it clearly when the menu is displayed.

USE A PICTURE IN YOUR TABLE

You can add pictures to your table. The picture will be entered into a cell. If need be, you can enlarge the picture by merging cells.

1. Select the cell to contain the picture.

2. On the Table Tools Design tab, click the **Shading** down arrow, and click **Picture** from the menu.

3. The Insert Picture dialog box will appear. Find the path to the picture you want, click the picture, and click **Insert**. The picture will be inserted into the cell.

Comparison of Sales for 2010
(in Millions)

	NW District	North District	West District	NE District	Total Sales
1st Qtr.	140	125	72	200	537
2nd Qtr.	340	420	427	200	1,387
3rd Qtr.	500	525	125	250	1,400
4th Qtr.	550	340	222	200	1,312
Total	1,530	1,410	842	850	4,632

Figure 5-11: Shaded columns and rows enable readers to find the totals more easily.

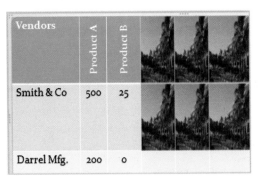

MERGE CELLS TO ENLARGE A PICTURE

You can select multiple cells that will hold the picture either at the beginning of the process or right before you merge the cells.

1. Select the cell or cells that will contain the picture.

2. On the Table Tools Design tab, click the **Shading** down arrow, and click **Picture** from the menu.

3. The Insert Picture dialog box will appear. Find the path to the picture you want, click the picture, and click **Insert**. The picture will be inserted into the cell, or, if multiple cells were selected, each cell will contain a copy of the picture.

4. To combine the pictures into a single large one, select the cells you want to contain the larger picture.

5. On the Table Tools Layout tab, click **Merge Cells** in the Merge group. The cells will be merged into one cell containing the picture.

DISPLAY OR HIDE INSIDE AND OUTSIDE BORDER LINES

To change the appearance of the borders (or cells) by controlling which inside or outside border lines appear:

1. Click the edge or border of the table to select it, or highlight the cells to select them. The Table Tools Design tab is displayed.

2. Click the **Borders** down arrow to see a menu of border selections, as shown in Figure 5-12.

3. Click the border option you want. If you selected the table, the whole table will conform to the new border selection. If you selected one or more cells, only the cells' outlines will change.

Work with Borders

You can vary the style (solid versus dotted line, for example), weight or thickness, and color of table borders.

NOTE

When you click the Border button on the Table Tools Table Styles group without clicking the down arrow, the selected cells or table will conform to the currently selected border.

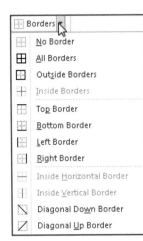

Figure 5-12: Borders of a cell or entire table can be set with the Borders tool on the Design tab.

CHANGE BORDER STYLE

To change the style or appearance of a border:

1. Click the border or edge of the table to select it. The Table Tools Design tab is displayed.

2. On the Table Tools Design tab, click the **Pen Style** button in the Draw Borders group.

3. Select the style of line you want. The pointer will morph into a pencil.

Product A		$250,000
Product B		$55,000

4. With the pencil icon, click or draw along the borders you want to have the new style. Click **ESC** when finished.

CHANGE BORDER WEIGHT

To change the thickness or weight of a border:

1. Click the border or edge of the table to select it. The Table Tools Design tab is displayed.

2. On the Design tab, click the **Pen Weight** button in the Draw Borders group.

3. Select the weight of line you want. The pointer will morph into a pencil.

4. With the pencil icon, click or draw along the borders you want to have the new weight. Click **ESC** when finished.

CHANGE BORDER COLOR

To change the color of a border:

1. Click the border or edge of the table to select it. The Design tab is displayed.

2. On the Table Design tab, click the **Pen Color** down arrow in the Draw Borders group. A dialog box appears, shown in Figure 5-13.

3. Select the line color you want. The pointer will morph into a pencil.

4. With the pencil icon, click or draw along the borders or lines on which you want to change the color.

Use the Table Layout Tab

Tables are managed and manipulated using the Layout tab. It contains commands to select, insert, and delete rows and columns; merge and split them; manipulate cell size; and align text within cells. Table 5-2 shows the commands on the Layout tab.

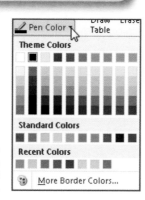

Figure 5-13: The Pen Color dialog box presents a palette of color options for the borders and lines of your table.

GROUP NAME	TOOL NAME	DESCRIPTION	SEE THIS SECTION FOR MORE INFORMATION
Table			
Select	Select	Allows you to select a table, column, or row.	"Selecting Table Components"
View Gridlines	View Gridlines	Display or hide gridlines on the table.	"Show or Hide Gridlines"
Rows and Columns			
Delete	Delete	Delete selected tables, rows, or columns.	"Deleting Columns and Rows"
Insert Above	Insert Above	Insert a row above the selected row.	"Insert Columns and Rows"
Insert Below	Insert Below	Insert a row below the selected row.	"Insert Columns and Rows"
Insert Left	Insert Left	Insert a column to the left of the selected column.	"Insert Columns and Rows"
Insert Right	Insert Right	Insert a column to the right of the selected column.	"Insert Columns and Rows"
Merge			
Merge Cells	Merge Cells	Merge selected cells into one cell.	"Merging or Splitting Cells"
Split Cells	Split Cells	Split selected cells into rows and columns.	"Merging or Splitting Cells"
Cell Size			
Height:	Height	Type the height of the cell. Changes the height of all cells in selected rows.	"Change the Size of Columns and Rows"

Table 5-2: Tools on the Table Layout Tab

GROUP NAME	TOOL NAME	DESCRIPTION	SEE THIS SECTION FOR MORE INFORMATION
Width: 1.69"	Width	Type the width of the cell. Changes the width of all cells in selected columns.	"Change the Size of Columns and Rows"
Distribute Rows	Distribute Rows	Make the height of the selected rows equal.	"Change the Size of Columns and Rows"
Distribute Columns	Distribute Columns	Make the width of the selected columns equal.	"Change the Size of Columns and Rows"
Alignment			
Align Horizontally icons	Align Horizontally	Left-align, center, or right-align within a cell.	"Aligning Text"
Align Vertically icons	Align Vertically	Top-align, center vertically, or bottom-align within a cell.	"Aligning Text"
Text Direction	Text Direction	Rotate or stack text within a cell.	"Rotating Text in Cells"
Cell Margins	Cell Margins	Set cell margins.	"Set Cell Margins"
Table Size			
Height: 3.33"	Height	Type the height of a table.	
Width: 5.33"	Width	Type the width of a table.	
Lock Aspect Ratio	Lock Aspect Ratio	Ensure proportional changes as height and width changes are made.	
Arrange			
Bring Forward	Bring Forward	Bring the selected object one position forward on the stack of objects; clicking the down arrow gives a choice of advancing one object to the top or going directly to the top.	
Send Backward	Send Backward	Put selected object one position backward on the stack of objects. Clicking the down arrow gives a choice of going back one position or going directly to the bottom.	
Selection Pane	Selection Pane	Display a task pane to work with objects more easily.	
Align	Align	Display all column and row alignment options; provide grid options.	
Group	Group	Options for grouping or ungrouping selected objects.	
Rotate	Rotate	Rotate objects.	

*Table 5-2: **Tools on the Table Layout Tab (Continued)***

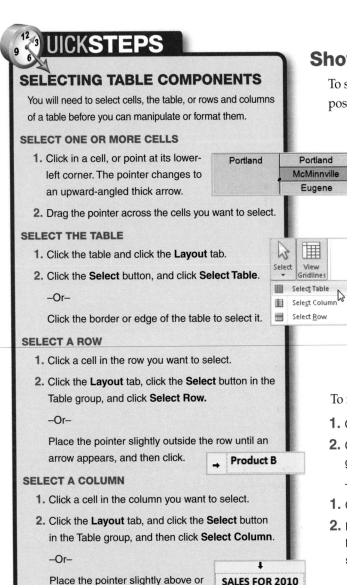

SELECTING TABLE COMPONENTS

You will need to select cells, the table, or rows and columns of a table before you can manipulate or format them.

SELECT ONE OR MORE CELLS

1. Click in a cell, or point at its lower-left corner. The pointer changes to an upward-angled thick arrow.

2. Drag the pointer across the cells you want to select.

SELECT THE TABLE

1. Click the table and click the **Layout** tab.

2. Click the **Select** button, and click **Select Table**.

   –Or–

   Click the border or edge of the table to select it.

SELECT A ROW

1. Click a cell in the row you want to select.

2. Click the **Layout** tab, click the **Select** button in the Table group, and click **Select Row.**

   –Or–

   Place the pointer slightly outside the row until an arrow appears, and then click.

SELECT A COLUMN

1. Click a cell in the column you want to select.

2. Click the **Layout** tab, and click the **Select** button in the Table group, and then click **Select Column**.

   –Or–

   Place the pointer slightly above or below the column, and then click.

Show or Hide Gridlines

To show or hide gridlines so that you can see the cells more clearly or to position objects more precisely:

1. Click the border or edge of the table to select it.

2. Click the **Layout** tab.

   - Click **Align** in the Arrange group, and click **View Gridlines** to display the gridlines.

   - Repeat the action to hide them. When the check mark is clear, the gridlines are hidden.

Insert Columns and Rows

You may find that you need to add rows or columns to your table.

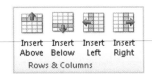

To insert a row:

1. Click in the row above or below where the new row is to be inserted.

2. Click the **Layout** tab, and click **Insert Above** or **Insert Below** in the Rows & Columns group.

   –Or–

1. Click in the row above or below where the new row is to be inserted.

2. Right-click the table and click **Insert**. A context menu will be displayed. Click **Insert Rows Above** or **Insert Rows Below**. The row will be inserted above or below the selected row.

DELETING COLUMNS AND ROWS

You can easily delete rows or columns on your table.

1. Click in the row or column, or highlight multiple rows or columns to be deleted by dragging over them.

2. Click the **Layout** tab, and click the **Delete** button.

- To delete selected columns, click **Delete Columns**.

- To delete selected rows, click **Delete Rows**.

   –Or–

- Highlight one or more rows or columns to be deleted, right-click, and select **Delete Rows** or **Delete Columns** from the context menu.

You can click **Undo** on the Quick Access toolbar (or you can press **CTRL+Z**) to reverse the previous action. You can undo up to 20 previous actions in this way.

To insert a column:

1. Click in the column to the left or right of where the new column is to be inserted.

2. Click the **Layout** menu, and click **Insert Left** or **Insert Right** on the Rows & Columns group.

   –Or–

1. Click in the column to the right or left of where you want the new column inserted.

2. Right-click the table and click **Insert**. From the context menu, click **Insert Columns To The Left** or **Insert Columns To The Right**. The column will be inserted to the right or left of the selected one.

Change the Size of Columns and Rows

You can change the width of columns and the height of rows manually by dragging the border of the column or row, you can type the specific height or width, or you can let PowerPoint do it automatically.

CHANGE COLUMN WIDTH

To adjust the size of the column, first click inside the table to select it.

- Place your pointer on the right border or edge of a column so that it morphs into a two-headed arrow. Drag the border right or left to increase or decrease the size, respectively.

   –Or–

- Click the **Layout** tab, and then click **Distribute Columns** in the Cell Size group. This makes the columns the same width and adjusts the contents to fit.

   –Or–

- Place your pointer on the right border of a column so that it morphs into a two-headed arrow. Double-click the column border to have PowerPoint adjust it to match the width of the longest piece of content within the column.

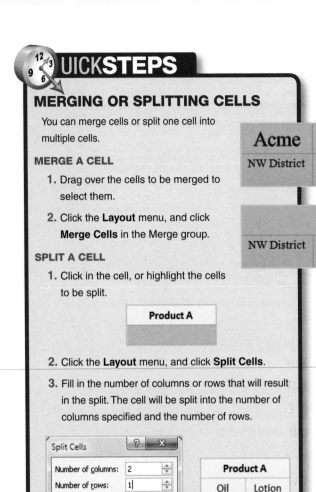

QUICKSTEPS

MERGING OR SPLITTING CELLS

You can merge cells or split one cell into multiple cells.

MERGE A CELL

1. Drag over the cells to be merged to select them.

2. Click the **Layout** menu, and click **Merge Cells** in the Merge group.

SPLIT A CELL

1. Click in the cell, or highlight the cells to be split.

2. Click the **Layout** menu, and click **Split Cells**.

3. Fill in the number of columns or rows that will result in the split. The cell will be split into the number of columns specified and the number of rows.

CHANGE ROW HEIGHT

To adjust the size of rows, first click outside the table to deselect any cells.

- Place your pointer on the lower border of a row so that it morphs into a two-headed arrow. Drag the border up or down to decrease or increase the size, respectively.

  –Or–

- Click the table. Click the **Layout** tab, and then click **Distribute Rows** on the Cell Size group. This makes the rows the same height and adjusts the contents to fit.

NOTE

To set a specific height and width for selected cells (which will affect all cells in the row or column), select the cells, click the **Layout** tab, and click the **Height** or **Width** spinners in the Cell Size group.

Chapter 6
Using Clips, Photos, and Other Images

This chapter looks at how you can add some pizzazz to your presentation by using *images*, such as clip art, photos, screenshots, and photo albums, to make your presentations more interesting. By adding colorful elements to your presentations, you keep your viewer's attention, balancing the narrative parts with visual effects.

Work with Clip Art

PowerPoint is installed with many "clips." Clips can be media files, such as sound, graphics, videos, and animation. In this section, we look at *clip art*, which comprises photos, drawings, and bitmaps. You will see how to find clip art on your own computer and online, then how to insert it, position it, and modify it to get the results you want. You will see how to place clip art using a grid and ruler lines to help you position it more precisely. You will see how to change

UNDERSTANDING OBJECTS

PowerPoint arranges art and graphic objects into three categories: images, illustrations, and tables. Many of the rules for manipulating these categories are the same. In this book, we often group them into a "super category" called *objects*. Therefore, an object, as mentioned in the "Working with Objects" QuickSteps, can be clip art, photos, a graph or chart, a table, a drawing, text, and so on.

UNDERSTAND IMAGES

Images include pictures, clip art, screenshots, and photo albums. The following are explored in this chapter:

- **Pictures** are separate files, typically photos, in formats such as .jpg, .gif, and .bmp.

- **Clip art** consists of separate files, generally small drawings and icons, located in collections on your computer or found on Office Online.

- **Screenshots** are graphic "captures" of what is displayed on your screen, such as windows, toolbars, and portions of Web pages. (The illustrations in this book are mostly screen captures.)

- **Photo albums** are slide shows of photographs and images in an album format. You select pictures and appearance options, such as display layout, captions, and frames for the photos.

UNDERSTAND ILLUSTRATIONS

Illustrations, covered in Chapters 7 and 8, include shapes, SmartArt, and charts.

- **Shapes** are prebuilt, simple graphics of common building-block drawings, such as circles, lines, arrows, flowchart elements, and callouts. Integrated with shapes is WordArt, a tool to add graphic artist–type effects to associated text.

Continued . . .

the image color, resize it, crop photos to refine the image, and delete clip art when necessary. You will also learn how to improve an image by increasing or decreasing contrast and brightness, and about the Clip Organizer, which enables you to find clips easily.

Find and Insert Clip Art

With your presentation open, you find clip art using the Clip Art task pane.

1. Click the **Insert** tab. Click **Clip Art** in the Images group. The Clip Art task pane will open, as shown in Figure 6-1.

2. In the **Search For** text box, type keywords for the subject you are looking for (for example, meetings, family, cars, or holidays).

3. Click the **Results Should Be** down arrow to open a menu of media types. Verify that the appropriate check boxes are selected. If a check box is selected, that media type will be searched for. (By default, all choices are selected.)

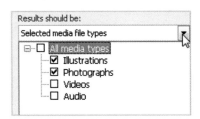

4. Click **Go** to start the search.

*Figure 6-1: **The Clip Art task pane allows you to search for clip art.***

UNDERSTANDING OBJECTS *(Continued)*

- **SmartArt** are shapes that have been enhanced and grouped together with text elements to provide prebuilt templates to demonstrate common interrelations, such as processes, cycles, and hierarchies.

- **Charts** are graphic representations of data contained in tables. They can be imported from applications such as Microsoft Excel or created directly in PowerPoint. The charts are used to bring life and visibility to numbers in presentations.

UNDERSTAND TABLES

Tables, a category all to itself, is covered in Chapter 5. Tables, whether imported from a spreadsheet program such as Excel or created in PowerPoint, organize data into rows and columns.

PowerPoint 2010 continues the trend of recent Office releases of blurring the distinction between various types of graphics and making working with them a more unified experience. The result is a tightly integrated grouping that shares similar formatting, sizing, and other attributes. No need to wonder whether you are working with images, illustrations, or tables. Simply select the object, and contextual tabs are displayed on the ribbon, providing quick access to many galleries of prebuilt designs, styles, and other tools. You can change the component elements of these prebuilt offerings (such as fill, outline, and special effects), or you can use a common Formatting dialog box that then lets you modify the formatting attributes in fine detail.

OLE (Object Linking and Embedding) objects, such as a spreadsheet, are either linked or embedded from another application, such as Microsoft Excel, work in a slightly different way, and are covered in Chapter 5.

5. The search results will be displayed as thumbnails in the preview pane, as shown in Figure 6-1. Scroll through the list. Click the thumbnail of the picture you want to insert, and it will be placed on the selected slide. (Alternatively, you can either right-click a selected thumbnail or click the down arrow on the thumbnail, and click **Insert**.)

Change the Color of Clip Art

You can change the color of clip art to be a different color, grayscale, sepia, washout, or dark and light variations on a color. You can even make a color transparent. To change the color of clip art in a presentation:

1. Click the clip art whose color you want to change. That will make the Picture Tools upper-level tab available to you. Click the **Format** tab, if it is not already displayed.

2. In the Adjust group, click the **Color** button. A menu of color choices will be shown, as you can see in Figure 6-2.

- As you point to a color, you can see how it would change the selected clip art. Under Recolor, you can see color as well as grayscale, sepia, and washout options. You can vary the intensity of a color.

- Click **More Variations** to see additional color choices.

- Click **Set Transparent Color** to turn the pointer into a pencil-and-arrow icon, which you can use to click the color you want made transparent. For example, clicking the red color of the clip art shown in Figure 6-2 turns the color transparent.

- Click **Picture Color Options** to open the Format Picture dialog box.

3. Click a color to select it.

Insert a Picture

Insert a picture using the Insert tab, as you did with clip art.

1. Click the **Insert** tab, and then click the **Picture** button in the Images group. The Insert Picture dialog box will appear.

2. Find and click the picture you want, and click **Insert**. The picture will be inserted on your slide.

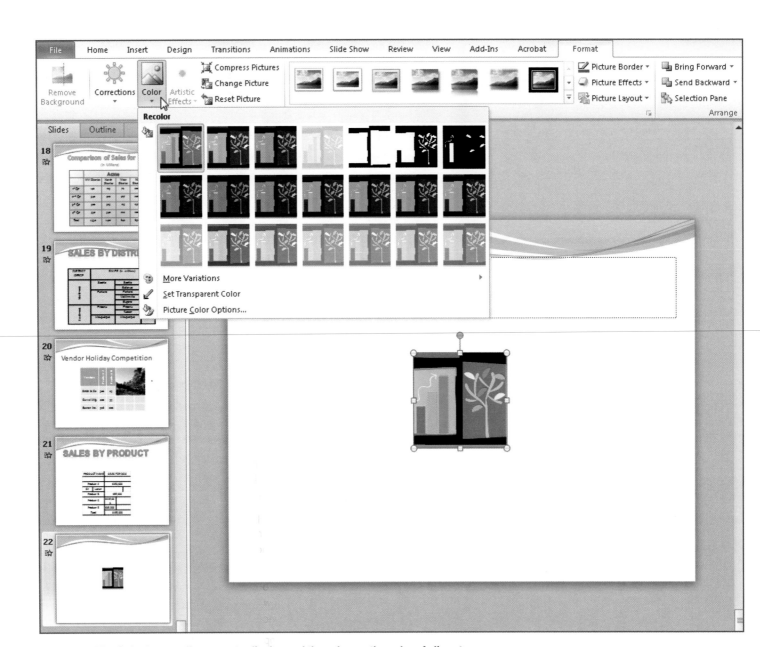

Figure 6-2: *The Color button allows you to display and then change the color of clip art.*

QUICKSTEPS

WORKING WITH OBJECTS

An object (see the "Understanding Objects" QuickFacts) is something added to a slide that can be selected, such as clip art, photos, a graph or chart, a drawing, or text placeholders.

SELECT OBJECTS

- Click an object to select it. You will know it is selected when the sizing handles and rotating handle are visible.

  –Or–

- Press **TAB**. If several objects are on the screen, press **TAB** until the one you want is selected.

MOVE OBJECTS

1. Select the object by clicking it.
2. Place the pointer on the selected object (but not on the sizing handles). The pointer will morph into a four-headed arrow.
3. Drag the object to its new location.

RESIZE OBJECTS

1. Select the object by clicking it.
2. Place the pointer on any of the sizing handles so that the pointer arrow morphs into a two-headed arrow. Then hold down the mouse button until the pointer morphs into a cross.
3. Drag the border of the object inward, outward, or diagonally to the size you want. Press **SHIFT** while you drag to size it proportionally.

DELETE OBJECTS

Select the object by clicking it, and then press **DELETE**.

Crop Objects

Cropping clip art or a picture allows you to zero in on the essential elements. You can cut the irrelevant part of the picture and retain the part you want to focus on.

1. Click the picture to be cropped to select it so that you can see the sizing handles on all four edges. The Picture Tools upper-level tab is now available as well.

2. Click the **Format** tab, and then click the upper half of the **Crop** button in the Size group. (The lower half of the Crop button contains a down arrow, and if you click that, just click **Crop** again from the menu.) Cropping marks will appear where the sizing handles are, and the pointer will morph between a four-headed arrow (when the pointer is within the picture) and a cropping tool, depending on where it is pointing. To use the cropping tool:

- Place the four-headed arrow on top of the cropping handles. It will turn into a cropping tool (an "elbow" or "T" shape, depending on the cropping handle it is on top of) when it is accurately placed.

Before pointer is placed correctly over crop handles   **After pointer is correctly placed**

- To cut an unwanted portion from one side of the picture, place the crop tool on a cropping handle, and drag it inward (vertically or horizontally) until the picture is reduced to what you want to see.

- If you want to cut unwanted portions equally from both sides of the picture (vertically or horizontally), press **CTRL** while dragging the crop tool. You can also press **SHIFT** to crop proportionally. Figure 6-3 shows an example of a picture being cropped.

- You can drag the image around the outer cropped background to get the image positioned exactly as you want. Place the pointer over the image until the four-headed arrow appears, and then drag.

3. When you have finished cropping your picture, click outside the cropped image to clear the cropping tool mode, and save your presentation. (Or click Crop again to turn it off.)

TIP

As the picture is reduced in size by cropping, you might alternate between resizing the picture and cropping it to gain a better idea of what else to crop. To do that, you need to click outside the picture to change from cropping to sizing, click the picture, drag the sizing handle, click the **Crop** tool, perhaps drag the internal image or drag the cropping handles, and so on.

NOTE

An image may be a bitmap or a vector image. If you draw a picture, for instance, depending on the drawing product and the choices you make about the saved image, your image may be saved as a group of pixels that define the image as a set of points only (bitmap image) or as mathematical expressions that define the image by a series of lines and points (vector image). Files extensions of .tif, .jpg, .bmp, and .gif are common bitmap files. Common vector extensions are .eps, .cdr, .wmf, and .emf.

NOTE

You may be asked to download an add-on/ActiveX control before you can access the page.

*Figure 6-3: **Cropping a picture lets you narrow the focus to exactly what you want to see.***

Search for Clip Art on the Internet

To search the Internet for clip art:

1. Click the **Insert** tab, and click **Clip Art** in the Images group.

2. On the Clip Art task pane, you have two options:

   - Select the **Include Office.com Content** check box. Specific search results will include Office.com matches.

   - Click the **Find More At Office.com** link to search for what you want and see what's available online.

3. Your browser will open the Microsoft Office Online clip art site. Continue searching for the art you want.

QUICKSTEPS

CHANGING CONTRAST AND BRIGHTNESS

You can adjust the contrast, brightness, sharpness, and softness of an object all from one menu. See Figure 6-4 for examples of contrast and brightness.

ADJUST CONTRAST AND BRIGHTNESS

1. If the Format tab is not selected, click the picture to select it.

2. Click the **Corrections** button in the Adjust group. The current settings for sharpen, soften, brightness, and contrast are selected in the menu by default.

   - Move your pointer over the settings in the Sharpen and Softness options to see how your picture will change.

   - Move your pointer over the settings in the Brightness and Contrast options to see the differences there.

3. When you find the setting you want, click the thumbnail, and your picture will be changed.

CHANGE BRIGHTNESS AND CONTRAST PRECISELY

1. If the Picture Tools Format tab is not showing, click the picture to be altered.

2. In the Picture Tools Format tab, click **Corrections** in the Adjust group.

3. Click **Picture Corrections Options** at the bottom of the menu. The Format Picture dialog box appears.

4. For the Picture Corrections option, drag the sliders, type a percentage, or click the respective spinners to apply the Sharpen And Soften or Brightness And Contrast settings. Figure 6-4 shows an example. Click **Close** when you're done.

Before applying any corrections | After contrast is increased by 40%, brightness by 2% | After brightness is increased by 20%, sharpen by –66% (i.e., for background image)

Figure 6-4: *Examples of before and after changing settings for sharpness, contrast, and brightness.*

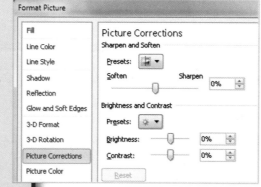

Display a Grid and Guides

Grids and guides can help you align objects precisely.

1. Right-click the slide. Select **Grid And Guides** from the context menu. The Grid And Guides dialog box appears.

2. Select one or more of the following options by clicking the relevant check box:

- **Snap Objects To Grid** aligns objects to a gridline.
- **Snap Objects To Other Objects** aligns objects to adjacent objects.
- The **Spacing** combo box offers options to specify exact grid spacing, as well as allowing you to type your own.
- **Display Grid On Screen** displays the grid on the screen.
- **Display Drawing Guides On Screen** displays horizontal and vertical guide lines on the computer screen.
- **Display Smart Guides When Shapes Are Aligned** displays the guide lines when shapes are aligned.
- **Set As Default** makes your current grid and guide settings the default settings.

3. Click **OK** to close the Grid And Guides dialog box.

Use Format Painter

Use the Format Painter to copy attributes from one object to another. All attributes will be copied, such as color, border formatting, and text formatting. If the object is not ungrouped (see Chapter 8 for a discussion on grouping/ungrouping), the entire image will receive the copied attributes.

1. Select the object containing the attributes to be copied, whether it is a picture, clip art, shape, or WordArt.
2. On the Home tab, click the **Format Painter** button in the Clipboard group.
3. Click the object where you want the formatting to be copied.

Create a Photo Album

To create a photo album with options for layout and captions:

1. Click the **Insert** tab, and on the Images group, click the **Photo Album** down arrow and then click **New Photo Album**. The Photo Album dialog box appears.

2. Click **File/Disk** to find and select the images you want to include in the album. Click **Insert** to place the selected images in the album. Figure 6-5 shows an example of an album being created.

Figure 6-5: You can create a custom photo album and display it as a slide show.

When you insert a text box in a photo album page, it can change the layout of the page. For instance if you choose two pictures per page and a text box, you'll get one picture per page with a text box. You might want to wait and insert the text box after the photo album is created by clicking **Picture Tools**, clicking **Format**, clicking **Insert**, and clicking **Text Box**.

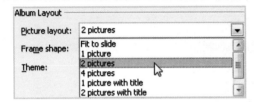

3. You have these options:

- To have a caption beneath all images in the album, click **Captions Below ALL Pictures**. If this option is grayed or unavailable, change the Picture Layout to something other than Fit To Slide.

- Click **ALL Pictures Black And White** to strip the color from all images. You can make changes to individual images when the photo album is created with the Picture Tools commands.

- Click **New Text Box** if you want to insert a narrative with some or all of the images. This inserts an item in the Pictures In Album list. Click the **Up** and **Down** arrows beneath the list to move the text box where you want it in the list. The text box can be moved around on the page, and a varying amount of text can be entered.

- Under Album Layout, click **Picture Layout** to determine how the album pages will be laid out—for instance, one image to a page or more. The thumbnail on the right reflects the selected layout.

- Click **Frame Shape** to create a border around the images or change their edges. The thumbnail to the right shows the effect of the choice.

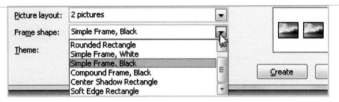

- To find and select a theme for your photo album, click **Browse**. It can be one that comes with PowerPoint or a custom theme you have created.

- The toolbar beneath the Preview image contains the following tools for making limited changes:

  - **Rotate Left, Rotate Right** rotates the image a quarter rotation to the left or right.

  - **Increase Contrast, Decrease Contrast** increases or decreases the contrast between colors.

  - **Increase Brightness, Decrease Brightness** increases or decreases the light or brightness in the image.

4. Click **Create** when your options are set. The album will open as an in-work PowerPoint presentation with all the tools and effects you have with a slide show. Figure 6-6 shows an example.

*Figure 6-6: **The completed photo album is simply a PowerPoint presentation with all the tools and special effects of a slide show.***

Snap a Screenshot

If you want to capture a screenshot of a program open on your desktop, you can use Screenshot. This command creates an image from an open program (not minimized in the taskbar), either captured automatically and made available to you or captured by you. There are two ways you can acquire screenshots.

CAPTURE AN OPEN WINDOW

If you have an open window on your desktop, it will be automatically available to you as a screenshot.

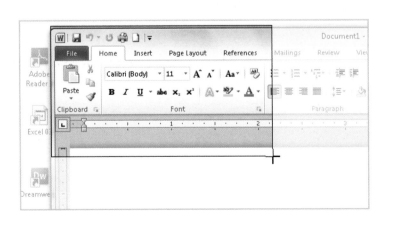

1. Open the program, or arrange your desktop to contain the programs or icons you want to capture with Screenshot.

2. In PowerPoint, click the slide where you want the screenshot to appear.

3. Click **Insert** and click **Screenshot**. A menu is displayed. Under Available Windows, click the image you want. It will be placed on your slide.

DEFINE A PARTIAL SCREENSHOT

In this case, you arrange your desktop with the windows you want, and then you clip or outline the part of it you want to capture.

1. Open the program, or arrange your desktop to contain the programs or icons you want to capture with the Screenshot command.

2. In PowerPoint, click the slide where you want the screenshot to appear.

3. Click **Insert**, click **Screenshot**, and then click **Screen Clipping**. PowerPoint will be replaced with a whitened desktop and a + pointer.

4. Drag the pointer over the items you want to capture, and release the pointer. PowerPoint is redisplayed with the captured image on your slide.

5. Drag the image where you want it on the slide.

Chapter 7
Using Charts in a Presentation

You add graphs and charts to make your presentations more interesting and informative. With these tools, you can add visual information to your presentation, making it more easily absorbed and understood. You reach more viewers with complete information, as it is easier to absorb pictures than numbers or words.

In this chapter you will see how to insert and format charts in your presentation. You will insert charts from scratch or import them from Microsoft Excel. You will learn how to perfect them by entering your own data, selecting your own type of chart, and formatting chart components—such as titles, data series, x- and y-axes, plot area, text, and axis numbers.

Work with Charts

You can create a chart or graph from scratch within PowerPoint or import one from Excel. In this book, graphs and charts are the same thing. When you first create a chart or graph in PowerPoint (and if you have Microsoft Excel 2007/2010 installed), you'll see a model chart displayed on the selected slide and the data creating it contained in a separate Excel window. If the data or chart comes from Excel 2007/2010, that application is opened and its ribbon and toolbars are available in a separate window, integrated with the PowerPoint ribbon and toolbars, to modify its own component. You can embed the chart, wherein the data is totally contained within PowerPoint, copy or paste the Excel chart as an image (it cannot be edited), or you can link the chart back to an Excel worksheet, where it is updated when the original worksheet is modified.

Insert Charts

When you first insert a chart, PowerPoint inserts a sample chart with a separate window containing an Excel worksheet. You replace the data in the worksheet with your own data, and it is reflected in the PowerPoint chart. You can also replace the chart with one of a different type, that is, a pie graph for a bar chart. A chart can contain *data series*—a group of related data points that are plotted on a chart. Each data series contains data points defining unique values in the series. You'll have plenty of room—you don't need to worry about running out of room for all your chart elements.

INSERT A CHART FROM WITHIN POWERPOINT

When you insert a chart using PowerPoint's tools, you are embedding a chart; that is, the data defining the chart is wholly contained within PowerPoint, even though you use Excel to define the data. To insert a graph within PowerPoint:

1. Click the slide that is to contain the chart or graph. Find a layout that contains the layout format and enough space for the chart you want.

2. If the layout contains a chart icon, click the **Insert Chart** icon 📊 . Otherwise, click the **Insert** tab, and in the Illustrations group, click **Chart**.

3. An Insert Chart dialog box will appear. Choose the type of chart you want, and click **OK**. A sample chart will be inserted in the Slide pane and a separate window containing a worksheet in Excel 2010 will open, as shown in Figure 7-1.

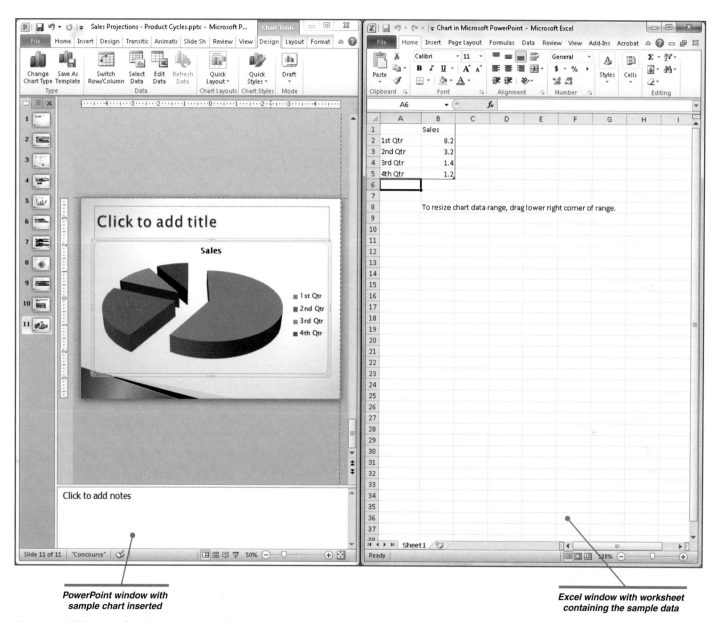

PowerPoint window with sample chart inserted

Excel window with worksheet containing the sample data

Figure 7-1: **When you first insert a chart in PowerPoint, a model of a chart is displayed, with a separate Excel window containing the data for it.**

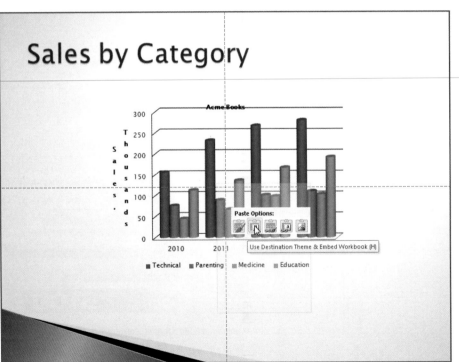
4. Modify the chart and worksheet as needed. (See "Enter Chart Data.")

5. Save the Excel worksheet and then the PowerPoint presentation.

COPY AND PASTE A CHART FROM EXCEL USING SMARTTAG

Excel is primarily a data collection and analysis program; PowerPoint presents data and other information. You can use Microsoft Office 2010 to achieve the best of both worlds by using Excel to retain and manipulate the data and then copying the charts to PowerPoint for use in presentations. You have several options as to the relationship between the data in Excel and the charts in PowerPoint. (We recommend *Microsoft Office Excel 2010 QuickSteps*, published by McGraw-Hill, for learning about Excel.)

1. In Excel, first create, format, and then select the chart. Click **Home** and click **Copy** in the Clipboard area, or use one of several alternative copying techniques, such as right-clicking a blank area on the chart to display the context menu.

2. Open PowerPoint 2010. Find the slide you want, right-click where you want the Excel chart inserted, and click one of the Paste options, as shown in Figure 7-2. You have these options:

   - **Keep Source Formatting & Embed Worksheet** — Retains the original Excel formatting and embeds the chart and workbook data into the destination file so that both the chart and data can be changed independently of the source workbook.

   - **Use Destination Theme & Embed Workbook** — Changes the formatting to that of the PowerPoint presentation, allowing the chart to be compatible with the rest of the presentation, and embeds the chart and workbook data into the destination file so that both the chart and data can be changed independently of the source workbook.

Figure 7-2: Charts are easily copied from Excel to PowerPoint, where you can link to the data or insert the worksheet into the destination file.

VIEWING AND CHANGING SOURCE DATA

You can easily navigate between the data contained in an Excel worksheet and the chart in PowerPoint.

EDIT THE CHART DATA

To display the Excel worksheet containing the data for a chart so you can edit it:

1. Click the chart to display the Chart Tools ribbon.

2. On the Chart Tools Design tab, click **Edit Data** in the Data group. The Excel window will open, displaying the chart data.

EDIT THE DATA SOURCE ATTRIBUTES

To change the attributes of the data itself:

1. Click the chart to display the Chart Tools ribbon.

2. On the Chart Tools Design tab, click **Select Data** in the Data group. The chart data is displayed and the Select Data Source dialog box will appear, as shown in Figure 7-3.

   - To change the data range included in the chart, either select a new range or type over the range in the Chart Data Range text box. (To manipulate the worksheet more easily, click the **Collapse** button ![icon] to minimize the dialog box; click it again to maximize it.)

   - To switch the x- and y-axes, click the **Switch Row/Column** button. The data previously plotted horizontally in rows will now be plotted vertically in columns.

   - To work with the data series entries, click **Add** to add a new series (a new legend entry), click **Edit** to edit the current data series, or click **Remove** to delete a data series.

Continued . . .

- **Keep Source Formatting & Link Data** — Copies the chart with its Excel formatting and maintains a link with the source workbook, so changes made to the data are updated in the PowerPoint chart as well (assuming the link isn't broken by removing the workbook or deleting the data). Updates are made automatically when both source and destination documents are opened, unless default settings have been changed.

- **Use Destination Theme & Link Data** — Copies the chart and changes the formatting according to the PowerPoint presentation. The link with the source workbook is maintained, so changes made to the data are updated in the PowerPoint chart as well, as described in the previous bullet.

- **Picture** — Inserts the chart as a standalone picture. No changes to the component are allowed by the destination program, and no data updates are provided by Excel.

3. You can redo this by clicking the **Paste Options SmartTag** in the lower-right corner of the chart. The five Paste options described in Step 2 are available.

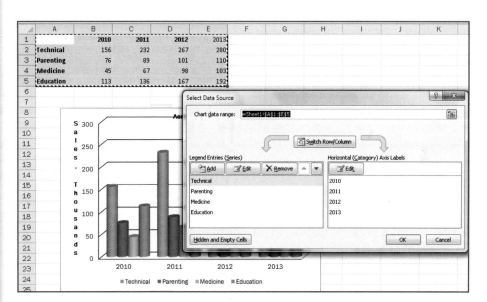

Figure 7-3: **Use the Select Data Source dialog box to change attributes of the source data, such as its range, labels, row-and-column orientation, and how empty and hidden cells will be plotted.**

QUICKSTEPS

VIEWING AND CHANGING SOURCE DATA *(Continued)*

- To rearrange the legend entries, click the **Move Up** or **Move Down** arrow.

- To edit the range of cells included in the category axis labels, click **Edit**.

- To establish how empty cells will be plotted and whether the data contained in hidden rows and columns will be plotted as well, click **Hidden And Empty Cells**.

3. Click **OK**.

NOTE

The new terms for axes are more "horizontal" and "vertical" and less x/y or value/category. Excel determines which axis is x and which is y based on which is greater (the greater one becomes the "horizontal/x/category" axis). Click **Switch Row/Column** in the Select Data Source dialog box (see Figure 7-3) to change this, if necessary.

TIP

The intersection between a horizontal row and a vertical column is a *cell*. You can identify it by the column and row letter/number designation for all charts, such as A1, or by the column and row labels for a particular chart, for example, Technical 2010.

Enter Chart Data

When inserting a new chart, you will need to replace the sample data in the chart with your own data. Be sure to replace all the data and delete the contents of any leftover cells; otherwise, any remaining data will be used to generate the chart.

1. If the Microsoft Excel 2010 window is not open, in PowerPoint, click the chart to display the Chart Tools ribbon. Click the **Design** tab, and click the **Edit Data** button in the Data group. Figure 7-4 shows the Excel window with the datasheet automatically inserted.

2. To clear the current contents, highlight the area of the spreadsheet that you want to replace, and in the Excel Home tab, click the **Clear** down arrow in the Editing group, and click **Clear Contents**.

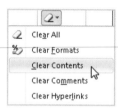

3. Enter your legend titles on the leftmost column. Enter the titles of your horizontal axis on the top row by clicking in a cell and typing. As you make your changes, you will see the chart instantly change.

4. Enter the data series points, that is, the series of data pertaining to one row or column on the datasheet.

Select the Type of Chart

When you insert a chart or graph, you are asked what type of chart you want to create. You can select the type of chart you want to create from several options, depending on your data and how you want it displayed, and you can change this later if need be.

1. Click the chart to display the Chart Tools ribbon. On the Design tab, click the **Change Chart Type** button in the Type group.

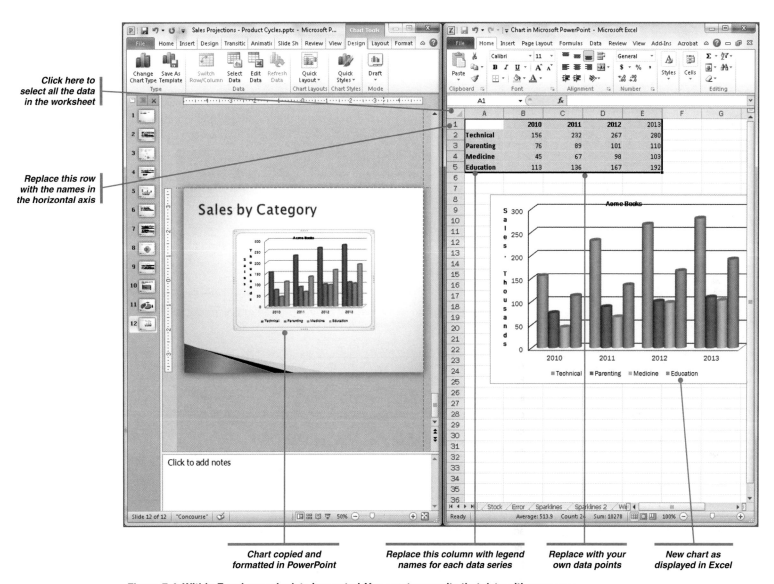

Click here to select all the data in the worksheet

Replace this row with the names in the horizontal axis

Chart copied and formatted in PowerPoint

Replace this column with legend names for each data series

Replace with your own data points

New chart as displayed in Excel

Figure 7-4: **Within Excel, sample data is created. You must overwrite that data with your own.**

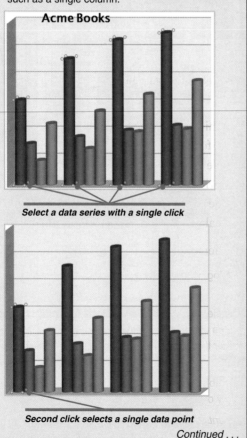

QUICKSTEPS

SELECTING CHART ELEMENTS

Depending on the type of changes to be made, there are several ways to select the chart element you want. Either:

- Click the element. In some cases, you may have to click more than once to get a single element out of a group. For instance, click the first time to select all elements of a certain type, such as the data series (columns in a bar chart, for instance). Click a second time to select only a single element, such as a single column.

Acme Books

Select a data series with a single click

Second click selects a single data point

Continued . . .

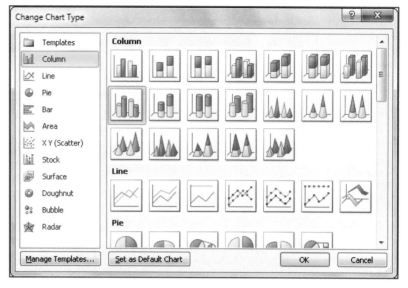

Figure 7-5: **You can choose from among many different chart types and variations among each type.**

–Or–

- Right-click in a background area of the chart, and choose **Change Chart Type**. (If you don't see that option in the context menu, right-click in a different spot on the chart.) The Change Chart Type dialog box displays a menu of chart type options, as shown in Figure 7-5.

2. Click a chart type on the left of the menu. You will see the variations available for that type.

3. Choose the variation you want by clicking it. Then click **OK**.

Format Charts

Formatting is used to change color, contents, text font and size, chart lines, and plot area. The formatting options vary, depending on the type of chart. This chapter primarily discusses formatting for bar and column charts. Other chart types are similar, but not exactly the same as what is discussed here.

QUICKSTEPS

SELECTING CHART ELEMENTS

(Continued)

–Or–

* Click the **Chart Tools Format** tab, and from the Current Selection group, click the **Chart Elements** down arrow. From the menu of elements, click the one you want. (When you use this approach, you then select the changes you want by clicking **Format Selection** from the Current Selection group to open the Format *element* dialog box for formatting choices.)

NOTE

To see a selection of built-in "designer" charts, click the **Design** tab on the Chart Tools ribbon, and then click the Chart Styles **More** button in the Chart Styles group (if you are viewing a less than full-size screen, a Quick Styles button will be present, not the thumbnails of the styles themselves). A menu of specially formatted charts will be displayed for the current chart type that you can use to add some excitement to your presentation.

TIP

The element displayed in the Chart Elements button on the Chart Tools Format tab changes as you select an element on the chart. For example, when you select a column, the option will be Series *name*; when you select an axis, the option will be *named* Axis; when you select the legend, the option will be Legend.

Most formatting is available:

* From the Chart Tools Format tab

  –Or–

* By choosing the **More** *element* **Options** menu, listed in the menus of the layout commands in the Labels, Axes, and Background groups found on the Chart Tools Layout tab (for example, click **Chart Title** in the Labels group, and select **More Title Options**).

Use Format Dialog Boxes

When you right-click an element, the context menu will contain two types of options. First, you'll see a Format *element* option, which contains options unique to an element. This displays the same dialog box as when you choose More *element* Options on the menus of commands on the Chart Tools Layout and Format tabs. These unique options are described in the appropriate "Format *element*" sections.

Here we discuss the second type. This option type is common to the elements it modifies, since, for the most part, for a certain type of element, these options are similar. In other words, you have the same options for modifying lines— whether they are on the plot area, gridlines, or legend—as you do for text, whether the text is in the legend, the labels, the title, or the axes. See Table 7-1 as a reference. Figure 7-6 shows the dialog boxes referenced in the table.

To use the common formatting options:

1. To display the Format *elements* dialog box, right-click the element and choose the **Format** *element* option.

   * Click *element* **Options** (if available) to set unique element options. (For example, for chart legends, Legend Options offers two unique options: where to position the element on the chart and whether the legend can overlay the chart. The following sections explore these options.)

   * Click an option as described in Table 7-1 and displayed in Figure 7-6. These are the common options shared by many of the chart elements.

2. Click **OK** to close the Format *elements* dialog box.

FORMATTING OPTIONS	DESCRIPTION	APPLY TO
Fill	Provides options for gradient, picture, or texture/pattern fill, as well as color choices and degrees of transparency. Each option displays unique content in the dialog box.	Axis, chart area, data labels/series, legend, plot area, titles, walls/floors
Border Color	Offers solid or gradient lines, as well as color choices, degrees of transparency, and gradient options. Choose No Line, Solid Line, and Gradient Line (or the default Automatic.)	Axis, chart area, data labels/series, error bars, gridlines, legend, plot area, titles, trendlines, walls/floors
Border Styles	Provides options for changing width, dashed, and compound (multiple) lines, as well as styles for line ends and line joins (and Rounded Corners for Chart Area)	Axis, chart area, data labels/series, error bars, gridlines, legend, plot area, titles, trendlines, walls/floors
Shadow	Provides preset shadow styles and controls for color, transparency, size, blur, angle, and distance	Axis, chart area, data labels/series, legend, plot area, titles, trendlines, walls/floors
3-D Format	Adds 3-D effect to shapes; provides top, bottom, material, and lighting presets and controls for depth contours and color. For instance, you can format the element with a bevel effect, changing the shape, depth, color, contours, and surface material and lighting.	Axis, chart area, data labels/series, legend, plot area, titles, walls/floors
3-D Rotation	Changes the rotation of the chart, whether the text is rotated or flat, the object's position from the ground of the chart, and the chart scale for a chart wall or floor (its depth and height as a percentage of the base or whether it is automatically scaled). Provides angular rotation and perspective adjustments, as well as positioning and scaling controls.	Walls/floors
Number	Provides the same number formats as the Format Cells Number tab, such as for currency, accounting, dates and time, percentages, fractions, etc. Also, you can establish whether the number is linked to a source worksheet.	Axis, data labels
Alignment	(Sometimes called Text Box.) Changes the text layout: vertically aligns, rotates, and stacks text; determines whether AutoFit should be applied to the text (the text box resized for the text or the text resized for the text box); and what the internal margins are within the text box.	Axis, data labels, titles, legends
Glow and Soft Edges	Adds glow or soft-edged effects; varying color; and size, transparency, and degree of emphasis	Titles, legends, data labels, chart area, plot area, series/labels, walls/floors, axis

Table 7-1: **Formatting Options for Chart Elements**

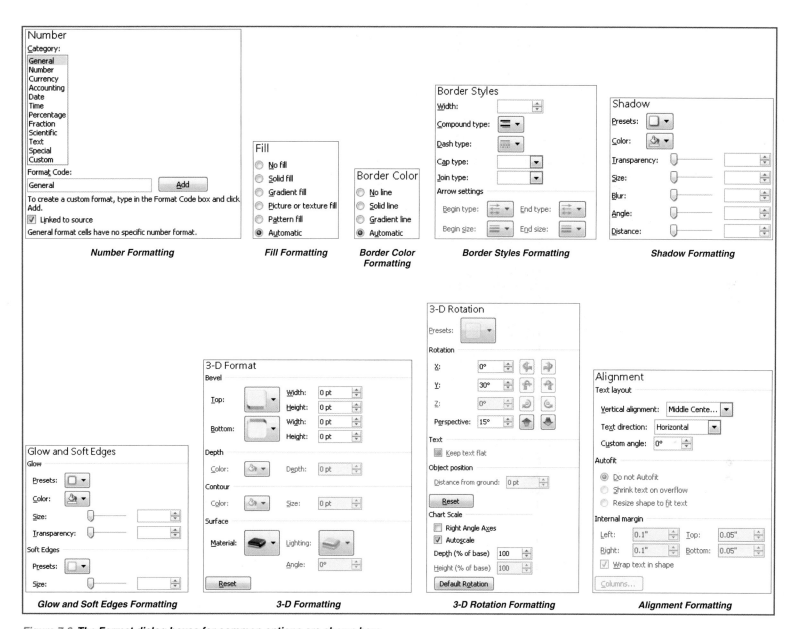

Figure 7-6: The Format dialog boxes for common options are shown here.

Format Legends

1. After selecting the chart, click the **Chart Tools Layout** tab, and click **Legend**. A menu will open, as shown in Figure 7-7.

2. Click one of the options to hide the legend or position it on the chart.

   –Or–

   Click **More Legend Options** to open the Format Legend dialog box. Under Legend Options, you can establish where on the chart the legend will be placed and whether it will be permitted to overlay the chart itself. See "Use Format Dialog Boxes," Table 7-1, and Figure 7-6 for detailed information on other formatting options.

Alter a Chart Title

To change the title of a chart:

After selecting the chart, right-click its title and select **Format Chart Title**. The Format Chart Title dialog box appears. See "Use Format Dialog Boxes," Table 7-1, and Figure 7-6 for detailed information on the formatting options. Click **Close** to exit the Format Chart Title dialog box.

–Or–

Click the chart to display the Chart Tools tabs, click the Layout tab, and click **Chart Title** in the Labels group. From the menu, click one of these options:

- Click **None** to hide the chart title.

- Click **Centered Overlay Title** to center the title on the chart and to overlay contents, if needed.

- Click **Above Chart** to display the title at the top of the chart and to avoid overlaying the contents by reducing the size of the chart.

- Click **More Title Options** to open the Format Chart Title dialog box. See "Use Format Dialog Boxes," Table 7-1, and Figure 7-6 for detailed information on other formatting options. Click **OK** to close the Format Chart Title dialog box.

–Or–

To just change the title contents and the text attributes, highlight the title to select it, type over the title, click the **Home** tab, and use the tools in the Font group. However, if you are changing a linked chart, you'll have to make any revisions to the source data in the Excel worksheet.

Figure 7-7: **You can modify the legend of a chart by changing its position on the chart or by formatting its lines and text.**

Format a Data Series

To format a data series for a bar chart:

1. Click the chart to display the Chart Tools tabs. Click the **Layout** tab.

2. Click the **Chart Elements** down arrow in the Current Selection group (it will have the name of the last element selected) to see a list of elements on the chart. Click the data series you want to change. The element will be selected, as you can verify on the chart.

3. Click **Format Selection** in the Current Selection group. The Format Data Series dialog box appears.

4. Select from these options:

- In Series Options, drag the **Gap Depth** slider to set the distance the data series is from the front of the chart (only available for 3-D charts).

- In Series Options, drag the **Gap Width** slider to set the width of the gap between sets of data series, adjusting the width of each series element accordingly, as shown in Figure 7-8.

5. See "Use Format Dialog Boxes," Table 7-1, and Figure 7-6 for detailed information on other formatting options.

6. Click **Close** to exit the dialog box.

Gap Depth establishes how far back the data series rests on the chart

Gap Width sets the width of the gap between sets of data series, adjusting the width of the data series to compensate

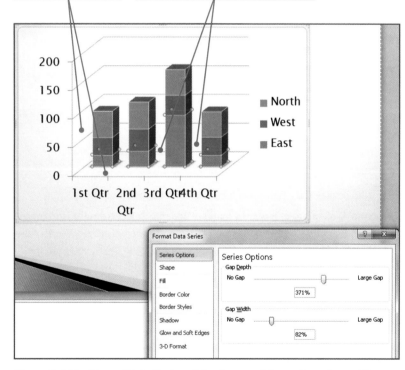

Format Data Labels

To format the data labels:

1. Click the chart to display the Chart Tools tabs. Click the **Layout** tab.

2. Click **Data Labels** in the Labels group to display a menu of options.

- Click **None** to hide or turn off data labels. They cannot be selected when this option is selected.

- Click **Show** to show or turn on the data labels so that they can be selected (select specific data series first if you only want labels to appear on them).

Figure 7-8: The Format Data Series dialog box contains options to position the data series from the front of the 3-D chart and to set the width of the gap between sets of data series.

Showing leader lines in a pie chart connects the chart to data labels, which identify the data being viewed. To add leader lines, right-click the "pie" elements on the chart, and click **Add Data Labels**. When the values appear on the pie chart, click them and drag them where you want them outside of the chart (they need to be sufficiently far from the chart to appear—you may need to move them around a bit to find out where they appear). You'll want to right-click the chart and select **Format Data Labels**, to make sure that **Show Leader Lines** is selected.

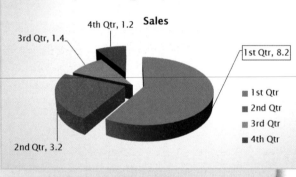

3. Click **More Data Labels Options** for additional formatting options. In the Label Options category, select from among the following:

- **Series Name** indicates that the label will contain the name of the data series.
- **Category Name** includes the category in the label.
- **Value** includes the value in the label. Value is the default label content.
- **Show Leader Lines** enables a line connecting data labels to the relevant element in the chart. (This option is available when you have added data labels to an appropriate chart, such as a pie chart.)
- **Reset Label Text** restores the default of Value only.
- **Include Legend Key In Label** places the key (identifying color, for example) in the label.
- **Separator** indicates how multiple elements in the label will be separated. A comma is the default.

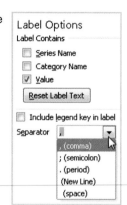

4. See "Use Format Dialog Boxes," Table 7-1, and Figure 7-6 for detailed information on other formatting options.

5. Click **Close** to close the dialog box.

Format an Axis

To format an axis for a chart and define the maximum, minimum, and incremental values; set tick marks; positioning; and more:

1. Click the chart to display the Chart Tools tabs. Click the **Layout** tab.

2. Click **Axes** in the Axes group to display a menu of options. Select **Primary Horizontal Axis** (the x-axis), **Primary Vertical Axis** (the y-axis), and, when available, **Depth Axis** (the z-axis). With the Primary Horizontal Axis option of a column chart, you have the following choices:

- Click **None** to hide or turn off the axis.
- Click **Show Left To Right Axis** to display vertical labels on the left edge of the chart and to start the category axis on the left.
- Click **Show Axis Without Labeling** to suppress the labels and tick marks.
- Click **Show Right To Left Axis** to display vertical labels on the right edge of the chart and to start the category axis on the right.

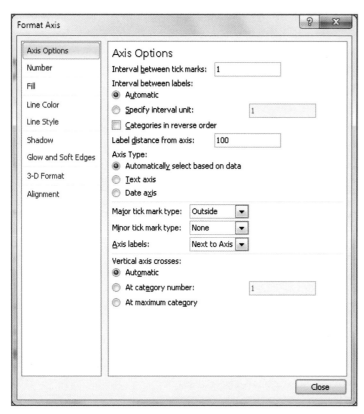

Figure 7-9: *The Format Axis dialog box is used to define the attributes of a selected axis. This example shows the options for the horizontal axis (the category axis) of a column type chart.*

3. If you click **More Primary Horizontal Axis Options**, you'll see a dialog box of additional formatting options. (Step 4 explains the More Primary Vertical Axis Options menu.) These options are shown in Figure 7-9. In the Axis Options category, you have the following options:

- **Interval Between Tick Marks** sets the number of units between tick marks.

- **Interval Between Labels** can be set in two ways. Select **Automatic** to have PowerPoint determine the interval between labels; click **Specify Interval Unit**, and then type a number if you want to refine the interval.

- **Categories In Reverse Order** displays the x-axis categories in reverse, from right to left.

- **Label Distance From Axis** sets how many units are between the label and the axis.

- **Axis Type** determines whether the axis is numeric, dates, or text. Select **Automatically Select Based On Data**, **Text Axis**, and **Date Axis**.

- **Major Tick Mark Type** and **Minor Tick Mark Type** determine whether the tick marks are inside the axis, outside the axis, or positioned across it.

- **Axis Labels** indicates where the labels are in relation to the axis: **Next To Axis** places them adjacent to the axis; **High** places them on the top of the chart; **Low** places them beneath the axis; **None** causes no labels to be displayed.

- **Vertical Axis Crosses** establishes where the y-axis will intersect with the x-axis. Normally, they cross at the left or right end of the horizontal axis. You can have them cross somewhere within the middle of the plot area, based the choices offered. Select **Automatic** to let PowerPoint determine the crossover, select **At Category Number** to manually set the crossover, or select **At Maximum Category** to establish the point on the y-axis where the largest value will cross the x-axis.

4. Click **Primary Vertical Axis** to see a menu to display the axis (or not), or to choose units for the vertical (y) axis. You can also choose to display the

Format Axis

Axis Options

- Axis Options
- Number
- Fill
- Line Color
- Line Style
- Shadow
- Glow and Soft Edges
- 3-D Format
- Alignment

Axis Options

Minimum: ⦿ Auto ○ Fixed 0.0
Maximum: ⦿ Auto ○ Fixed 200.0
Major unit: ⦿ Auto ○ Fixed 50.0
Minor unit: ⦿ Auto ○ Fixed 10.0

☐ Values in reverse order
☐ Logarithmic scale Base: 10
Display units: None ▾
☐ Show display units label on chart

Major tick mark type: Outside ▾
Minor tick mark type: None ▾
Axis labels: Next to Axis ▾

Floor crosses at:
⦿ Automatic
○ Axis value: 0.0
○ Maximum axis value

Close

*Figure 7-10: **The Vertical Axis Format Axis dialog box defines the attributes of the y-axis.***

axis using a logarithmic 10 scale. If you click **More Primary Vertical Axis Options** at the bottom of the Primary Vertical Axis menu, you'll see a different dialog box with additional formatting options, shown in Figure 7-10. You have the following choices:

- **Minimum** changes the lowest value automatically; or you can type a fixed value in the text box.

- **Maximum** changes the highest value automatically; or you can type a fixed value in the text box.

- **Major Unit** shows the largest increments displayed automatically; or you can type a value in the text box.

- **Minor Unit** shows the smallest increments displayed automatically; or you can type a value in the text box.

- **Values In Reverse Order** displays the largest value at the bottom of the axis and the smallest at the top.

- **Logarithmic Scale** displays the values in a logarithmic relationship rather than in an arithmetic one.

- **Display Units** shows a menu of units that can be displayed. If you select a quantity, you can select **Show Display Units Label On Chart**.

Display units: None ▾
☐ Show displa None
                Hundreds
                Thousands
                10000
                100000
                Millions
                10000000
                100000000
                Billions
                Trillions

- **Major Tick Mark Type** and **Minor Tick Mark Type** determine whether the tick marks are inside the axis, outside the axis, or positioned across it.

- **Axis Labels** indicates where the labels are in relation to the axis. **Next To Axis** places them adjacent to the axis; **High** places them on the top of the chart; **Low** places them beneath the axis; **None** causes no labels to be displayed.

- **Floor Crosses At** establishes the point or value on the vertical axis where the horizontal axis will cross it. Select **Automatic** to have PowerPoint determine this, select **Axis Value** to set the value yourself, or select **Maximum Axis Value** to establish the point on the horizontal axis where the largest value will cross the vertical axis.

5. Click **Close** to close the dialog box.

Format the Plot Area

The chart area encompasses the total chart area, whereas the plot area is a subset of the total chart area. The plot area is the background upon which the chart rests. It can be formatted with color and fill effects, and its border can be formatted to take on a different style, thickness, or color.

1. Click the chart to display the Chart Tools tabs. Click the **Layout** tab.

2. Click the **Chart Elements** down arrow in the Current Selection group, and click **Plot Area**. Then click **Format Selection** in the Current Selection group. The Format Plot Area dialog box appears.

3. See "Use Format Dialog Boxes," Table 7-1, and Figure 7-6 for detailed information on the formatting options.

4. Click **Close** to close the dialog box.

Format Text

You can format text in a chart by changing its font, font style, font size, and color. If you are changing data in a linked file from Excel, for example, you must make the changes in the source worksheet. However, text in a label is changed in PowerPoint.

1. Select the chart element that contains the text to be formatted.

2. Click the **Home** tab, select the text to be changed, and use any of the tools in the Font group.

   –Or–

   Use the options on the mini toolbar that floats over selected text.

Format Gridlines

To make gridlines less obvious or more apparent (usually in order to help viewers visually):

1. Click the chart to display the Chart Tools tabs.

2. Click the **Layout** tab, and click **Gridlines** in the Axes group. A menu is displayed.

3. Choose from among these options:

- **Primary Horizontal Gridlines** displays or hides major and minor horizontal (or x-axis) gridlines.

- **Primary Vertical Gridlines** displays or hides the major and minor vertical (or y-axis) gridlines.

- **Depth Gridlines** (only for some chart types, such as Surface) shows or hides the major depth and minor depth (or z-axis) gridlines.

4. For any of the gridlines, click **More** *type* **Gridlines Options** to display the Format Gridlines dialog box, where you can change the line and line styles. (See "Format Dialog Boxes," Table 7-1, and Figure 7-6 for detailed information on the options.)

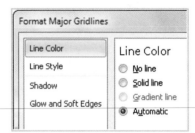

5. Click **Close** when you have made your choices.

How to...

- *Transition Between Slides*
- *Learning About Animation*
- *Animate Objects and Slides*
- *Understanding Animation Effects*
- *Increasing Performance*
- *Use Fills for Shapes or Backgrounds*
- *Add Special Effects to an Object*
- *Change Outlines of Shapes*
- *Removing Effects*
- *Work with WordArt*
- *Draw a Shape*
- *Type Text Within a Shape*
- *Working with Curves*
- *Combine Shapes by Grouping*
- *Create a Mirror Image Using Rotate*
- *Positioning Shapes*
- *Choose SmartArt Categories*
- *Insert a SmartArt Graphic*
- *Aligning Shapes*
- *Change SmartArt Designs*
- *Change SmartArt Formatting*

Chapter 8
Using Special Effects and Drawing Shapes

This chapter works with two interesting and creative aspects of PowerPoint: its special-effects capabilities and its drawing features. Special effects make your slides more interesting, allowing transitioning between slides, animating objects or slides, and creating engaging backgrounds. With the drawing features, you can create shapes or use predefined shapes to design your own diagrams, charts, clip art, and other objects to enhance your presentations. Also in this chapter is a special type of shapes, called SmartArt. Using SmartArt adds artistic elements to your presentations that make them look more professional and "finished."

Work with Transitions and Animations

Transitions and animations are special effects to add that touch of "professionalism" for dressing up your presentation. Transitions, defining what happens between slides, are easy to implement and add interest when moving from one slide to the next. Animation also makes a presentation come alive by adding action to your slides.

Transition Between Slides

Transitions are used to lead from one slide to the next. For example, you can have one slide dissolve and another emerge, have slides slip in from the side, or have them emerge from the center. There are many more possibilities— all easy to implement. You can also add sounds, vary the speed of transitions, and vary the effect on each slide. Or, you can make all transitions the same. Figure 8-1 shows the transition commands available in the Transitions tab.

1. First, display the slides in Slide Sorter view by clicking **Slide Sorter** view 🔲 on the status bar. This will make it easier to see the slides to which you will apply the transitions.

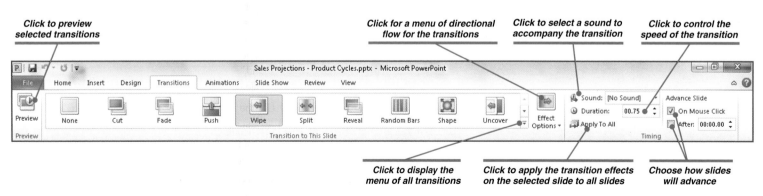

Click to preview selected transitions

Click for a menu of directional flow for the transitions

Click to select a sound to accompany the transition

Click to control the speed of the transition

Click to display the menu of all transitions

Click to apply the transition effects on the selected slide to all slides

Choose how slides will advance

Figure 8-1: **The Transition To This Slide group on the Transitions tab displays the commands for adding a transition between slides.**

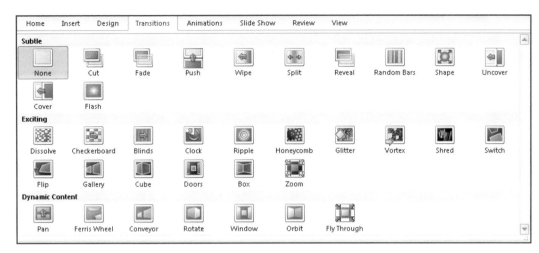

Figure 8-2: **The Transitions tab contains the special effects you can apply to slide transitions.**

2. Select one or more slides that will have the transition effect. To select adjacent slides, hold down **SHIFT** while you click the first and last slides in the range. To select noncontiguous slides, hold down **CTRL** while you click the desired slides.

3. Click the **Transitions** tab on the ribbon, and then click the **More** button in the Transition To This Slide group. The menu shown in Figure 8-2 will be displayed.

4. Select from these options:

- Scroll through the list of transitions, as shown in Figure 8-2, and click a transition for the slides selected in step 2. The effect is increasingly bold within a range of effects that are subtle, exciting, or dynamic.

- In the Timing group, click the **Sound** down arrow, and scroll through the sounds available. As you place your pointer over the menu item, its sound will play. Choose a sound to accompany the transition. "No Sound" is the default. (If you click "Other Sound," you can browse for and install a sound file of your own.)

- Click the **Duration** spinners for the length of time you want the transition to last.

- Click **On Mouse Click** if you want to advance to the next slide by clicking the mouse.

- Click **After** and fill in the time if you want the slides to automatically advance after a certain period.

- Click **Apply To All** to assign the transition effects and sound to the whole presentation. Otherwise, the effects will be applied only to selected slides.

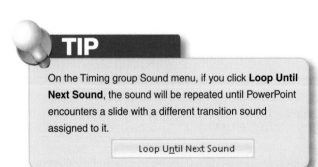

TIP

On the Timing group Sound menu, if you click **Loop Until Next Sound**, the sound will be repeated until PowerPoint encounters a slide with a different transition sound assigned to it.

Loop Until Next Sound

LEARNING ABOUT ANIMATION

You apply animations to text or objects on a slide both to add interest and to help the speaker in his or her presentation or to ease the viewer's task in following the presentation. Animations can be subtle, such as text simply appearing on the screen, or emphatic, such as an object spinning around on the slide. You can apply animation to all the text, bullets, and graphics on a slide as a whole or to selected objects, such as one line of text. (To apply animation selectively, see "Add Custom Animation.") You can animate text or an object one way when entering the slide, animate it during its appearance on the slide, and then animate it again upon exit. For example, in a speaker's presentation, you can cause the text on a slide to fly in from the left one paragraph at a time, diminish its font size or change color after it has been discussed, upon a mouse click have the next paragraph fly in similarly, and then have all text fly off the slide to the right upon exit before the next slide is displayed.

5. Click the **Preview** button in the Preview group to see the effects for one slide.

6. Click **Slide Show** 💻 on the status bar to view the slide show with transition effects.

Preview

Animate Objects and Slides

Transitions apply when one slide is advanced to another. Animation, on the other hand, is applied to objects on a slide. You can animate text, graphics, charts, and other objects. You can apply animation to master slide placeholders as well, such as for titles, for example, to have all titles appear on the slides in the same way. The effects are applied roughly according to when you want to see them.

- **Entrance Effects** animate text and objects as they are first displayed on a slide, such as flying or bouncing in.

- **Emphasis Effects** animate text and objects while on display, such as growing and shrinking or changing color.

- **Exit Effects** animate text and objects as they disappear or leave the slide, such as sliding off in some direction or fading out.

- **Motion Path Effects**, applied at any time, move text and objects along a path, such as in a circle or star pattern.

The approach for applying animations is to use the Animation group to apply one animation and for changes, and use the Advanced Animation tools to add additional effects to a slide. It is somewhat confusing. Here is a summary of how you use the commands:

- **To add the first animation** Use the Animation group gallery or Add Animation in the Advanced Animation group.

- **To replace existing animations** Use the Animation group gallery only.

- **To add subsequent animations after the first** Use Add Animation in the Advanced Animation group only.

- **To modify the attributes of animations** Use Effect Options in the Animation group, Animation Pane or Trigger in the Advanced Animation group, or the Timing group commands.

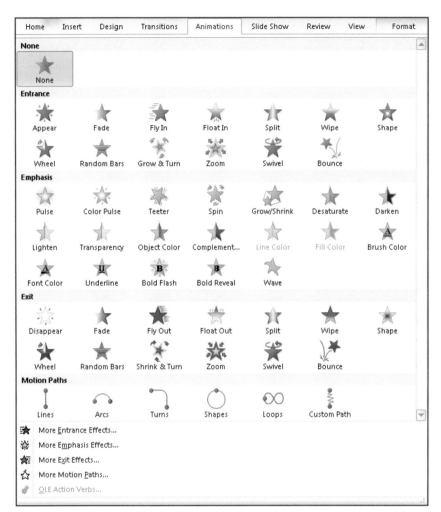

Figure 8-3: *You can animate objects or text as a whole on a slide simultaneously. This figure shows the menu for text, which can be animated as a whole or by paragraphs.*

ADD OR CHANGE AN ANIMATION WITH THE ANIMATION GALLERY

The animation gallery gives you quick access to the animation effect. You can animate all objects or text on a slide to have some action while the slide is being displayed, or to affect its exit before the next slide is displayed. When you apply the first animation to a slide but not subsequent animations, you can use the Animation group gallery, although you can also use the Advanced Animation group to add all your animations, as explained in the next section, "Add Advanced Animations." You also use the Animation group, but not Add Animation, to replace existing animations.

1. Display the slide in Normal view 🔲 so that you can easily see what needs to be animated. Select the placeholder containing the objects or text on the slide that you want to animate as a whole.

2. On the Animations tab, click the **More** down arrow in the Animation group. A menu is displayed, an example of which is shown in Figure 8-3. The menu options will vary with the type of placeholder (text is different from a chart, for instance). So you will see some options grayed out, or unavailable.

3. If you have selected text and want to select a unique way for it to enter the slide, choose from among the Entrance, Emphasis, Exit, or Motion Paths options. As you place your pointer over the option, you'll see the action reflected in the slide. Examples of Entrance options are shown here—you can point to other options to see examples of Emphasis, Exit, or Motion Paths.

- **None** removes all animation effects from the selection.

- **Fade** causes the selected object to fade in.

- **Wipe** causes the selected object to appear bit by bit, from the bottom of the object to the top.

- **Fly In** causes the selected object to fly into position from the bottom of the slide.
- **More Entrance Effects**, **More Emphasis Effects**, and **More Exit Effects** display dialog boxes with additional choices. You can choose Basic, Subtle, Moderate, or Exciting animations.
- **More Motion Paths** allows you to move the object or text in a specific pattern. This command displays a dialog box with Basic, Lines & Curves, and Special choices.

4. Click **Effect Options** in the Animation group to choose a further definition of the animation. The options will vary, depending on whether you've selected text or graphics to animate. Here are some examples of what you may see:

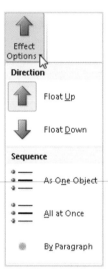

- **Direction** options specify where and how the effect is to move. In this example, the Float In animation was chosen, so the Float Up or Float Down directions are available.
- **As One Object** applies the animation as if the selected objects and text were one object.
- **All At Once** applies the selected animation to the entire selected placeholder. For example, all lines in the selected text will fade in at one time. Or, if you have several selected objects, they will be treated as one for the animation.
- **One By One** applies the animation to each selected element, one at a time. For example, if you have four objects selected and apply an entrance animation to the group, they will appear one at a time.
- **By Paragraphs** applies the selected animation to paragraphs, one at a time.
- **By Series, By Category, By Element In Series, By Element In Category** applies the animation to selected parts of a graph.

5. Click **Preview** in the Preview group to see the animations played on the selected slide.

6. Click **Slide Show** to play the presentation.

ADD ADVANCED ANIMATIONS

The Advanced Animation and Timing groups contain options for applying multiple animations to a slide and using more control over animations. You use the various commands together. For instance, you add an animation using Add Animation, view it and modify the effects using the Animation pane, and control what triggers the animation event using Trigger. The Timing group controls when the various animation effects take place. Once you have defined an animation, you can copy it to other objects or text using Animation Painter.

TIP

To replace an animation once it has been applied, select it by clicking its tag on the slide or in the Animation pane. Then click **More** in the Animation pane and click the replacement animation.

TIP

The numbers assigned to an item depend on the relationship between the effects. Each separate effect is numbered sequentially. Each effect related to the effect above it carries the same number. For example, effects initiated with mouse clicks are separate. Effects initiated "with" the previous effect or "after" it are related to the previous effect and will carry the same number.

TIP

If you place the pointer over an effect in the task pane, you will see a tooltip describing the effect. The effects are listed and numbered in the sequence in which they will occur, and the corresponding slide items contain tags with the same numbers. So you can look at the tags on the slide and identify which effect controls each item.

1. Display the slide in Normal view ⊞.

2. Select the object or text to be animated. For instance, if you want all text in a text box to be animated as one effect, click in the text box. If you want to separate the object or text into animated segments (such as differing effects or timing for each bulleted item), select just the individual object or bullet.

3. On the Animations tab, in the Advanced Animation group, click **Add Animation**. The menu of animation effects will display, similar to that shown in Figure 8-3. You can choose to use animation for an entrance or exit or for emphasis, or to determine which direction a motion will take. If you do not see the animation you want, click one of the **More *type* Effects** listed at the bottom of the menu. Each of these displays a dialog box with several animation choices. You may see a fifth choice, OLE Action Verbs, if you select an object (such as a linked table). Click the animation you want.

Small numbered rectangles will appear on your slide, as seen in Figure 8-4. To view the details of the animation and to make changes, use the Animation pane, as described in "Use the Animation Pane."

USE THE ANIMATION PANE TO CHANGE ATTRIBUTES

After you have applied animations to your slide, you may want to control several aspects of it, such as to give directional and sequence instructions.

1. Select the slide containing the animations to be changed.

2. In the Advanced Animation group, click **Animation Pane** to open it. Figure 8-4 shows the task pane with a group of animations. See the "Understanding Animation Effects" QuickFacts to see what the various icons and graphics mean.

3. To change or delete an animation, first select the effect to be changed from the Animation Pane list. (You can also click the tag number of the effect on the slide.)

4. Click the down arrow on the selected item to open the menu, as seen in Figure 8-5. Then select from these options:

   ● Click **Start On Click** to instruct the animation to be activated on the click of the mouse.

   ● Click **Start With Previous** to activate the animation at the same time as the previous effect in the list.

   ● Click **Start After Previous** to activate the animation after the previous one in the list.

   ● Click **Effect Options** to open a dialog box with various options, depending on the animation.

8

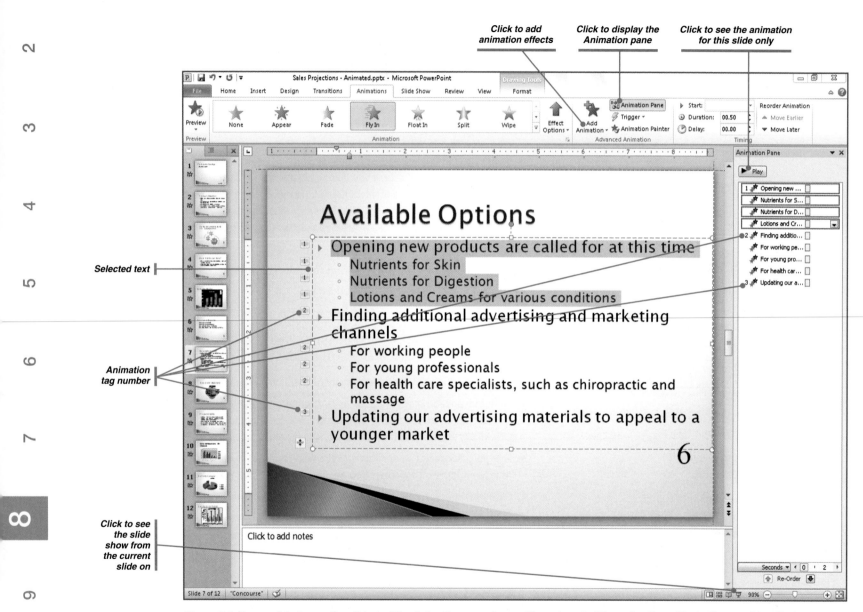

Click to add animation effects

Click to display the Animation pane

Click to see the animation for this slide only

Selected text

Animation tag number

Click to see the slide show from the current slide on

Figure 8-4: *You work between the slide and the Animation pane to modify and control the animation effects. You can identify the associated item on the slide by its selected tag number.*

QUICKFACTS

UNDERSTANDING ANIMATION EFFECTS

As you add animation effects, you see them displayed in the Animation pane in a scrollable list. Between the tooltips and the icons, it's fairly easy to tell what an effect does and which object or line of text it relates to. The icons describe the effects: The number tab identifies the object or text the effect applies to—a yellow star for "emphasis," a green star for "entrance," a red star for "exit," a white star for "motion path," and cogs for "object actions." To complicate things, you can have many different Emphasis icons— Underline is different from Font Color, for instance. A selected effect contains a down arrow for accessing the Animation pane effects menu, as shown in Figure 8-5.

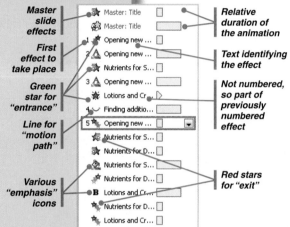

Master slide effects

First effect to take place

Green star for "entrance"

Line for "motion path"

Various "emphasis" icons

Relative duration of the animation

Text identifying the effect

Not numbered, so part of previously numbered effect

Red stars for "exit"

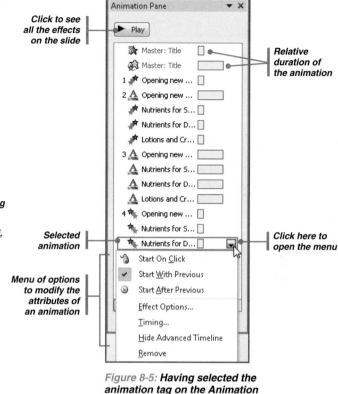

Click to see all the effects on the slide

Relative duration of the animation

Selected animation

Click here to open the menu

Menu of options to modify the attributes of an animation

Figure 8-5: *Having selected the animation tag on the Animation pane, you can open the related menu and select which attribute you wish to change.*

TIP

On the Animations tab Advanced Animation group, the Animation Pane button is a toggle. Clicking it turns the Animation pane on and off.

- Click **Timing** to display a dialog box to specify how the animation starts, whether there is a delay before it is activated, how long it lasts, whether it should be repeated, and whether it should rewind when through (for an audio effect, for example). The Trigger options are also accessible from here.

- Click **Hide Advanced Timeline** to hide the graphic revealing the relative time duration of the animation.

- Click **Remove** to delete the selected animation.

6. Click **Play** to see the effect played out for the current slide.

Click **Slide Show** on the status bar to see the presentation from this slide on.

QUICK**FACTS**

INCREASING PERFORMANCE

Animations can degrade the performance of your presentation significantly if you don't use some commonsense actions. When you are adding animation to your slides, consider these performance-enhancing actions:

- Reduce the size of the objects being animated.

- Run animations in sequence rather than simultaneously.

- Don't animate individual elements of an object; animate the whole object. For instance, don't animate the individual letters or words in a title or subtitle; animate the whole word, title, or subtitle.

- Reduce the use of animations that manipulate the object on the slide, such as with fading, resizing, or rotating.

- Use solid-color fills instead of gradients or other settings.

In addition to these PowerPoint actions, you can perform some hardware and operating systems actions, such as changing to a lower resolution (lowering 1280 × 1024 to 1024 × 768, for instance), increase your available disk space, empty your Windows/TEMP file, or ask about how video cards for your computer could enhance the performance.

NOTE

You will not see any animations based on "Start On Click" until you view the presentation with the Slide Show view. Clicking Play does not show them.

ANIMATE BULLETED TEXT

You can animate a bulleted list so that it displays one bullet at a time, allowing you to finish speaking about one item before moving to the next. Using this procedure, each bullet will be displayed on a click of the mouse button in the sequence you choose. The bulleted text will be displayed in a different color when you have moved on to the next bullet.

1. Display the slide in Normal view ⊞.

2. Select the text in the first bullet to be animated.

3. Click the **Animations** tab, and then click **Animation Pane** in the Advanced Animation group.

4. From the Advanced Animation group, click **Add Animation** and choose an Entrance style.

5. Click the down arrow on the new animation listed in the Animation pane. Click any other options as needed; for instance:

- Click **Start On Click**.

- Click **Effect Options** and choose the options you want for the animation you have. For this Fly In effect, the dialog box is set to fly in from the upper right with an arrow sound and a change in the font color to red after the animation. (See "Use Effect Options for Animations" for more details.) Click **OK**.

6. Repeat steps 3–5 for each bulleted item. Be sure to choose **Start On Click** in step 5.

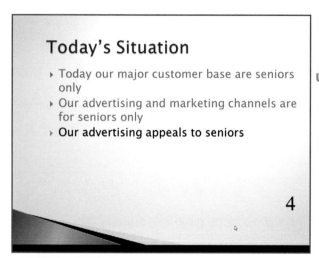

Today's Situation

▸ Today our major customer base are seniors only

▸ Our advertising and marketing channels are for seniors only

▸ **Our advertising appeals to seniors**

4

Figure 8-6: ***The third bullet is currently being discussed and will turn the same color as the other two bullets when the presenter clicks the mouse. A fourth bullet is yet to be displayed.***

Figure 8-7: ***Use the Effect Options dialog box to fine-tune the effect of your animation.***

7. When you are finished, click **Slide Show** to see how it works. Click the screen or slide image, and then click for each new bullet and for the next slide to be displayed. Figure 8-6 shows an example.

USE EFFECT OPTIONS FOR ANIMATIONS

For any animation, you can specify a number of effects and timing considerations using the Effect Options dialog box. You can find the Effect Options dialog box in two locations:

1. Click the **Animation** tab, and then click **Effect Options** from either of these locations:

   ● On the Animation group, click the **Effect Options Dialog Box Launcher**.

   ● In the effect listing on the Animation pane, click the selected effect's down arrow, and click **Effect Options**.

2. Click the **Effect** tab (an example for a Wipe Entrance effect is shown in Figure 8-7), and select among the options for that effect. The options will differ, depending on what animation is selected. In this case:

   ● Click the **Direction** down arrow, and choose how the animation will travel across the slide.

   ● Click the **Sound** down arrow, and scroll through the list of possibilities. Click the sound you want to accompany the effect.

   ● Click the **After Animation** down arrow, and select among these options: Choose whether to have sound after the animation, select a color to replace the current color when the animation is complete (for example, for text), choose **More Colors** if the color you want is not displayed, choose not to dim the effect after it has been played, and choose whether to hide the object or text after the animation or with the next click of the mouse.

   ● Click the **Animate Text** down arrow to choose how the line of text will be animated: All At Once, By Word, or By Letter (the latter two are not recommended in most cases).

3. Click **OK** to close the dialog box.

USE TIMING EFFECTS FOR ANIMATIONS

The timing effects are used to control when an animation begins, how long it lasts, and whether there is to be a delay before it starts. You also can repeat the effect or rewind it in some cases or set triggers.

1. Click the **Animations** tab, and then click **Effect Options** from either of these locations:

   - On the Animation group, click the **Effect Options Dialog Box Launcher**. Click the **Timing** tab.

   - In the effect listing on the Animation pane, click the selected effect's down arrow, and click **Timing**.

   Effect Options...
   Timing...
   Hide Advanced Timeline
   Remove

2. You have these options:

   - Click the **Start** down arrow, and choose **On Click**, **With Previous (Effect)**, or **After Previous (Effect)**.

   - Click the **Delay** spinner to set how many seconds the animation is to be delayed before beginning.

   - Click the **Duration** down arrow, and click the speed at which the animation is to occur, from Very Fast to Very Slow.

   - Click the **Repeat** button to set how many times or until which action occurs to repeat the animation. None (No Repeat) is the default.

   Repeat: (none)
   Rewind   (none)
              2
   Triggers   3
              4
              5
              10
              Until Next Click
              Until End of Slide

   - Click the **Rewind When Done Playing** check box to cause the audio or video effect to rewind.

   - Click the **Triggers** down arrows, and set what other events may activate the animation. For example, if it is activated as a result of being clicked itself (the default), of some other object being clicked, or when another animation is initiated.

   Triggers
   ⦿ Animate as part of click sequence
   ○ Start effect on click of:
   ○ Start effect on play of:

3. Click **OK** to close the dialog box.

Use Special Effects for Backgrounds and Objects

Using the fill, outline, and special effects, you can make your slides unique and interesting. For instance, you can fill a background with a picture or rotate a beveled shape after changing the color of it and its outline. These effects, for the

most part, can be applied to clip art, pictures, shapes, placeholders, text, tables, and charts. Because the commands to apply these effects are similar, regardless of the object type, you'll be able to use the steps for one type with the other types as well. For example, the Picture Effects, Shape Effects, Text Effects, and Effects for Tables offer much the same options for all object types, although not identical in all cases.

Use Fills for Shapes or Backgrounds

You can use special effects—such as gradient color, texture, and pattern fills—in shape or placeholder backgrounds. See "Draw and Use Shapes in PowerPoint" later in this chapter for how to draw and work with shapes.

FILL BACKGROUNDS

1. Select the placeholder or shape you want to fill with a color or effect. The Drawing Tools Format tab is displayed.

2. On the Format tab, click the **Shape Fill** button in the Shape Styles group.

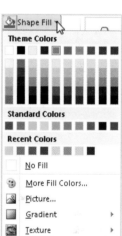

   - To apply color to a shape or placeholder background, point to the colors in the menu (the color of the shape or background will change) until you find one you want, and then click it.

   - To remove fill from a shape or placeholder, click **No Fill**.

   - To access additional colors, click **More Fill Colors**. The Colors dialog box will appear. You can choose between the Standard and Custom tabs.

   - Click the **Custom** tab if you want to work with RGB (Red, Green, and Blue) or HSL (Hue, Saturation, and Luminosity) settings. This dialog box can be seen in Figure 8-8. Click the color palette to set the approximate color, or drag the **Colors** slider to get a more exact shade. Drag the **Transparency** slider to make the fill more transparent. Click **OK** when you're done.

   –Or–

   - Click the **Standard** tab to access a standard set of colors, as seen in Figure 8-9. Click a unit of color, and see the difference in the New preview box compared with the current color. Drag the **Transparency** slider to manage the transparency of the fill. Click **OK** when you're done.

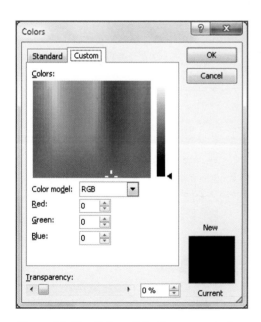

*Figure 8-8: **The Colors dialog box, accessed by clicking the Custom tab, allows you to precisely work with color through RGB- and HSL-specific settings.***

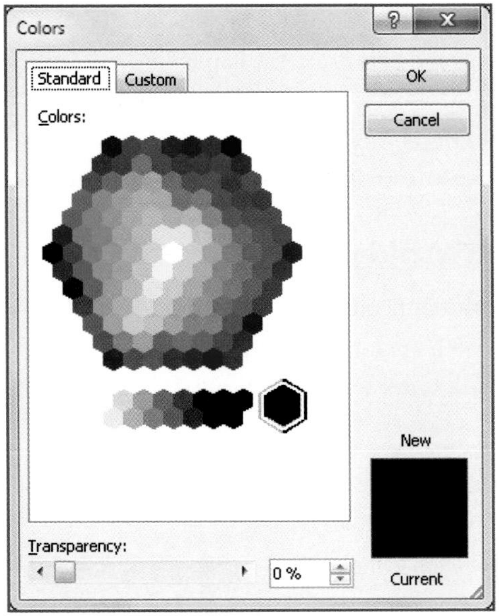

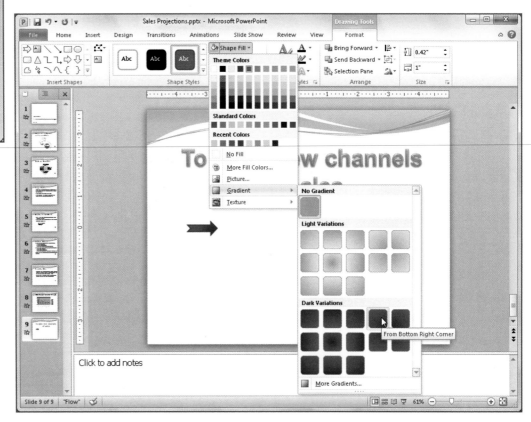

Figure 8-9: *Use the Standard tab to find more "Web-friendly" color selections which are supported by most browsers.*

CREATE A GRADIENT BACKGROUND FOR YOUR SLIDES

A gradient background lets you fill a placeholder or shape with a blend of colors. Figure 8-10 shows the Gradient menu, which you use to employ this special effect.

1. Select the placeholder or shape to contain the gradient effect. The Drawing Tools Format tab is displayed.

Figure 8-10: *You can point to the variations of gradient patterns on the Gradient menu and see the effects in the selected placeholder or shape.*

2. Click the **Format** tab, and click **Shape Fill**. Then click **Gradient** to see the menu shown in Figure 8-10.

3. To select a gradient pattern on the menu, point to it and see the preview results on the shape or placeholder. When you find the one you want, just click it.

4. To have more control over the gradient possibilities, click **More Gradients** on the bottom of the gradient menu. The Format Shape dialog box appears. On the Fill category, click **Gradient Fill** and choose one of these options:

   ● Click the **Preset Colors** button to select one of the gradient color schemes from the Preset Colors drop-down menu.

   ● Click the **Type** down arrow to display a menu of patterns for the gradient effect. Choose **Linear**, **Radial**, **Rectangular**, or **Path**.

   ● Click the **Direction** button to set the way the pattern sweeps or moves.

   ● Click the **Angle** spinner to rotate the angle of the gradient fill within the shape.

   ● **Gradient Stops** sets a nonlinear distribution of the color within the pattern. The color will not be graduated from one color to another. Instead, it goes from the first color you specify to each of the colors in the stops. Each stop consists of a color; a stop position, which defines where each color stops and the next begins; a brightness, which defines the lightness of the color; and a transparency, which indicates how transparent the gradient pattern is. Set these four components, and click the **Add Gradient Stop** icon on the right. To remove a stop, select the stop and click **Remove Gradient Stop**.

   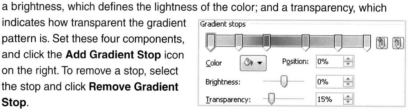

   ● Click the **Rotate With Shape** check box if you want the gradient fill to rotate within the shape's rotating context.

5. Click **Close** when you are through.

CREATE A TEXTURED BACKGROUND FOR YOUR PLACEHOLDER OR SHAPES

To create a background or shape with a textured background:

1. Click the placeholder or shape that you want to fill with texture. The Drawing Tools Format tab will be displayed.

2. Click **Shape Fill** and then, from the menu, click **Texture**. A popup menu will be displayed, as seen in Figure 8-11.

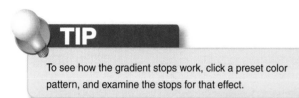

To see how the gradient stops work, click a preset color pattern, and examine the stops for that effect.

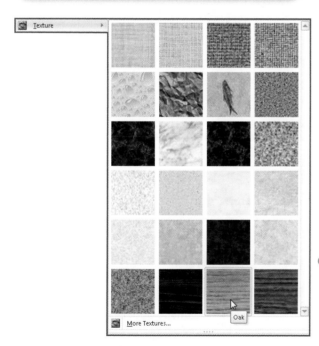

*Figure 8-11: **Select a texture to fill the background of a placeholder or shape.***

NOTE

A quick way to copy an object is to press **CTRL** while you drag it. A copy will be moved, not the original object.

Applying 3-D Rotation (Perspective Contrasting Left)

Recent Colors

No Outline

More Outline Colors...

Weight ▸

Dashes ▸

3. Point at the various textures until you find the one you want. You'll see the effects of the texture in the placeholder or shape as you point at them. When you find the one you want, click it.

USE A PICTURE AS THE BACKGROUND ON A SHAPE OR PLACEHOLDER

You can add a picture to your placeholder or shape as a background effect. Another way to think of this, depending on your intent, is that you can change the shape of a picture by inserting it into a shape.

1. Select the shape or placeholder that will contain the picture. The Drawing Tools Format tab will be displayed.

2. On the Format tab, click the **Shape Fill** button in the Shape Styles group. A menu is displayed.

3. To place a picture in the placeholder or shape, click **Picture**. The Insert Picture dialog box appears. Fill in the path information to select the picture you want. Click **Insert**.

Add Special Effects to an Object

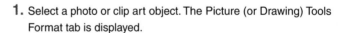

When you select an image or shape object, you will see the Picture (or Drawing) Tools Format tab. It contains commands to add special effects, such as a shadow, reflection, glow, soft edges, bevel, or 3-D rotation effect, to a photo, clip art, or shape.

Preset ▸

Shadow ▸

Reflection ▸

Glow ▸

Soft Edges ▸

Bevel ▸

3-D Rotation ▸

1. Select a photo or clip art object. The Picture (or Drawing) Tools Format tab is displayed.

2. On the Format tab, click **Picture Effects** (or **Shape Effects**) in the Picture Styles (or Shape Styles) group.

3. Click an option, such as **Shadow**, for a menu of choices. On the menu, click the effect you want. The special effect will be applied to the selected object.

Change Outlines of Shapes

You can outline a shape with a different color, a weighted line, or a dashed line.

1. To apply an outline, select the shape and click the **Shape Outline** button in the Shape Styles group of the Drawing Tools Format tab. A menu similar to that shown earlier in Figure 8-10 is displayed, except the options apply to lines instead of fill.

2. Select a color, weight of line, or a dash or arrow style from the submenu.

Work with WordArt

You can add special effects to text by applying WordArt containing unique character styles; a text fill of varying colors, gradients, textures, and pictures; a text outline with varying colors, weights, and dashes; and text effects of shadows, reflections, glows, bevels, 3-D rotation, and "transform," which curves and distorts the character shapes.

APPLY A WORDART EFFECT

Special effects can be added easily to text using WordArt to give a graphic artist's professional touch.

1. Select the text to which you want to apply the WordArt. The Drawing Tools Format tab is displayed. Click the **Format** tab. Within the WordArt Styles group are the special effects commands.

The more button

2. Click the WordArt **More** button to display the WordArt gallery of text styles, shown in Figure 8-12.

3. Select a style you want. The WordArt style will be applied to the text.

FILL AND OUTLINE TEXT

You can add fill to WordArt or text using color, pictures, gradient colors, and texture. In addition, you can outline text with a different color, a different weighted line, or a dashed line. The technique used is basically the same as described earlier for shape fills (see "Use Fills for Shapes or Backgrounds") and shape outline effects (see "Change Outlines of Shapes"). While you can add pictures, gradients, and so on to plain text, you really can't see much until you apply a WordArt style to give the text some width to see the change.

APPLY TEXT EFFECTS

The Text Effects option allows you to apply really interesting effects, such as shadows, reflections, glows, bevels, 3-D rotations, and transforming distortions of the character shapes.

1. Select the text to contain the special effect by highlighting it. The text can be WordArt-styled or other text. The Drawing Tools Format tab is displayed.

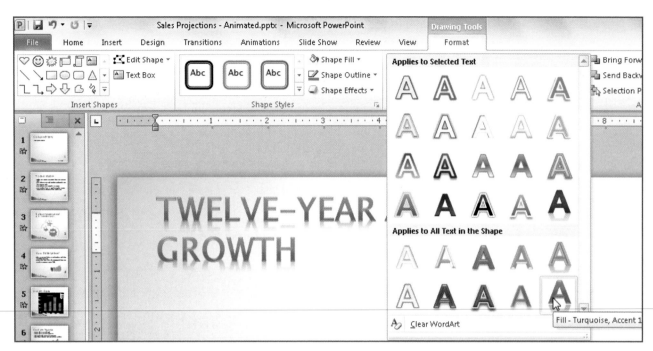

Figure 8-12: *The WordArt styles gallery displays a variety of styles that you can apply to text to give it a professional and artistic look.*

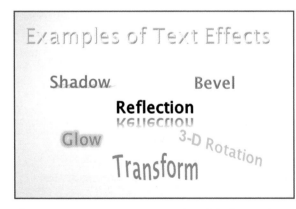

Figure 8-13: *Here are some examples of the interesting effects that the Text Effects command in the Drawing Tools Format tab can create.*

2. Click **Text Effects** in the WordArt Styles group. A menu is displayed. Click the effect you want. A submenu will be displayed. Click the effect to be applied. Figure 8-13 shows examples of the various effects.

Draw and Use Shapes in PowerPoint

The drawing feature in PowerPoint enables you to create line drawings and art with simple-to-use tools. It also presents "canned shapes" that you can use to draw lines, circles, rectangles, and other common shapes. It contains predefined shapes for inserting a variety of arrows and other connecting symbols, flowchart

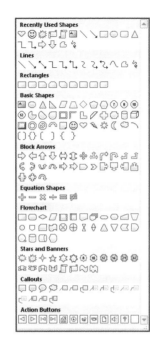

Figure 8-14: *These are the "canned" shapes you can create in PowerPoint.*

symbols, callouts, stars and banners, and other useful shapes. Figure 8-14 shows the drawing shapes available. You can edit these canned shapes, making them uniquely yours. Within the toolbox for shapes are the colors and special effects that add interest and a professional look to your shapes.

Draw a Shape

You can draw a variety of shapes using the Shapes menu. The procedure that follows can be used as a model for drawing whatever shape you want.

1. Click the **Home** tab, and in the Drawing group, click the **More** button. The gallery of shapes is displayed, as shown in Figure 8-14. (You can also click **Insert** and click **Shapes**.)

2. Click the shape that you want to create. When you click the shape, your pointer will become a crosshair.

3. Place the crosshair pointer where you want the edge of the shape to begin. Drag the pointer diagonally across the slide, creating the shape. Release the pointer by releasing the mouse button.

Type Text Within a Shape

You type text into a shape by inserting a text box within it. You can both center and control the word wrap within the shape by varying the size and shape of the text box. You might want to insert text within a shape for a label, for instance. (If you need to draw a shape first, see "Draw a Shape.") To type text in a shape:

1. Click the shape to select it, and then click the **Drawing Tools Format** tab.

2. Click the **Text Box** button in the Insert Shapes group. The pointer will become an insertion point, which you drag to form the text box. Drag the insertion point so that the text box conforms to the size of your shape.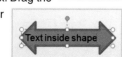

3. Type your text.

4. Point to the text box, and when the pointer becomes a four-headed arrow, drag the text box to position it within the shape and resize it as needed to fit the shape.

WORKING WITH CURVES

Tools are available to draw curved shapes. They are found on the Insert tab, on the Shapes menu in the Illustrations group, under the Lines option, and in the Drawing Tools Format tab in the Insert Shapes group.

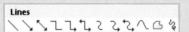

CREATE A CURVE

On the Drawing Tools Format tab, in the Insert Shapes group, click the **More** button for the Shapes menu. Then beneath the Lines option, click one of the following:

● **Curve** ⌒ creates flowing shapes. Click the cross pointer to establish the curve's starting point. Move the pointer and click to continue creating other curvatures. Double-click to set the end point and complete the drawing.

–Or–

● **Freeform** ⌓ uses a combination of curve and scribble techniques. Click the cross pointer to establish curvature points, and/or drag the pencil pointer to create other designs. Double-click to set the end point and complete the drawing.

–Or–

● **Scribble** ⸾ creates pencil-like lines. Drag the pencil icon to create the shape you want. Release the mouse button to complete the drawing.

ADJUST A CURVE

1. Select the curve by clicking it. Click the **Drawing Tools Format** tab. Click **Edit Shape** in the Insert Shapes group.

Continued . . .

Combine Shapes by Grouping

You can combine shapes for any number of reasons, but typically, you work with multiple shapes to build a more complex drawing. So you don't lose the positioning, sizing, and other characteristics of these components, you can group them. They are then treated as one object.

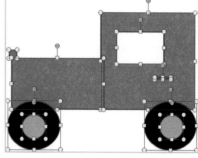

GROUP SHAPES

1. Select the shapes to be grouped by clicking the first shape and then holding **CTRL** while selecting the other shapes.

2. On the Drawing Tools Format tab, click the **Group** button on the Arrange group. A menu is displayed. Click **Group**. A single set of selection handles surrounds the perimeter of the combined shapes. Coloring, positioning, sizing, and other actions now affect the shapes as a group, instead of individually.

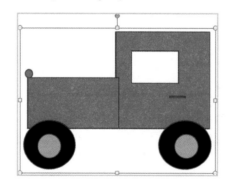

UNGROUP AND REGROUP SHAPES

● **To separate a group into individual shapes** again, select the group and on the Drawing Tools Format tab, click the **Group** button on the Arrange group, and click **Ungroup**.

● **To regroup shapes after separating them**, select any shape that was in the group, click the **Drawing Tools Format** tab, and click the **Group** button on the Arrange group. Click **Regroup**.

WORKING WITH CURVES *(Continued)*

2. Click the **Edit Points**
   option. Black rectangles
   (called *vertices*) appear
   at the top of the curvature
   points.

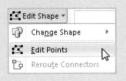

3. Drag a vertex to
   reconfigure the curve's
   shape.

4. Change any other vertex, and click outside the
   curve when finished.

ROTATE A CURVE

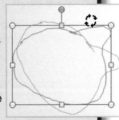

1. Click a curve to select it. A
   green rotate handle will appear
   above the selection box.

2. Place the pointer over the
   handle, and drag it to rotate the
   curve in the way you want.

NOTE

If you cannot easily ungroup an image, it may be a
bitmap, which can't be ungrouped and converted to an
object. In this case, use an imaging program to edit the
image before placing it back into your slide.

Create a Mirror Image Using Rotate

You can create a mirror image of a shape using some of the rotate or flip Shape
tools. Rotating is turning a shape clockwise or counterclockwise by a specific
amount. Flipping is turning it upside down, either vertically or horizontally. If
you click Rotate (Right or Left) 90° twice, you will turn the shape 180 degrees;
three times, 270 degrees; four times, 360 degrees, or back to the original
position. Similarly, if you flip a shape twice, it will
return to its original position. To rotate or flip a shape,
use the Rotate command in the Arrange group of the
Drawing Tools Format tab.

1. Select the shape (not a placeholder) you want to be half of
   the mirror image, right-click the middle of the shape, and
   from the context menu, click **Copy Here**. A second copy of
   the image is placed on top of the original and is selected.

2. On the Drawing Tools Format tab, click the **Rotate** button,
   and click **Flip Horizontal** or **Flip Vertical**, depending on
   how you want the image to look.

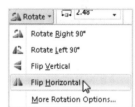

3. Press **SHIFT** and select the original graphic. (You may need
   to separate the two images in order to select both of them.)
   Both graphics should be selected.

4. Click the **Align** button, and
   click **Align Selected Objects** so that
   the two are aligned to each other rather
   than to the slide. Then click an applicable
   alignment to make the graphics even.
   (In Figure 8-15, the Align Top command
   was used.) See the "Aligning Shapes"
   QuickSteps later in the chapter.

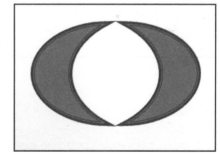

5. If you need to, select one shape, press
   and hold **CTRL**, and press the applicable
   arrow key to nudge the shape into a
   mirrored position.

Figure 8-15: **This mirror image was flipped
horizontally and then aligned using the
Align Top command to get facing shapes.**

Choose a SmartArt Graphic

List

Basic Block List

Use to show non-sequential or grouped blocks of information. Maximizes both horizontal and vertical display space for shapes.

- All
- List
- Process
- Cycle
- Hierarchy
- Relationship
- Matrix
- Pyramid
- Picture

OK   Cancel

*Figure 8-16: **SmartArt graphics offer you many choices for adding professional-looking and complex "working" graphics to your presentation.***

TIP

If you cannot select the shape you want, send the shapes on top of the stack to the back until the one you want is on top.

QUICKSTEPS

POSITIONING SHAPES

Shapes can be positioned by just dragging them, a technique with which you are probably familiar. However, PowerPoint also provides a number of other ways to help you adjust where a shape is in relation to other shapes and objects.

MOVE SHAPES INCREMENTALLY

Select the shape or group, and press the arrow key in the direction you want to move the shape in larger increments; hold down **CTRL** and press the arrow key to move the shape in smaller increments.

Continued . . .

Use SmartArt Graphics

PowerPoint provides predefined graphics for inserting many flexible and professional-looking diagrams and connecting symbols. Figure 8-16 shows the categories, such as the "Cycle" category, of SmartArt graphics that are available. Each category contains a description of the selected graphic and several variations.

Choose SmartArt Categories

Some of the SmartArt categories you can choose from include:

- **List:** Shows a list format. Items in the list may contain more text than other categories, and do not necessarily show relationships or processes, although they can. An example would be an artistic bulleted list.

- **Process:** Shows a step-by-step relationship, such as a process moving from one task or situation to the next to accomplish a goal. Variations show processes emerging from a center, for example.

- **Cycle:** Shows a circular relationship, where items are on the same level, or priority. Variations can show overlapping processes or relationships to a central core.

- **Hierarchy:** Shows a hierarchical relationship with levels—for example, higher levels with lower ones reporting up, as in a traditional corporate organization.

- **Relationship:** Shows a variety of related items, some very complex—from A + B = C to a Venn diagram, and more.

- **Matrix:** Shows a relationship of parts to a whole, such as four quadrants to a whole.

- **Pyramid:** Shows a pyramid-shaped relationship, where a larger base supports an increasingly smaller tip (or the reverse, where the top is larger).

- **Picture:** Contains pictures as an important part of the graphic. The picture may be the main element (such as a sequence of pictures), or it may be an element in showing informational relationships (such as a picture used as a bullet).

To choose the right category, you must be clear on what you are trying to show, what structure best displays the data, and how much data there is to display (some of the graphics do not hold a lot of text).

QUICKSTEPS

POSITIONING SHAPES (Continued)

REPOSITION THE ORDER OF STACKED SHAPES

You can stack graphics by simply dragging one on top of another. However, sometimes it is difficult to edit or format a shape within the stack. To reposition the order of the stack, display the Drawing Tools Format tab, and in the Arrange group:

- Click the **Bring Forward** down arrow, and choose to move the graphic to the top, or forward, in the stack.

- Click the **Send Backward** down arrow, and choose to move the graphic to the bottom, or backward, in the stack.

USE THE SELECTION PANE TO ORDER THE STACK

1. On the Drawing Tools Format tab, click the **Selection Pane** button in the Arrange group. A Selection And Visibility pane will open, as shown in Figure 8-17.

   - Click the **eyeball** icon to hide the object from the pane if it is not part of what you are trying to re-order.

   - Click **Show All** to show all the objects on the slide.

   - Click the **Bring Forward** and **Send Backward** arrows to re-order the objects.

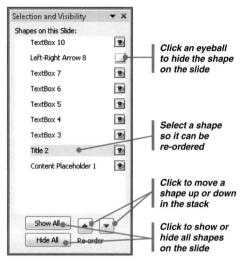

Click an eyeball to hide the shape on the slide

Select a shape so it can be re-ordered

Click to move a shape up or down in the stack

Click to show or hide all shapes on the slide

Figure 8-17: **The Selection And Visibility pane allows you to identify all the objects on a slide, even stacked objects, and to re-order them as needed.**

Insert a SmartArt Graphic

You can insert a SmartArt graphic and then add artistic elements to it, as described in "Change SmartArt Designs." To first select and insert a SmartArt graphic:

1. Click the **Insert** tab, and click **SmartArt**. The Choose A SmartArt Graphic dialog box appears (see Figure 8-16).

2. Click the category on the left, and then select a graphic on the right. When you click a graphic, a display of it is previewed on the right along with a description.

3. When you find the graphic you want, select it and click **OK** to close the dialog box and insert the graphic. The SmartArt Tools tabs, Design and Format, are now available on the ribbon.

4. In the Type Your Text Here text box, click a bullet and type your text. As you type, the text will be recorded in the appropriate shape. You may need to click the small sidebar on the left of the graphic to display the Type Your Text Here dialog box, or click **Text Pane** in the SmartArt Tools Design tab Create Graphic group.

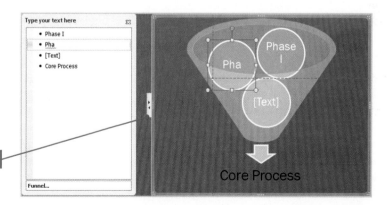

Click here to open and close the text box

ALIGNING SHAPES

Aligning shapes enables you to position shapes more precisely with the aid of an invisible grid and guides, as well as by aligning shapes horizontally or vertically in relationship to each other.

ALIGN SHAPES WITH GRIDS AND GUIDES

To align a shape to an invisible grid, select the shape, click the **Drawing Tools Format** tab, and click the **Align** button in the Arrange group. Click **Grid Settings**. The Grid And Guides dialog box appears.

- To align a shape to an invisible grid (only invisible if the Display Grid On Screen check box is cleared), select the **Snap Objects To Grid** check box.

- To align shapes to one another, select the **Snap Objects To Other Objects** check box. The shapes will be "attracted" to each other when they are moved close to each other. This is useful for stacking objects or for selecting and moving them as a unit.

- To display the grid or guides and establish grid and guide settings, set the appropriate settings in the Grid Settings and Guide Settings areas.

EVENLY SPACE SHAPES

To align objects so that they have equal space above and below or to the left and right on a slide, you can use the Distribute commands. Select one or more shapes, click the **Drawing Tools Format** tab, click the **Align** button on the Arrange group, and click **Distribute Horizontally** or **Distribute Vertically**.

Change SmartArt Designs

When you click a SmartArt object, the SmartArt Tools Design and Format tabs are made available. The SmartArt Tools Design tab contains several ways to change and enhance your SmartArt object.

1. Click the SmartArt object, and click the **SmartArt Tools Design** tab.

2. Select the specific element within the SmartArt graphic that you want to change or duplicate. If you want to work with multiple elements, select them while pressing **CTRL**. The ribbon SmartArt Tools Design options are shown in Figure 8-18.

   - Click the **Add Shape** down arrow in the Create Graphic group to add another shape to the graphic. It may be another text box, circle, layer, bullet, or whatever shape makes up the design. Click the placement option you want.

   - Click **Add Bullet** in the Create Graphic group to add another label or bullet to the text box. The bullet is initially added as a sub-bullet to an existing shape.

- Click **Text Pane** to display or hide the Type Your Text Here text box, as seen in Figure 8-19, where the Text Pane button is selected and the text box is displayed.

- Click the **Promote** and **Demote** buttons in the Create Graphic group to move the selected circle, level, text box, or whatever the shape is to a higher or lower level. For example, in Figure 8-19, promoting "Core Process" would move it up as a subtopic under "Phase 1."

- Click **Right To Left** to orient the shape in the opposite direction. For some shapes, as in Figure 8-19, this command is irrelevant.

- Click **Reorder Up** or **Reorder Down** to switch places with the item above or below it. For example, in Figure 8-19, Reorder Up switches places between the selected "Core Process" and "Phase I."

- Click **Layout** to work with organization layouts—for example, to change chart branch layouts if you have selected that type of chart from the Hierarchy category.

- In the Layouts group, either click a thumbnail for an alternative layout option for the selected graphic or click the **More** down arrow to display a menu of options. Point to the options to see the effects on your graphic.

- Click **Change Colors** in the SmartArt Styles group to change the colors of the design. Note that when you insert another SmartStyle of the same type, it reverts to the default theme colors.

- Click a **SmartArt** thumbnail in the SmartArt Styles group to change the style of the graphic, as was done in Figure 8-19.

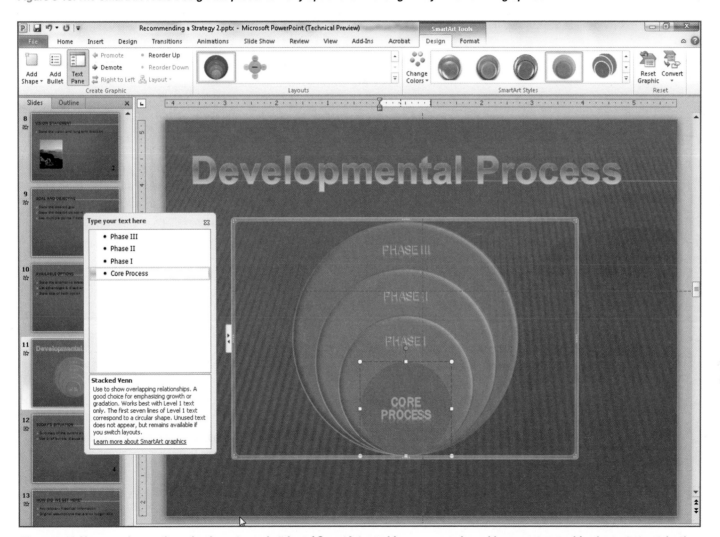

Figure 8-18: **The SmartArt Tools Design tab presents many options for working with your SmartArt graphics.**

Figure 8-19: **You can change the color, layouts, and styles of SmartArt graphics; you can also add or remove graphic elements to make them fit your needs.**

- In the Reset group, click **Reset Graphic** to remove formatting that you have made to the graphic and return it to its original state.

- Click **Convert** to change a SmartArt graphic to an ordinary shape or text. In this way, you can change, delete, or add to the graphic.

3. Click outside the graphic to deselect it and see the results of your design changes.

Change SmartArt Formatting

The SmartArt Tools Format tab, shown in Figure 8-20, contains many familiar tools to change the graphic, such as Shape Fill, Shape Outline, and Shape Effects. Most of the tools are discussed in other chapters. There are a few, though, that are tailored to the SmartArt feature.

1. Click the SmartArt object, and click the **SmartArt Tools Format** tab.

2. Click the specific element within the SmartArt graphic that you want to change or duplicate. If you want to work with multiple elements, select them while pressing **CTRL**. The ribbon SmartArt Tools Format options are shown in Figure 8-20.

- **Edit In 2-D** allows you to edit a three-dimensional shape in order to move or resize it.

- **Change Shape** displays a menu of shapes that can replace the selected shapes. Click the shape you want.

- **Larger** and **Smaller** resizes the selected shape to be larger or smaller. Click the button, and the shape is resized slightly with each click.

- **Shape Styles** change the color, outline, and effects of the current SmartArt selection. When you click the Shape Styles More button, you'll see additional possibilities.

- **WordArt Styles** are also discussed under "Work with WordArt."

- The **Arrange** group is discussed in the "Positioning Shapes" QuickSteps.

- **Shape Height** and **Shape Width** in the Size group allow you to precisely change the dimensions of a shape or object. Click the **More** button for the dialog box settings.

3. Click outside the object to deselect it and see the effects of your formatting.

Figure 8-20: *The SmartArt Tools Format tab provides tools to change and enhance SmartArt graphics.*

Chapter 9
Working with Multimedia and the Internet

Multimedia files and presentations on the Internet are two features that lend impact to your presentations. In this chapter you will see how to insert and play audio and video files in your presentation. You will see how to manage your sound files. You will then actually record sound files and package all linked files together with the presentation. Using the Internet, you will be able to make your presentation available to others who may not have PowerPoint. You will learn how to store the presentation on the SkyDrive server so that those without PowerPoint can view the presentation with a browser.

Use Multimedia Files in Your Presentation

Music, sound, and video clips can be inserted on a slide or object on a slide. The clips can come from files on your computer, Microsoft's Clip Organizer, the Internet, or from another network. You can record your own sounds and add them to the presentation. The sounds you insert can be made to start automatically when the slide is displayed or to start when you click the mouse.

Insert Sounds from Audio Clip Art

PowerPoint provides an inventory of sounds that you can use for your slides, or you can use files from Office.com.

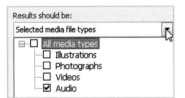

1. In Normal view, select the slide that will have the sound.

2. Click the **Insert** tab, and click the **Audio** down arrow in the Media group. A menu will be displayed.

3. Click **Clip Art Audio**. The Clip Art task pane is displayed, as shown in Figure 9-1. It contains a gallery of canned sounds. You may want more options.

4. Under Search For on the Clip Art task pane, type the subject, such as laugh, airplane, or fireworks, for which you want a sound.

5. In the Results Should Be drop-down list box, **Audio** should be selected (if it is not, select it) to find audio types of files (AIFF, MIDI, or WAV, for instance). To extend the selection of files to the Web, make sure the **Include Office.com Content** check box is selected.

6. Click **Go**.

7. When the sound files are displayed in the preview of thumbnails, click the down arrow on the side of a thumbnail, and click **Preview/Properties** to hear the sound. The Preview/Properties dialog box appears, and the sound is played.

8. If you want to hear it again, click the **Play** button, shown in Figure 9-2. Click **Close** when you are satisfied with the sound.

9. To insert the sound, on the Clip Art task pane, double-click the thumbnail of the audio file you want. (It may take a minute to download.)

Figure 9-1: *The Clip Art task pane contains canned sounds, and you can search for additional possibilities.*

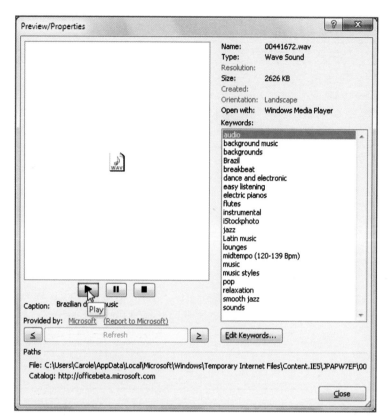

Figure 9-2: *You can find and preview sounds before you choose the one that fits your needs.*

10. A selected audio icon is displayed along with the mechanism to play the file, adjust the timing, notice the duration, and adjust the volume. Click **Play** to listen to the sound. When you're satisfied with the sound you've chosen, drag the icon to an "out-of-the-way" spot on the slide.

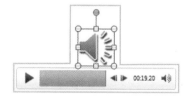

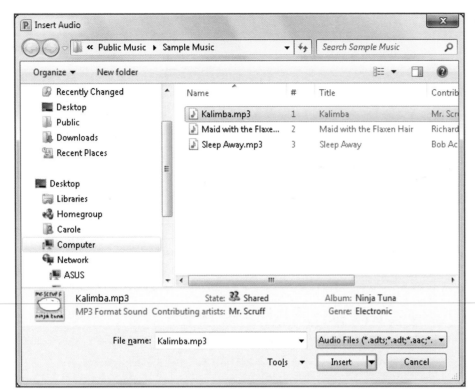

Figure 9-3: *You can insert sound files from your own computer or a computer on a network.*

Insert a Sound from a File

On your computer or network, you may have your own sounds. You can also insert them in your slides.

1. In Normal view, select the slide that you want to have the sound.

2. Click the **Insert** tab, click the **Audio** down arrow in the Media group, and click **Audio From File**.

3. The Insert Audio dialog box will appear, as shown in Figure 9-3.

4. Find and select your sound file, and click **Insert**. The selected audio icon is displayed along with the mechanism to play the file, adjust the timing, notice the duration, and adjust the volume.

5. Click **Play** to listen to the sound.

6. When you're satisfied, drag the icon to an "out-of-the-way" spot on the slide.

Work with an Audio File

You can perform several tasks with the commands found on the Audio Tools Playback tab, shown in Figure 9-4, which is displayed when a sound file is selected. To work with the sound file:

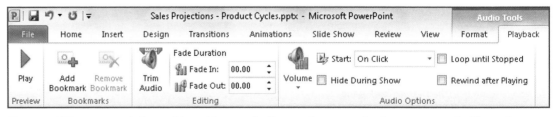

Figure 9-4: *The commands for working with an audio file permit you to tailor how you want the file to play.*

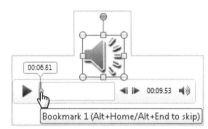

1. Insert your audio file onto the slide where you want it, and make sure it is selected.

2. Click the **Audio Tools Playback** tab. You have these options available to you:

   - In the Preview group, click **Play** to begin the sound clip. This is needed for several of the other commands in the Playback tab to be used.

   - In the Bookmarks group, click **Add Bookmark** to insert a marker or bookmark in the audio file at the current time. A small circle that turns yellow when it is selected, will be inserted into the sound clip. You can use the bookmark to advance the clip or soundtrack to a designated place before it plays. To do this, click the **Animations** tab, click **Trigger** in the Advanced Animation group, click **Bookmark**, and select the specific one. To delete a bookmark, click it and click **Remove Bookmark** in the Playback tab Bookmarks group.

   - In the Editing group, click **Trim Audio** to trim some amount of sound from the beginning or end of the file. See "Trim an Audio File."

   - In the Editing group, click the **Fade Duration** spinners to set a time when the clip will begin to fade in or fade out.

   - In the Audio Options group, click the **Volume** down arrow, and click the volume you want played.

   - Click the **Start** down arrow to set what will activate the sound clip to play. You can choose a mouse click, automatically when the slide is displayed, or playing continuously across slides.

   - Under Audio Options, click **Hide During Show** if you want the audio icon to be hidden during the actual presentation.

   - Under Audio Options, click the **Loop Until Stopped** check box if you want the audio clip to repeat itself until you click the mouse.

   - Click **Rewind After Playing** to set the clip to rewind after it has played.

Trim an Audio File

To cut extra sound from the beginning or end of a sound file, use the Trim Audio command.

1. Insert the audio file in your presentation, and click it to select it.

2. Click the **Audio Tools Playback** tab, and in the Editing group, click **Trim Audio**. The Trim Audio dialog box will appear, as shown in Figure 9-5.

TIP

You may want to set the sound to play over a number of slides. The audio will stop when the number of slides is over. Click the **Animations** tab, and click **Animation Pane** in the Advanced Animation group. The Animation pane is displayed. Click the audio effect from the Effects list, click the down arrow, and click **Effect Options**. On the Effect tab, under Stop Playing, click the **After ___ Slides** check box to insert a check mark. Click the spinner to set the number of slides, and click **OK**.

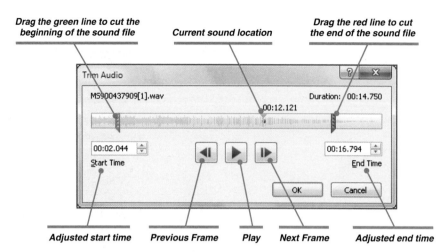

Drag the green line to cut the
beginning of the sound file

Current sound location

Drag the red line to cut
the end of the sound file

Adjusted start time   Previous Frame   Play   Next Frame   Adjusted end time

Figure 9-5: *Trim Audio is used to cut the beginning or end of a file
sound to adjust it so that the sound fits the slide perfectly.*

3. Click **Play** to play the audio file.

4. Drag the left green line segment to the position where the sound is to start. You can use the start time as a guide to where that is.

5. Drag the right red line segment to where the sound is to end. You can use the end time as a guide to that position.

6. Click on the audio bar to reposition the current position (the blue marker).

7. Use the **Previous Frame** and the **Next Frame** to reposition the current location on the file.

8. Click **OK** to close the dialog box when you're finished.

Use Animations to Set Sound Effects

You may find it more convenient to use the Animations tab to set sound effects using the Animation pane instead of using the Playback tab (see "Work with an Audio File"). Once a sound has been inserted onto a slide, you can use the Animation pane to change or refine how and when it plays. (Chapter 8 contains additional information about animations.)

1. Select the sound icon for which you want to set options. Click the **Animations** tab, and in the Advanced Animation group, click **Animation Pane**.

TIP

To apply sound to an animation, select the animated object, click the **Animations** tab, and click **Animation Pane** in the Advanced Animation group. The Animation pane is displayed. On the Effects list, click to select the effect, and then click its down arrow. Click **Effect Options** on the menu. Under Enhancements on the Effect tab, click the **Sound** down arrow, and click a sound, or click **Other Sounds** to search for an audio file. Click **OK**. See Chapter 8 for more information about special effects and animation.

Figure 9-6: *The Animation pane allows you to select additional options for sound files.*

Figure 9-7: *The Play Audio dialog box is where you set specific performance, timing, and other sound attributes.*

2. On the Animation pane, click the sound effect in the Effects list, and click its down arrow. A menu will open, as shown in Figure 9-6.

3. Click **Effect Options** and click the **Effect** tab to open the Play Audio dialog box, shown in Figure 9-7. The options may vary, depending on the type of sound file you have selected.

4. You may have these options:
   - Under Start Playing, click **From Beginning** to start playing the sound clip from the beginning.
   - Click **From Last Position** to continue playing the sound clip from the previous location on the track.
   - Click **From Time** and click the spinner to set the number of seconds to advance into the sound clip before beginning to play.
   - Under Stop Playing, click **On Click** to stop the sound when the slide is clicked.
   - Click **After Current Slide** to stop playing when the next slide is displayed.
   - Click **After** and click the spinner to set the number of slides during which the sound continues to play before stopping.

5. On the **Timing** tab:
   - Click the **Start** down arrow, and select **On Click** (the sound starts when you click the sound icon), **With Previous** (the sound starts at the same time as another effect), or **After Previous**.
   - Set the **Delay** spinner with the number of seconds that are to pass after the slide is displayed but before the sound plays.
   - Click the **Repeat** down arrow, and select the number of times the sound is to repeat.
   - Click the **Rewind When Done Playing** check box to return the sound clip to the beginning when the clip has completed playing.
   - Click the **Triggers** down arrows, and click **Animate As Part Of Click Sequence** if the sound is to be part of another effect or group of effects, click **Start Effect On Click Of** to connect the sound with the click of another effect, or click **Start Effect On Play Of** to connect the sound with the play of another effect. Click the down arrow to choose the other effect.

Total playing time: 00:20
File: [Contained in presentation]

NOTE

When you are inserting multiple sound clips on a slide, the default is to play them in the order in which they are inserted. You can change this order in the Effect and Timing tabs of the Play Audio dialog box.

CAUTION

One potential problem with linked files is that if you move the presentation from its current location, you may lose linked sound files. So it is important to keep the presentation and sound files together, in the same folder if possible. See "Package Presentation Files" later in the chapter.

TIP

To compress media files, click **File**, click **Info**, and click **Compress Media**. Select the quality you want for the compressed files.

6. On the Audio Settings tab:

- Click **Sound Volume** to set the slider to the volume you want.

- Click the **Hide Audio Icon During Slide Show** check box to hide the sound icon while the presentation is being played.

- Use the **Information** area to learn how long the sound clip plays and the path to the source file listed.

7. Click **OK** to close the Play Audio dialog box.

Record Sound Files

There are at least three reasons you might want to record a narrative for your slide show. First, recording prior to the presentation enables the slide show to run without your presence. You can produce a Web-based presentation or a kiosk trade show presentation this way. Second, recording during the presentation saves a record of your comments and the audience's response, if you choose. Finally, you might want to record short comments on just a few slides to note a change you'd like to make or to emphasize an important point. Before recording, however, you may need to set up and test your microphone equipment.

RECORD A NARRATIVE FOR YOUR PRESENTATION

You use the Slide Show tab to record a narrative for your presentation. The narrative will play as the slide show is presented. You can record and re-record to get the timings correct for each slide. You can record on selected slides or all slides. You use the timings to see how long your presentation will be, judge the time you should spend on any given slide, and perfect the message and the length of the presentation.

1. Select the slide on which you will begin the narration.

2. Click the **Slide Show** tab, and click the **Record Slide Show** down arrow. A menu is displayed.

3. Choose between **Start Recording From Beginning Slide** and **Start Recording From Current Slide**. In either case, the Record Slide Show dialog box appears.

Click to advance slide action   **Records current slide time**   **Records cumulative time**

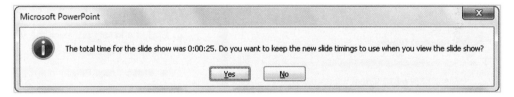

Pause recording   **Repeat previous action**

4. Select **Narrations And Laser Pointer**, and click **Start Recording**. The Recording dialog box will appear on the activated slide show.

5. Talk into the microphone as your slide show proceeds.

   ● Be sure the microphone is on. Speak into it. The narration for your slide show will be recorded as you speak.

   ● To move from one slide to the next when you are finished recording on one, click **Next** on the Recording toolbar, or right-click and click **Next**.

   ● To temporarily pause recording, click **Pause** on the Recording toolbar, or right-click the slide and click **Pause Recording**.

6. If you end the recording session, or if it ends naturally, you will see a message informing you that the timings, or the record of how long each slide took, will be saved with the slide. You can see the timings under each slide in the Slide Sorter view. Click **Yes** to save the timings. Click **No** to discard the timings.

Microsoft PowerPoint

ⓘ The total time for the slide show was 0:00:25. Do you want to keep the new slide timings to use when you view the slide show?

[Yes]   [No]

7. To continue recording after clicking Pause, click **Resume Recording** on the Recording Paused dialog box.

8. Refer to "Work with an Audio File" earlier in the chapter to set up the directives for how your narrative will be played in the slide show. For example, if you want the slides to play automatically, all but the first can be set to Start After Previous. You may set the first to On Click.

Microsoft PowerPoint

ⓘ Recording paused.

[Resume Recording]

RECORD SHORT COMMENTS

To record a short comment on a single slide:

1. Select the slide that will have the comments.

2. Click the **Insert** tab, click the **Audio** down arrow, and click **Record Audio**. The Record Sound dialog box appears.

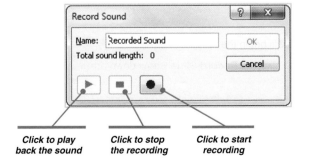

Record Sound

Name: Recorded Sound   [OK]
Total sound length: 0   [Cancel]

Click to play back the sound   **Click to stop the recording**   **Click to start recording**

CHANGING VIDEO OPTIONS

These options, set on the slide, determine how the video portion of your slide show will run. The Video Options group is accessed from the Video Tools Playback tab, which appears when the movie is clicked or selected.

LOOP OR REWIND A MOVIE

To cause a movie to play repeatedly or to rewind, click the movie to select it, and then click the **Video Tools Playback** tab. In the Video Options group:

- Click the **Loop Until Stopped** check box to cause the movie to repeat.

- Click the **Rewind After Playing** check box to return to the beginning of the movie.

FILL THE SCREEN WITH THE MOVIE

To run the movie at full-screen size, click the **Video Tools Playback** tab, and click the **Play Full Screen** check box in the Video Options group.

RESIZE THE MOVIE

Occasionally, a video may look fuzzy at full-screen size. To fix this, you can resize the movie so that it plays in a smaller screen area during the slide show. To resize a movie, making it larger or smaller, select the movie and drag the sizing handles of the picture to the size you want.

–Or–

Set the size you want in the Size group on the Video Tools Format tab.

Continued . . .

---

3. Type a name for the recording.

- To begin the recording, click **Record**.
- To stop, click **Stop**.
- To play back the recording, click **Play**.

4. Click **OK** when you are done.

Use Video Files in Your Presentation

As with sound files, you can insert video files and set options to vary the start, stop, timing, and other attributes of videos in your presentation. When you insert a video, you will see a picture of the beginning of the video rather than an icon.

INSERT A VIDEO

1. Select the slide that will contain the video.

2. Click the **Insert** tab, click the **Video** down arrow in the Media group, and from the popup menu, click the source of your video file.

- **Video From File** to insert a video file from your own collections, not from part of the Clip Organizer collection
- **Clip Art Video** to select from Microsoft's collection of clip art videos
- **Video From Web Site** to insert a video clip from online collections

3. Find your video file, and insert it into the selected slide.

4. Click the **Video Tools Playback** tab to set how to start the movie. In the Video Options group, click the **Start** down arrow and:

- Click **Automatically** to start the movie when the slide displays.
- Click **On Click** to start the movie when the mouse button is clicked.

5. To preview the video on this slide, click **Preview** on the Preview group. To see the whole slide show, press **F5**.

QUICKSTEPS

CHANGING VIDEO OPTIONS *(Continued)*

SET THE VOLUME

To set the volume for the movie:

1. Click the Video Tools Playback tab, and click the Volume button in the Video Options group.

2. Click the volume level you want.

SET A FADE IN/FADE OUT TRANSITION

1. To set a period of fade in/fade out on either side of the video, click the **Video Tools Playback** tab.

2. In the Editing group, click the **Fade Duration** spinners to set the period of time that will be used for the fade-in/fade-out transition.

CAUTION

If you have a recorded sound, such as a song in the background, and are recording a narrative over it, be sure the transition timings for both sounds are compatible. For instance, you'll want to set the background song to play over a given number of slides so that the transition to the next slide will not have to wait until the song has totally played, but will advance when your narration has finished, as set by After *recorded timing* (in the Transitions tab Timing group).

TIP

The narrative timings automatically time your slide display without you clicking to advance the slides. They can be turned off and on as you wish. (Click the **Slide Show** tab, and click **Use Timings** to select or clear the check box to display the slide show without or with control by timings.)

CHANGE START OR PLAY TIMES

You can delay the start of the video until a certain time after a slide has been displayed or after a certain click sequence.

1. Display the slide containing the video effect.

2. To display the Animation pane, click the **Animations** tab, and click **Animation Pane** on the Advanced Animation group. The Animation pane will open.

3. In the Effects list of the task pane, select the effect for the video, and click the down arrow. Select **Timing**. The Pause Video dialog box is displayed with the Timing tab active.

- Click the **Delay** spinners to set the amount of time before the video is to start.

- To play the video in the normal sequence of click events, click the **Triggers** down arrows, and click **Animate As Part Of Click Sequence**. To delay the video until something on the screen is clicked, click **Start Effect On Click Of**, click the down arrow, and click the click-event that will start the video.

USE SPECIAL EFFECTS WITH VIDEOS

You may find that you want the video frame to be enhanced in some way. For instance, you can change the frame, the color casting, the frame shape, or add a special effect to the frame, such as a glow. You can do these with the Video Tools Format tab.

1. Click the video you want to change.

2. Click the **Video Tools Format** tab. You'll find several interesting options for working with the video's appearance.

   ● In the Video Styles group, click the **Video Shape** button, and click a shape. The video will be contained within the shape, such as you see with Figure 9-8.

   ● In the Video Styles group, click the **Video Border** button to select a color for the frame border. You can also change its style or weight.

   ● To add an artistic color cast to the video, in the Adjust group, click **Color** and select a color that will be imposed over the video, as shown in Figure 9-8.

Figure 9-8: When displaying a video in PowerPoint, you can add several custom effects shown here, such as the action button, shape containing the video, color cast over the video, colored border, and special effect, such as the glow.

SHARING YOUR PRESENTATION

PowerPoint provides ways for you to share your presentation with others. Your purpose may be to send your presentation to your e-mail contacts, save it on a server in order for people to access it using a browser, enable others to collaborate on it, broadcast it on a Web site, or publish it to a library so it can be managed.

To access sharing commands, click **File** and click **Share**.

SEND USING E-MAIL

Clicking this button allows you to send your presentation via e-mail. You can choose whether to send it as an attachment or link, a PDF, or XPS file, or to send it as an Internet fax. All use your e-mail program, except when sending an Internet fax, you must be signed up with a service provider. You can sign up here by clicking **Send As Internet Fax**.

SAVE TO SKYDRIVE

You can upload your file to SkyDrive, a server maintained by Microsoft, where anyone with a browser and the address can access it. You can load up to 50MB per file to a total of 25GB of data onto SkyDrive for free. You must have a Windows Live ID and a SkyDrive account, both of which can be obtained with the Save To SkyDrive command. After that, you simply save or drag your presentation to SkyDrive. It can either have a unique Web address that only those you give permission to can access, or it can be public to all with a browser. (See "Make Your Presentation Available Online.")

SAVE TO SHAREPOINT

If you are using SharePoint and want to collaborate on the development of a PowerPoint presentation or use it for some purpose within your SharePoint group, you can do so. You save the file to your SharePoint location

Continued . . .

Share

- Send Using E-mail
- Save to SkyDrive
- Save to SharePoint
- Broadcast Slide Show
- Publish Slides

● To add a special effect (discussed in Chapter 8), in the Video Styles group, click the **Video Effects** button, and select the type of special effect you might want, such as the glow as in Figure 9-8.

INSERT ACTION BUTTONS

Action buttons can be inserted on the beginning slide of a video to act as triggers for starting, pausing, or stopping the video. An example of one to start the video is shown in Figure 9-8. These replace the mouse clicks normally used to start, pause, and stop it. To insert an action button:

1. Click the slide containing the movie.

2. Add the buttons to the slide. To do this, click the **Insert** tab, click **Shapes**, and select a button that fits your video scheme (point to each button to see its function) under the Action Buttons list at the bottom of the popup menu (such as the Action Button: Movie 🎥):

Action Buttons

- Your pointer will become a cross. Drag it on the slide where you want the button shape. When you release the mouse, the Action Settings dialog box will appear.

- On the Action Settings dialog box, under Action On Click, click **None**. Then click **OK**.
- Repeat this for each button you wish on the slide.

3. To open the Animation pane, click the **Animations** tab, and in the Advanced Animation group, click **Animation Pane**. Select the movie on your slide.

4. Make the buttons the trigger for the actions you want. To do this:

- In the Effects list on the task pane, select each effect to be triggered by a button, such as the movie.

- Click its down arrow, and select **Timing**.

- Click the **Triggers** down arrow, click **Start Effect On Click Of**, and click the action button you want.

Triggers ⬍
○ Animate as part of click sequence
◉ Start effect on click of: Action Button: Movie 5 ▾
○ Start effect on play of: ▾

SHARING YOUR PRESENTATION

(Continued)

where those with access can view and edit the file. All SharePoint users can then access all versions; links are sent instead of attached documents, saving time and computer resources; and notifications are made when the presentation is modified.

BROADCAST A SLIDE SHOW

Broadcasting allows you to send a link of your slide show to others who can view it in real time without having PowerPoint. This service requires coordinating a time with viewers for when the broadcast will occur. When you click the Start Broadcast button after initiating the service, you will be given a link to share with others. You can copy the link to deliver to recipients via alternative means, or you can choose to send an e-mail automatically containing the link. You fill in the addresses of the recipients, and then you start the broadcast. It will be uploaded to a remote server. Those who receive the e-mail will be able to click the link and see the slide show as it is being broadcast. (No audio is available with broadcasted presentations.) During the broadcast, the presentation appears in a Broadcast tab (all the other tabs except File are unavailable during the broadcast), where you can control several aspects of the broadcast.

PUBLISH SLIDES

When you publish your presentation, you save it to a shared library (or SharePoint location) where others can access it. In the library, versions of the presentation are maintained so that you can find the most current version and see previous versions. If your Save option settings are activated, the check-in/check-out capability can be used to track edits. You will be notified when the file is edited by others. This is a simple way to manage viewing and editing of a file.

Package Presentation Files

You can copy all the presentation files to a folder or burn them on a CD (or DVD) in order to easily transport them to another computer to show a presentation. This is called packaging.

1. Open the presentation to be packaged.

2. Click **File** and click **Share**. Under File Types, click **Package Presentation For CD**, and then click the **Package For CD** icon. The Package For CD dialog box will appear. You may see a message that some of the files will be upgraded to compatible file formats for PowerPoint Viewer.

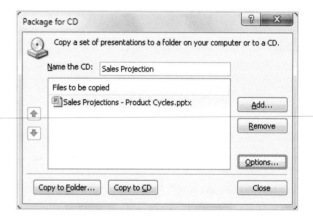

3. Type a name in the Name The CD text box.

4. Click **Add Files** if you need to add files other than those that are listed under Files To Be Copied (linked files and the PowerPoint Viewer are included by default, so they don't need to be added). The Add Files dialog box will appear. Browse for the files you want to include, and click **Add**. They will be added to the list of files to be copied.

5. Click **Options** to specify whether to include linked or embedded TrueType fonts and to protect the PowerPoint files with a password. You can have the presentation checked to verify that private information is not included. Click **OK** to close the Options dialog box.

   ● Click **Copy To Folder** to copy the files to a unique folder. After setting these options, click **OK**.

   –Or–

- Click **Copy To CD** to burn the files to a CD. If you have linked files, you will be asked if you want to include them in the package. Then you will be asked to insert a CD. A message will ask if you want to continue if comments and annotations are included in the slides. If you do, click **Yes**.

6. The files will be copied. If you want to copy the files to another folder or CD, click **Yes**.

7. Click **Close** to close the Package For CD dialog box.

Make a Video of Your Presentation

You can save your presentation as a .wmf file, creating a video of it.

1. Click **File** and click **Share**. Under File Types, click **Create A Video**. The right pane will show your options.

   - Click **Computer & HD Displays** to choose the destination of the video: to view on a computer monitor, projector, or high-definition display; to upload to a Web site; or to display on a portable device.

   - Click **(Don't) Use Recorded Timings and Narrations** to choose between recording the timings and narrations in the video or not. (Your option may be entitled without the "Don't.")

   - Click the spinners for the **Seconds To Spend On Each Slide** to set how long to pause on each slide in the video.

2. Click **Create Video**. In the Save As dialog box, name and locate your video. Click **Save**.

Use the Internet with Your Presentations

You can use the Internet in several ways. You can insert a hyperlink to a Web page that is embedded in your presentation. You can save your presentation to an FTP (File Transfer Protocol) location. You can save your presentation as a Web page on a local computer, an intranet, or the Internet. Others can then view your presentation with a Web browser. (See "Sharing Your Presentation" QuickFacts for other ways to use the Internet.)

Connect to Web Pages with Hyperlinks

PowerPoint makes it easy to incorporate information stored on Web sites as part of your slide show. A slide show can be published on the Internet or can provide the speaker access to Web pages when making the presentation. You can connect to a Web page by inserting a hyperlink directly into the presentation or by placing an action button in your slide, which connects to the Web page when clicked.

INSERT A HYPERLINK

To place a hyperlink directly on a slide:

1. Display the slide you want to contain the hyperlink in Normal view.

2. Type the text you want to become a hyperlink:

   ● If the text is the URL (Uniform Resource Locator) of a Web page, press **ENTER** or **SPACEBAR**, and the text will be recognized as a hyperlink, as shown here. Your task is done.

   www.cofinances.org

   ● If you want the hyperlink to be part of the text of the presentation, select the text by highlighting it to prepare for the next step.

   Click here for the current budget.

3. Click the **Insert** tab, and in the Links group, click **Hyperlink**. The Insert Hyperlink dialog box will appear.

   ● In the Address box, type or find the URL of the Web site, either Internet- or intranet-based, that will be linked to the selected text, as shown in Figure 9-9.

   ● Click **Existing File Or Web Page** to find a file on your computer, on an intranet, or on the Internet.

   ● Click **Place In This Document** to enter a hyperlink to another slide in the presentation.

   ● Click **Create New Document** to enter a hyperlink to a new document yet to be created (you can edit the new document now or later).

   ● Click **E-mail Address** to enter a link to an e-mail address. Enter the address and subject.

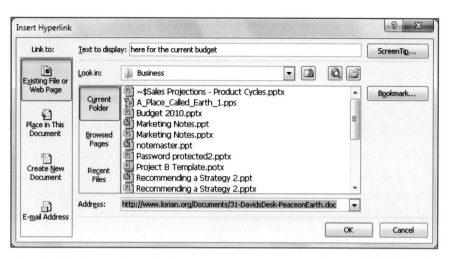

Figure 9-9: *To insert a hyperlink in your presentation, you need to identify the text that will be the hyperlink and the address to which it will be linked.*

4. Click **OK**. The text will be colored and underlined to show that it is a hyperlink, such as:

> Click <u>here for the current budget</u>

USE ACTION BUTTONS TO CONNECT TO A WEB PAGE

You can insert a hyperlink in the form of an action button on a slide that, when clicked, connects to a Web page.

1. In Normal view, display the slide that you want to contain the action button.

2. Click the **Insert** tab, and click **Shapes** in the Illustrations group. A popup menu will be displayed.

Shapes

3. Click an action button shape from the bottom of the menu. The pointer will become a cross, which you drag diagonally across the slide to form a button shape. When you release the pointer, the Action Settings dialog box will appear.

4. Click **Hyperlink To**.

5. Open the drop-down list box, and click the hyperlink connection. For a Web site, click **URL**.

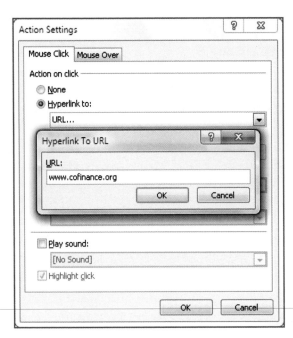

6. In the Hyperlink To URL dialog box, type the URL address, as shown in Figure 9-10 (you don't need to type http://), and click **OK**. Click **OK** again to close the Action Settings dialog box. The hyperlink is now attached to the action button.

7. Format the button as needed. (Figure 9-11 shows an example of a slide with an action button connecting to a Web page.)

- In the Drawing Tools Format tab, click **Shape Effects** in the Shape Styles group to create a custom shape, such as a bevel.

- Use the sizing handles to make the button the size you want.

- Click in the button shape and type the words you want to appear on it. Resize and position it on the action button as needed.

- Drag the button to where you want it placed on the slide.

*Figure 9-10: **The Action Settings dialog box allows you to connect to a Web site from an action button on your slide.***

*Figure 9-11: **The action button can be used to connect to a Web page on the Internet or intranet while you are giving a presentation.***

NOTE

To set up your SkyDrive credentials and upload a file, you must first establish a Windows Live ID and a SkyDrive account. To do this, click **File** and click **Share**. The Share pane appears. Click **Save To SkyDrive**, click **Sign Up**, and follow directions to establish a Windows Live ID and SkyDrive account.

Make Your Presentation Available Online

Using SkyDrive you can save your presentation to a remote server, enabling viewers who don't have PowerPoint to view the presentation with a browser. (See "Sharing Your Presentation" QuickFacts for an overview). Using this technique preserves the links, color schemes, and other design elements created with PowerPoint. The file and all the supporting objects are saved to a Web folder that you create on SkyDrive or to a public folder.

ADD A FOLDER TO SKYDRIVE

SkyDrive, shown in Figure 9-12, contains a number of folders to hold your presentations and other documents. Some of these are standard and are in the

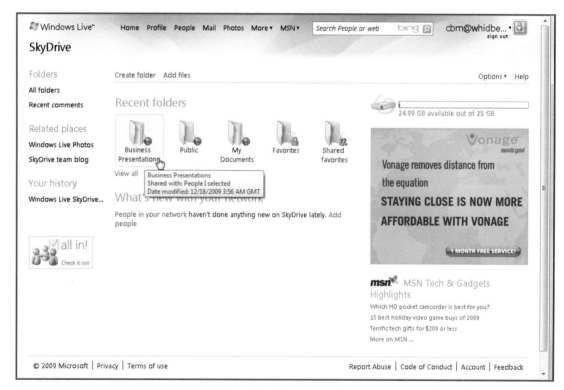

Figure 9-12: *You can save your presentations to SkyDrive where viewers can access them with a browser.*

account at the beginning. Others, such as the Business Presentations in Figure 9-12, are your personal folders that you create. (See "Understanding SkyDrive Folders" QuickFacts.)

To log on to SkyDrive and create a new folder to hold your documents:

1. From the Save To SkyDrive pane (click **File**, click **Share**, and click **Save To SkyDrive**), click either **SkyDrive** or **Sign Up** to see the SkyDrive window, shown in Figure 9-12.

2. Click **Create Folder** to add a new folder to the account. The Create A Folder view will appear.

3. Type the name for the folder.

4. Click **Share With** to choose those permitted to see the contents of the folder. Choose **Everyone (Public)**, **My Network**, **Just Me**, or **Select People**.

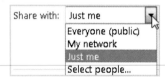

5. If you choose Select People, you'll be able to enter the e-mail addresses of those allowed in the Individuals text box. If you click Select From Your Contact List, you can choose the permitted viewers from your e-mail contact list.

6. Click **Next**. The Add Files to foldername dialog box is displayed. Follow the steps in "Add Files To SkyDrive" next.

ADD FILES TO SKYDRIVE

You can upload files to SkyDrive by dragging them from your computer to a designated folder.

1. Click **Add Files** on the SkyDrive home page. (If you have added a folder, you will see the Add Files To *foldername* when you click **Next**.) You will see a list of folders.

2. Click the folder you want to use. The Add Files To *foldername* window appears, as shown in Figure 9-13.

3. You can upload files in two ways:
   - If you have Windows Explorer open, click your file and drag it to the Add Files To *foldername* window.

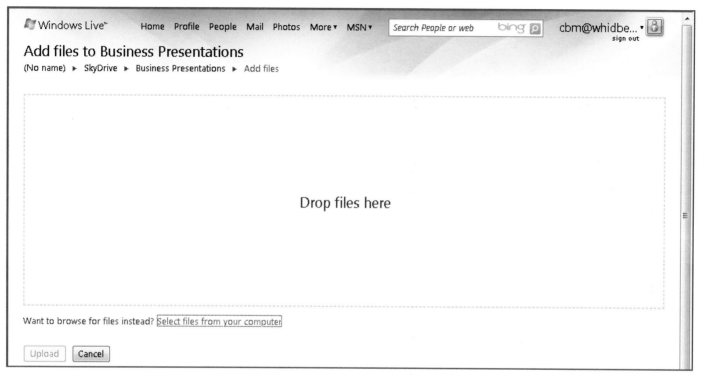

Figure 9-13: *Adding files to SkyDrive is as easy as dragging the files from Windows Explorer or using the browse function, Select Files From Your Computer.*

- Click **Select Files From Your Computer**, find your file, and click **Open** to place it into the SkyDrive window.

4. When all the files you want to be uploaded are displayed in the SkyDrive Add Files window, click **Upload**. You'll see a message informing you that the upload has been successful, along with icons of your other uploaded files.

How to...

Chapter 10
Printing and Running a Slide Show

This last chapter addresses how to display the output of a PowerPoint presentation. You may wish to present it as a slide show projected before an audience, on another monitor controlled by your laptop computer, or as a slide show running by itself on a standalone computer or kiosk. You may print it as transparencies, as a PostScript file for 35-mm slides, or simply as a printed handout. PowerPoint gives you a great deal of flexibility in how you offer your presentation.

Run a Slide Show

How you run your presentation depends, of course, on the circumstances around your need for creating it. There are really three types of slide shows:

- **Automatic Slide Show**   This type of slide show, which runs by itself, is useful for trade shows or other places where you want a presentation to automatically run repeatedly with no presenter. The viewer watches, with limited or no ability to intervene with the presentation. The presentation may entice hundreds of people to stop as they stroll through and watch it for a few minutes or the whole slide show.

- **Presenter View**   In contrast, the presenter has control over a "manned" presentation given before an audience ranging from a full auditorium of listeners, a classroom, a meeting, or a family gathering. This type of format offers a structured way of controlling the slide show. What is seen on the secondary monitor is the full-screen slide show. On the primary monitor, the laptop usually, is a reduced slide show with tools, thumbnails of the slides, and speaker notes.

- **Full Screen View**   This type is related to Presenter view but is more freeform. Both monitors see the full-screen slide show, but the presenter uses a context menu to access the pen and other tools. This menu can be seen by the audience as well or hidden.

In all three cases, you must set up to display on dual monitors and you must prepare the slide show.

Use a Laptop to Control Dual Monitors

If you have a dual-monitor display card installed in your computer (most laptops do) and are using a later version of Windows (XP, Vista, or Windows 7), you can have the same or different images of the slide show displayed on your primary monitor (most likely a laptop) and on a projector or secondary monitor. When you connect a laptop to a projector or a second monitor, you need to set up the controls between the two displays, and you may need to fine-tune the resolution and audio before you can run the presentation from your laptop as you normally would.

SET DISPLAY CONTROLS

1. Connect the cables from the projector or monitor to the laptop and the audio cables from the speakers to the laptop, according to your laptop documentation.

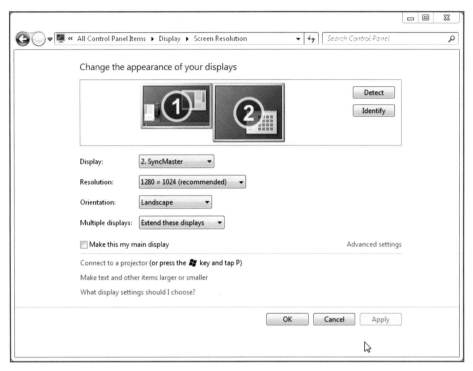

Figure 10-1: *Adjust the resolution using the Screen Resolution dialog box.*

2. Use the keys appropriate for your computer (**FN+F8** for a Dell computer) to synchronize the laptop to the monitor or projector so that both are on.

3. To set the controls on your laptop computer, right-click the **Desktop** and click **Personalize**.

4. Click **Display** in the Windows 7 window.

5. Click **Adjust Resolution** in Windows 7. The Change The Appearance Of Your Displays dialog box, shown in Figure 10-1, appears.

TIP

If you are not sure which monitor is configured to be number 1 or 2, click the **Identify** button. The numbers will be displayed in large size on your screen.

Identify

6. If your setup is accurate, you should see two thumbnails of monitors in the dialog box. Click the **number one image** to select it. This is your primary computer, which is the laptop. Click the **Display** down arrow, and choose **1. Mobile PC Display**. Click the **Make This My Main Display** check box. If the option is unavailable but is selected, that option is set by default.

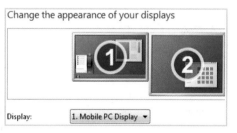

7. Click the **number two image** to select it. This is the monitor or projector that will reflect what is on the primary computer. Click the **Display** down arrow, and choose *Other Monitor type.*

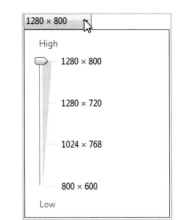

8. Click the **Resolution** down arrow, and drag the slider to the resolution that is common with the projector system (use 1024 × 768 if you are unsure). You can flip back and forth between the monitor boxes shown in the dialog box to adjust the settings for both.

9. With the secondary monitor selected, click the **Multiple Displays** down arrow, and choose one of these options:

- **Extend These Displays** This causes the display to be extended to the second monitor. Use this if you are using Presenter view where you will be manually manipulating the slide show. If you are using the full-screen slide show on both monitors, do not select this. Click **Apply**.

- **Duplicate These Displays** This causes the image on the primary monitor to be echoed in the secondary monitor. This is what you would use if you were setting up an automatic slide show, such as in a kiosk.

- You may have other options, such as Show Desktop Only On 1 (2), depending on your monitor.

10. Click **OK** to close the dialog box.

SET THE VOLUME

1. To set the volume, click the volume icon 🔊 on the taskbar. Start the presentation.

2. Drag the volume slider where you want it.

Set Up an Automated Slide Show

In an automated slide show, you rely on the timings in each slide to determine when to advance to the next slide. There are two ways to do this. In the first, you simply set a standard time for each slide. This is used when your slides do not require a variable amount of time to view. In the second way, you record and save the timings for each slide. This applies in those cases where each slide needs its own individual timing. Once you have established the timing, you set the slide show for an automatic display.

Open your presentation and click a slide to select it.

NOTE

You'll notice as you change the resolution that the size of the monitor images, noted as 1 and 2, change size relative to each other. The changes also depend on which monitor is selected.

NOTE

Another way to establish which screens are active when setting up dual computers is to click to the **Connect To A Projector** link.

USE STANDARD TIMING

To set a fixed time for each slide to display:

1. Click the **Transitions** tab, and then in the Timing group, click the **After** spinners to set the number of seconds; or you can select the displayed time and type the time you want.

2. In the Timing group, click **Apply To All**.

USE RECORDED TIMING

To record and save timings for each slide:

1. On the Slide Show tab, click the **Record Slide Show** button (not the down arrow, which displays a menu) in the Set Up group. The Record Slide Show dialog box will appear.

2. Click **Slide And Animation Timings**, and click **Start Recording**.

3. When the recording is finished for the slides you want, click **Close** in the Recording toolbar.

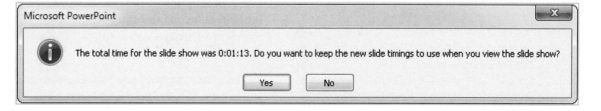

4. When you see a message informing you of the total time and asking if you want to save it, click **Yes**. Each slide for which you've recorded timing will display according to its time when the following controls are set.

QUICKSTEPS

SETTING UP A SLIDE SHOW

All the topics in this QuickSteps require that the Set Up Show dialog box be displayed. To do so, click the **Slide Show** tab, and click **Set Up Slide Show**. Figure 10-2 shows the Set Up Show dialog box. (The Multiple Monitors section of the dialog box is covered in "Use a Laptop to Control Dual Monitors.")

SHOW SELECTED SLIDES

The default for a slide show is to show all slides in the presentation. To show a range of slides, under Show Slides, click the **From** and **To** spinners to set the range. To show slides selected for a custom show, click the **Custom Show** check box, and click the name of the custom show you want from the drop-down list. (Note that you first must have created a custom show for it to be available to you. Click **Custom Slide Show** in the Start Slide Show group to begin.)

Continued . . .

SET THE SLIDE SHOW CONTROLS FOR AUTOMATIC PLAY

In addition to the timing, you need to set the slide show controls.

1. Click the **Slide Show** tab, and click **Set Up Slide Show** in the Set Up group. The Set Up Show dialog box appears.

   - Click **Browsed At A Kiosk (Full Screen)**. Loop Continuously is set by default and so is dimmed or unavailable to be changed.

     –Or–

   - Click **Browsed By An Individual (Window)**, and click **Loop Continuously Until 'Esc'** to have the slide show automatically repeat.

     –Or–

   - Click **Presented By A Speaker (Full Screen)**, and click **Loop Continuously Until 'Esc'** to have the slide show automatically repeat.

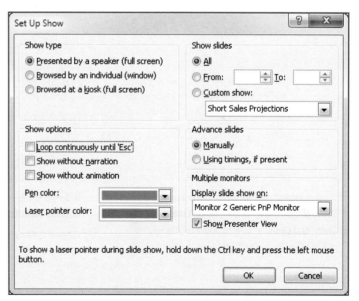

Figure 10-2: The Set Up Show dialog box controls many aspects of how a slide show is run.

SETTING UP A SLIDE SHOW (Continued)

DETERMINE THE TYPE OF PRESENTATION

To determine the type of presentation and how it will be run, select from among these choices:

- Click **Presented By A Speaker (Full Screen)** to display a full-screen slide show that will have a speaker controlling the slide display.

- Click **Browsed By An Individual (Window)** if the slide show will be run by the viewer.

- Click **Browsed At A Kiosk (Full Screen)** if the slide show is to run automatically with no intervention by the viewer.

USE TIMINGS TO ADVANCE SLIDES

To advance from one slide to the next, choose **Manually** for Presenter and Full Screen view slide shows. Click **Using Timings, If Present** to use previously set timings.

LOOP CONTINUOUSLY THROUGH THE PRESENTATION

Under Show Options, click **Loop Continuously Until 'Esc'** to cause the presentation to repeat until **ESC** is pressed. This is used for a trade show, for instance.

HIDE THE NARRATION DURING A SLIDE SHOW

To avoid playing the narration during the slide show, under Show Options, click **Show Without Narration**.

HIDE THE ANIMATION DURING A SLIDE SHOW

To hide any animation in the presentation, under Show Options, click **Show Without Animation**. This can make the slide show faster and easier to control. You do not have to click the mouse repeatedly to initiate various animations as well as to advance the slide show or wait for the animations to occur before continuing with the presentation.

2. Under Advance Slides, click **Using Timings, If Present**. This ensures that the slides advance by themselves without external manipulation.

3. Click **OK** to close the Set Up Show dialog box.

START THE PRESENTATION WITH POWERPOINT

Start the presentation exactly as you would on your own computer.

1. Start PowerPoint and open your presentation.

2. Click **Slide Show** and click **From Beginning** on the Start Slide Show group or press **F5**.

Use a Presenter View Slide Show

Presenter view offers a structured way of controlling the slide show. What is seen on the secondary monitor is the full-screen slide show. On the primary monitor is a reduced slide show with tools, thumbnails of the slides, and speaker notes. Figure 10-3 shows an example.

SET UP A PRESENTER VIEW WITH TWO MONITORS

After you have enabled the dual-monitor support, you can open your presentation to set up the slide show.

1. Open your presentation in PowerPoint.

2. Click the **Slide Show** tab, and click **Set Up Slide Show** in the Set Up group. The Set Up Show dialog box is displayed.

3. Under Show Type, click **Presented By A Speaker (Full Screen)**

4. Under Advance Slides, click **Manually**.

5. Under Multiple Monitors, click the **Display Slide Show On** down arrow, and click the monitor you want to be the one on which the presentation will be full-screen, usually **Monitor 2 Generic PnP Monitor**.

6. Click the **Show Presenter View** check box to make the Presenter view tools available to you on the primary monitor.

7. Click **OK**.

8. Click **Slide Show | From Beginning** on the Start Slide Show group, or click **Slide Show** 🖥 to test the display; or you can press **F5** to start the presentation from the beginning.

RUN A SLIDE SHOW IN PRESENTER VIEW WITH DUAL MONITORS

When the support for the dual monitors has been established and you start the presentation (press F5), you have different screens available on the primary and secondary monitors. Figure 10-3 shows what the primary monitor looks like and the Presenter view tools for helping the presenter walk through the slide show.

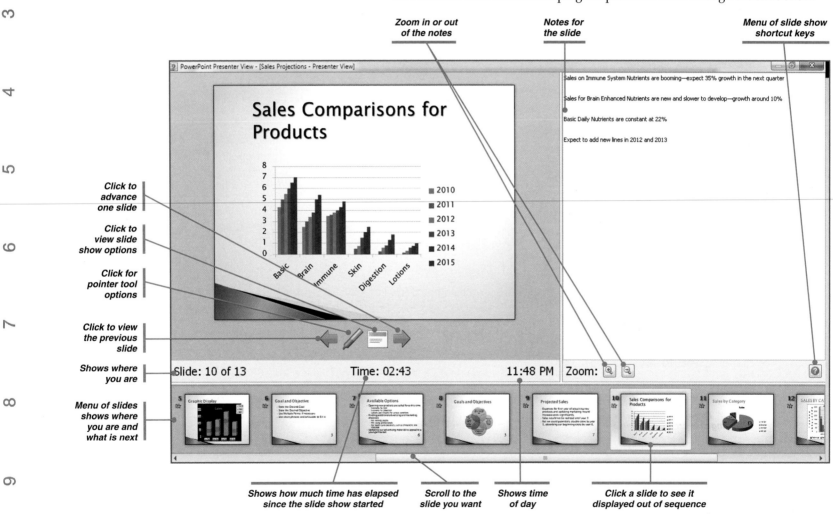

Zoom in or out of the notes

Notes for the slide

Menu of slide show shortcut keys

Click to advance one slide

Click to view slide show options

Click for pointer tool options

Click to view the previous slide

Shows where you are

Menu of slides shows where you are and what is next

Shows how much time has elapsed since the slide show started

Scroll to the slide you want

Shows time of day

Click a slide to see it displayed out of sequence

Figure 10-3: The primary monitor controls the presentation using Presenter view.

If you have set any animations to occur, they may also be included in the timing. For instance, if you have the automatic timing set for 10 seconds and also have a heading that will be displayed, the slide will be displayed first, the heading will be displayed after 10 seconds, and the next slide will appear 10 seconds after that. If the animation does not advance the way you expect, look to see if the start of the animation is set for "on click," requiring you to click the mouse to start the animation.

RUN A FULL-SCREEN SLIDE SHOW WITH DUAL MONITORS

The Full Screen method combines some of both the Automatic and the Presenter views. In this case, both monitors see the full-screen slide show, but the presenter can use pen tools and other tools available by right-clicking the screen. (See "Use a Pen Tool.") In Full Screen view, the presenter can be actively working with the slides while showing them. Figure 10-4 shows an example.

If you prefer to see a full-screen slide show and use the pen or other tools that are available with the context menu rather than the tools available with Presenter view (shown in Figure 10-4), make these changes:

1. Click **Slide Show** and click **Set Up Slide Show** in the Set Up group to show the Set Up Show dialog box.

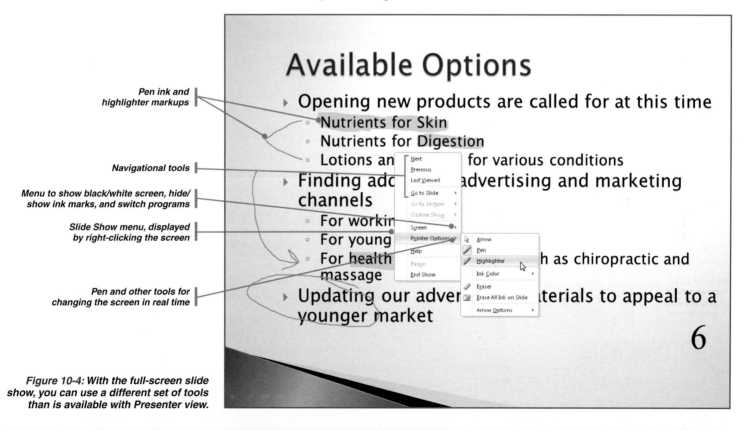

Figure 10-4: With the full-screen slide show, you can use a different set of tools than is available with Presenter view.

Figure 10-5: *You can use a pen tool to emphasize points during your presentation.*

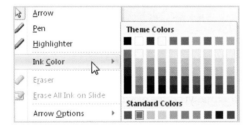

2. Make these changes:
   - **Show Type**   Set to **Presented By A Speaker (Full Screen)**
   - **Show Options**   As you wish, but probably none of them
   - **Pen Color**   Set the color you want the pen to show when you mark up the screen.
   - **Advance Slides**   Set to **Manually**
   - **Multiple Monitors**   Do not select the Show Presenter View check box. With that disabled, you will see the same display on both screens. You will also have the navigational buttons on the lower-left area of the screen and the slide show menu available when you right-click the screen, as seen in Figure 10-4.

3. Click **OK**.

4. Right-click the desktop, click **Personalize**, click **Display**, and click **Change Display Settings**. Click the **Multiple Displays** down arrow, and select **Duplicate These Displays**. (See "Set Display Controls.") Click **OK**, click **Yes** to keep the new settings, and close the Display window.

5. To start the slide show, press **F5** or click **Slide Show** and click **From Beginning** on the Start Slide Show group.

Use a Pen Tool

If you are not using Presenter view during a slide show, you can use a pen tool or highlighter to emphasize points, draw connecting lines, circle text you want to discuss, and more, as illustrated in Figure 10-5. Your marks will not be saved until you signal PowerPoint to do so. You must be in Slide Show view to do this.

1. With your presentation in Slide Show view, right-click the slide and click **Pointer Options**.

2. From the context menu, click **Pen**.

3. To select a different color, right-click the screen, click **Pointer Options**, select **Ink Color**, and click the color you want.

4. When the slide show is over, you will be asked if you want to keep your ink annotations. Click **Keep** to save the markings. Click **Discard** to do away with them.

QUICKSTEPS

NAVIGATING A SLIDE SHOW

If your slide show is not run automatically, you can use the following methods to navigate through it.

START A SLIDE SHOW

To start a slide show, do one of these:

- From within PowerPoint, click **Slide Show**  to start at the current slide.

- Click the **Slide Show** tab, and click **From Beginning** in the Start Slide Show group to view the presentation from the beginning; or click **From Current Slide** to view the presentation from the current slide on.

- Press **F5** to start at the beginning.

- In My Computer or Windows Explorer, find the .pptx or .ppt file, and double-click it.

- In Windows Explorer, right-click the file name, and click **Show** on the context menu.

ADVANCE TO THE NEXT OR PREVIOUS SLIDE

To get to the next slide (or the next animation, if it is started by a mouse click), do one of the following actions:

- Click the slide.
- Press **ENTER**.
- Press **PAGE DOWN**.
- Press **DOWN ARROW**.
- Right-click and click **Next**.

Continued . . .

Rehearse Your Timing

You can rehearse the length of time it takes you to present your slide show. You can experiment with the timings, either testing previously recorded narratives or your own presenter notes.

1. With your presentation in Normal or Slide Sorter view, click the **Slide Show** tab, and click **Rehearse Timings** in the Set Up group.

2. The presentation will begin with a full-screen slide show and the Recording dialog box in the upper-left corner of the screen.

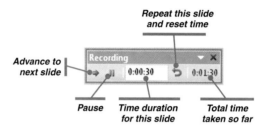

3. Go through your slide show as you expect to actually present it.

4. Click the **Next** arrow on the Recording dialog box to move to the next slide, or press **PAGE DOWN**. If you need to try a slide again, click **Repeat** and do it over. If you need to stop for a time, click **Pause**.

5. When you are done, click **Close** on the Recording dialog box, and click **Yes** to record the timings and create a timed presentation. The timings will appear on the bottom of the slides in Slide Sorter view. Click **No** to discard the timings.

Display a Blank Screen

As you are making a presentation, you may want to pause for a moment and hide the slide being displayed while you discuss a point further. You cannot be in Presenter view to do this.

1. For a white screen, press **W**; for a black screen, press **B**. (To restore the slide, click **W** or **B** again.)

–Or–

NAVIGATING A SLIDE SHOW *(Continued)*

To get to the previous slide (or previous animation, if it is started by a mouse click), do one of the following actions:

- Click **PAGE UP**.
- Press **UP ARROW**.
- Press **BACKSPACE**.
- Right-click and click **Previous**.

GO TO THE BEGINNING OR END OF A SLIDE SHOW

- To go to the beginning of a slide show, press **HOME**.
- To go to the end of a slide show, press **END**.

GO TO A PARTICULAR SLIDE

- To go to the previously viewed slide, right-click the current slide, and click **Last Viewed**.
- To go to a specific slide number, right-click the current slide, click **Go To Slide**, and click the slide you want.

    –Or–

- Type the number of the slide, and press **ENTER**.

EXIT THE SLIDE SHOW

To exit a slide show, press **ESC**, or right-click and click **End Show**.

TIP

Try these tricks to speed up your presentation: reduce the screen resolution; use graphic hardware acceleration, if it is available on your computer; reduce animation of individual objects and bullets or the size of animated pictures on a slide; simplify the animations you have; and avoid using background special effects, such as gradient, textured, or transparency enhanced backgrounds.

- In Slide Show view, press **SHIFT + F10** or right-click the slide. A menu will be displayed. Click **Screen** and select from these choices:
    - Click **White Screen** to display a totally white screen.
    - Click **Black Screen** to display a totally black screen.

2. When you are ready to continue, click **ESC**. Or right-click the screen, click **Screen**, and click **Unwhite Screen** or **Unblack Screen**.

Create a Custom Slide Show

You can create a custom show from your current presentation by adding, removing, or shuffling the slides. Your new custom presentation is a subset of the current one.

1. Click the **Slide Show** tab, and click **Custom Slide Show** in the Start Slide Show group. Click **Custom Shows**. The Custom Shows dialog box will appear.

2. Click **New** to create a new presentation. The Define Custom Show dialog box will appear, as shown in Figure 10-6.

3. Type a name in the Slide Show Name text box.

4. Select the titles of the slides you want from the Slides In Presentation list, and for each, click **Add**.

5. To re-order the slides, select a slide in the Slides In Custom Show list, and click the up and down arrows on the right of the dialog box.

6. To delete slides from the new slide show, select the slide from Slides In Custom Show, and click **Remove**.

7. When you are finished, click **OK**.

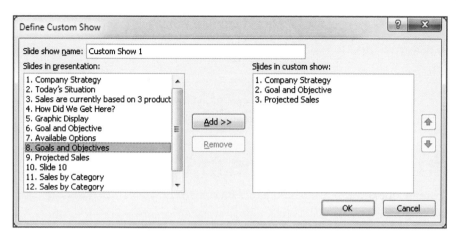

Figure 10-6: Create a new slide show from a current one by modifying the slides used and their order.

8. To review the new presentation, click **Show**; to finish without viewing the slide show, click **Close**.

9. You can run the custom show in the future by clicking its name on the Custom Slide Show menu.

Divide Your Presentation into Sections

You can divide your presentation into sections to group them into manageable sizes. This works particularly well if the presentation is being worked on by a number of people, helping to clarify responsibility, or to give greater visibility in the flow or logic of the presentation. Do this in Normal view (from the Slides tab) or Slide Sorter view.

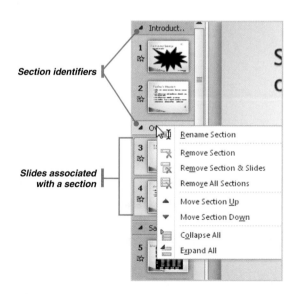

Section identifiers

Slides associated with a section

1. Right-click between the slides, and from the context menu, click **Add Section**.

2. Right-click the new section, and click **Rename Section**. On the Rename Section dialog box, type the name of the section, and click **Rename**. Repeat this for each section you want.

3. You have these options to work with sections by right-clicking a section:

   ● **Remove Section** removes the section identifier.

   ● **Remove Section & Slides** removes both the identifier and associated slides.

   ● **Remove All Sections** removes all identifiers.

   ● **Move Section Up** and **Move Section Down** move the section above or below the section next to it.

   ● **Collapse All** reduces the thumbnail images to just the section identifiers.

   ● **Expand All** expands the thumbnail images to include both identifiers and associated slides.

QUICKSTEPS

SETTING PRINT OPTIONS

Print options can be set in the Print view, which is displayed by clicking **File** and clicking **Print**. You will see the preview of the current slide.

SELECT A PRINTER

Under Printer, click the current selected option down arrow, and click the name of the printer you want to use.

PRINT ALL OR SELECTED SLIDES

To determine which slides will be printed, click the first down arrow under Settings, and select the slides you want to print—all slides, the current selected slide only, or a custom range.

- To enter a range of slides, click **Custom Range**, and in the Slides text box, type the first slide number, a hyphen, and the last slide number (for example, 5-15).

- To print individual slides, type the slide numbers separated by commas (for example, 1,3,6). Combine ranges and individual slides with a comma (for example, 1,3,5-10,20-22).

DETERMINE WHAT TO PRINT

To select what you will be printing, click the second down arrow under Settings, and choose what you want to print.

- Choose from printing full page slides, notes, an outline, or a selection of handout layouts.

- Click **Frame Slides** to see a border around the slides, or not.

Continued . . .

Place a Presentation Shortcut on Your Desktop

To place a shortcut to your presentation on the desktop:

1. Find the file using Windows Explorer.
2. Drag the file to the desktop with the right mouse button held down.
3. Release the button and click **Create Shortcuts Here**.

Print Presentations in Various Ways

A presentation can be printed on paper (in color or grayscale), on transparencies, or to a file for transfer to a 35-mm slide-service bureau or for high-resolution printing. In this section, you will learn how to print to a printer or file to produce these types of output.

As part of the print process, you can quickly preview your slides before printing them, as seen in Figure 10-7.

1. Click **File** and click **Print**, and the screen shown in Figure 10-7 will display.
2. Set your printer options as described in the "Setting Print Options" QuickSteps.
3. When you're ready, click **Print**.

Establish Print Color

To designate the color in which the slides will be previewed and printed:

1. In the Print view, click **Color**. A menu will display. Click one of these options:
   - **Color** for color slides (requires a color printer)
   - **Grayscale** for grayscale slides
   - **Pure Black And White** for no gray tones

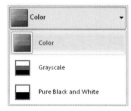

Hide or Print Comments, Markings, and Hidden Slides

Click the second drop-down menu under Settings, and click **Print Comments And Ink Markup**. A check mark beside the option means that hidden slides, comments, and ink markups will appear in the preview and be printed. To deselect the option, click the check mark to remove it. (If Print Comments And Ink Markup is dimmed, it means these are not in the presentation.)

Insert Headers and Footers

To insert a header or footer on a slide or on all slides, click **Edit Header & Footer** beneath the Color drop-down option. The Header And Footer dialog box will appear.

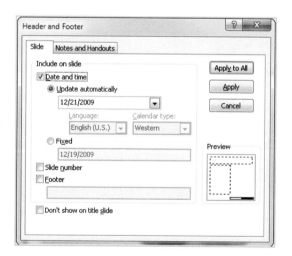

1. Select the **Date And Time** check box to include the date and time on the slide.

   - Click **Update Automatically** and click the down arrow to choose a style in which the current date and time should appear when automatically updated.

     –Or–

   - Click **Fixed** and type a date and time (or other text) that you want to appear on the slide without being updated.

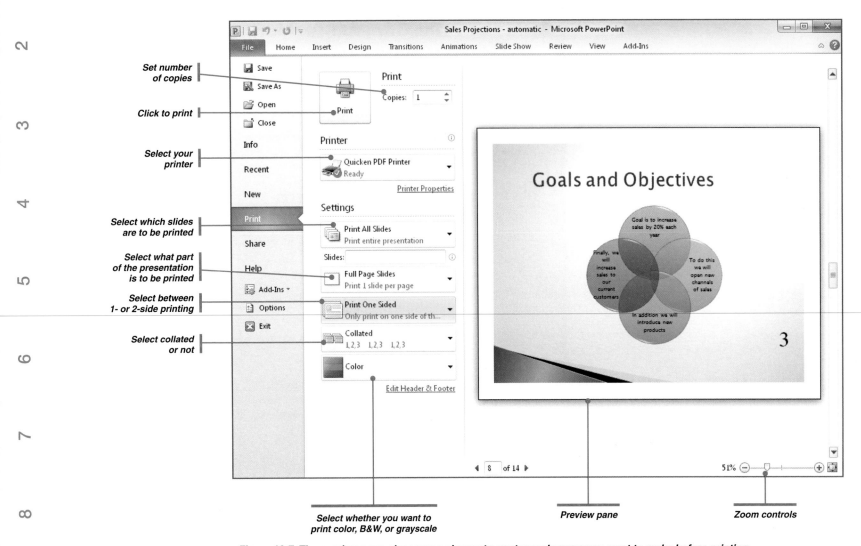

Figure 10-7: The preview pane gives you a chance to spot any changes you want to make before printing.

2. Click the **Slide Number** check box to have the slide number appear on the slide.

3. Click the **Footer** check box, and type the footer text in the text box.

4. Click the **Don't Show On Title Slide** check box to prevent the selected information from being displayed on the first or title slide.

5. Click **Apply** to apply the options to only the selected slide, or click **Apply To All** to apply the options to all slides.

See Chapter 3 for information about headers and footers for notes and handouts.

Scale Slides to Fit Paper

Since you can print the slides on a variety of paper sizes, you can scale the slides to fit the size, whatever it may be. To do so, click the second down arrow under Settings, and select the **Scale To Fit Paper** check box.

Configure Page Setup

Set up the slide width and height, page size, slide orientation, and the beginning slide number by using the Page Setup dialog box.

1. Click the **Design** tab, and click **Page Setup** in the Page Setup group. The Page Setup dialog box will appear, as shown in Figure 10-8.

2. Select from among these options:

   ● To select a page size, click the **Slides Sized For** down arrow, and click an option.

   ● To precisely enter the slide size, use the spinners to set the width and height.

   ● To set a starting slide number other than 1, click the **Number Slides From** spinner.

   ● Under Slides Orientation, click **Portrait** to set the slide orientation to tall. Click **Landscape** to set the slide orientation to wide.

   ● Under Notes, Handouts & Outline Orientation, click **Portrait** to set the orientation to tall. Click **Landscape** to set the orientation to wide.

3. Click **OK** to close the Page Setup dialog box.

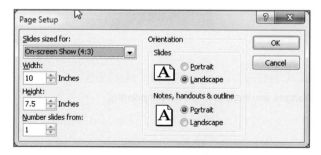

Figure 10-8: The Page Setup dialog box displays options for varying your slide printout.

Print Transparencies

You may want to print your slides on transparencies to present the slide show with an overhead projector. Use the Page Setup dialog box to set the type of output media. (Not all printers have a specified software option for printing transparencies. If yours doesn't, see your printer's manual for instruction on how to print transparencies.) PowerPoint will optimize your slides for the black-and-white or color printer that you choose.

1. Click the **Design** tab, and click **Page Setup**.

2. Click the **Slides Sized For** down arrow, and click **Overhead**.

3. Set the orientation and other options as needed.

4. Click **OK** to close the dialog box.

5. Print the slides as usual.

Print to Disk

To print a file to a disk instead of the printer:

1. Click **File** and click **Print**.

2. Click the **Printer** down arrow, and click the **Print To File** check box at the end of the list.

3. Set your printer options as described in the "Setting Print Options" QuickSteps.

4. When you're ready, click **Print**.

5. In the Print To File dialog box, type your file name and location where the slide show is to be saved.

6. Click **Save**.

Print a PostScript File for 35-mm Slides

You cannot print 35-mm slides using PowerPoint. However, you can create a PostScript file to take to a business that can then create 35-mm slides from that. To create PostScript files, you must have a color PostScript driver installed on your computer. Many come with the Windows operating system, but your

10

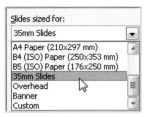

source for creating 35-mm slides may have specific file types that you need to produce. After receiving those specifications, you may print a PostScript file.

1. First, click the **Design** tab, and click **Page Setup** in the Page Setup group. The Page Setup dialog box will appear.

2. Click the **Slides Sized For** down arrow, and click **35mm Slides**.

3. Click **OK** to close the dialog box.

4. Click **File** and click **Print**. The Print view will appear.

5. Click the **Printer** down arrow, and click the name of your PostScript printer driver.

6. At the bottom of the Printer drop-down list, click the **Print To File** check box.

7. Click the options you want (some options are printer-specific, so your options may be different than these listed).

   - Under Settings, select the slides you want printed. Verify that the **Print Hidden Slides** check box is selected.
   - Select what part of the presentation is to be printed.
   - Select between one-sided and two-sided printing.
   - Select **Color** in the Color/Grayscale/Pure Black And White drop-down list box.
   - Select any other options you want.

8. Click **Print** to start the printing to a file. The Print To File dialog box will appear.

9. In the Print To File dialog box, type your file name and location where it is to be saved.

10. Click **Save**.

Stop Printing

To halt the printing of the slides while printing is in progress:

1. Double-click the printer icon in the taskbar. A dialog box for your printer will appear.

2. Click the presentation name to select it.

3. Click **Document** and click **Cancel**.

4. Click **Yes** to confirm that you want to cancel the print job.

5. Click **Close** to close the dialog box.

TIP

Since Windows adds a .prn file extension to the saved file, which may not be acceptable to some publishers or businesses, you may want to change the extension to .ps, for PostScript, since this is the file type more commonly used. You could do this by opening the .prn file in a program such as Adobe Acrobat Reader and saving it as a .ps file.

NOTE

If you do not have the required PostScript driver, get one from your source for 35-mm slides. Or, install a PostScript printer on your computer, which carries the drivers with it, knowing that you will only print to disk with it. Install it in Windows 7 by clicking **Start**, clicking **Devices And Printers**, and clicking **Add A Printer**. In Windows XP, click **Start**, click **Printers And Faxes** (your path to the Printers And Faxes Control Panel feature may vary, depending on your operating system), and click **Add A Printer**. Follow the instructions to add the new printer, for example, one of the HP printers that shows PS after its name/model.

TIP

Because the print queue empties to the printer so quickly, you may not be able to cancel the printing of all the slides. Also, if your presentation is short, the print icon will be present on the taskbar for a short time. You may not be able to click it fast enough.

NOTE

For more information on installing printers on the Windows Vista or Windows 7 operating systems, see *Windows Vista QuickSteps* or *Window 7 QuickSteps*, published by McGraw-Hill/Professional.

Change Printers

To print to a printer other than the default one for your computer:

1. Click **File** and click **Print**. The Print view will appear.

2. Click the **Printer** down arrow, and click the printer you want to use.

   - If you are on an Active Directory domain and the printer is not there, click **Add Printer** and follow the directions on the dialog box to search for and find the printer.

   - If the printer is not on the list—that is, it is not on your computer or network—you must add it. Click **Start** and find the Printer Control Panel—(your path may vary, depending on your operating system). Click the **Add A Printer** button. Follow the wizard or dialog box prompts to install the printer on your computer or network.

3. When the correct printer name is in the Print view and you have selected the options you want, click **Print** to begin printing.

charts (*Cont.*)
  identifying cells in, 130
  inserting, 126–129
  x-, y-, and z-axes in, 126
circle, creating, 161
clip art
  changing color of, 115–116
  converting to drawing objects, 120
  cropping, 117–118
  explained, 114
  finding and inserting, 114–115
  searching for on Internet, 118
Clip Art task pane, searching for sounds in, 170–171
Clipboard, using, 89–90
clips, types of, 113
Close option, choosing, 2
Color button, using with clip art, 115–116
color schemes, adding and changing, 32–33
color themes. *See* theme colors
colors, designating for slides, 204
Colors dialog box, accessing, 155
columns
  deleting in tables, 111
  inserting into tables, 111
  selecting in tables, 110
commands
  adding to Quick Access toolbar, 15
  displaying for outlines, 38
  in File button, 5
  in Quick Access toolbar, 5
  in ribbon, 5
comments
  hiding and printing, 205
  recording on slides, 177–178
compressing media files, 176
Contact Us feature, accessing, 20
contrast, changing for objects, 119
Control menu, location of, 3
copies for printing, selecting number of, 205

Copy command, using with slides, 49
copying
  attributes with Format Painter, 57
  objects, 158
  slides, 50
  slides between presentations, 48
  slides in presentations, 48
  text, 82
  text boxes, 78
  text selections, 85
copyright information, finding, 20
corrections. *See* AutoCorrect feature
Corrections button, using with objects, 119
cropping and sizing, changing between, 118
cropping objects, 117–118
CTRL key. *See* shortcut keyboard commands
curves
  adjusting, 162–163
  creating, 162
  rotating in cells, 163

D

data series, formatting in charts, 137
date
  displaying in footer, 57
  including in header for notes, 66
deleting
  animations, 149
  objects, 117
  slides, 43
  tables, 100
  text, 86
  text boxes, 78
Dell laptops, using secondary devices with, 192
design themes, applying, 49. *See also* themes
designs
  copying, 49
  using Browse command with, 49

desktop, creating shortcut on, 2
Dialog Box Launcher icon, using with groups, 6
disk, printing files to, 208
.doc files, inserting outlines from, 36–37
document information panel, displaying, 17–18
document properties, reordering, 18
drag-and-drop technique, using with text, 88
drawing tool, turning on and off, 95
dual monitors. *See also* monitors
  running full-screen slide shows with, 199–200
  running slide shows with, 198
  setting up Presenter view with, 197
Duplicate Slides command, using, 49
DVDs, burning presentation files on, 182–183

E

effects. *See also* animation effects
  adding to objects, 158
  applying, 53, 146
  displaying tooltips for, 149
  numbering, 149
  removing, 159
e-mail attachments, sending presentations as, 181
enterprise editions, availability of, 5
Excel
  copying and pasting charts from, 128–129
  editing chart data in, 129
  entering chart data in, 130–131
  using to create tables, 98
  x and y axes in, 130
Exit option
  choosing, 2
  using in File view, 8
eXtensible Markup Language (XML), overview of, 22–23

F

F keys. *See* shortcut keyboard commands
File button
    commands in, 5
    function of, 4
    location of, 3
file extensions, displaying, 31. *See also* "x"
file information, stripping from
    presentations, 40
File view
    exiting, 8
    finding, 6–8
fill backgrounds, creating, 155. *See also*
    backgrounds
Fill option
    using with chart elements, 134
    using with text boxes, 79
fills, removing, 159
Fit Slide to Current Window icon
    function of, 4
    identifying, 3
folders
    adding to SkyDrive, 187–188
    changing default for, 23–24
    saving templates to, 30
    saving to, 23
font attributes, changing in master slides, 72
Font dialog box, using, 82
font groups, using with tables, 99
font style, changing in slide master, 69–70
footers
    inserting on slides, 205, 207
    using on notes and handouts, 66
    using on slides, 56–57
Format elements dialog box
    displaying, 133
    options on, 136

Format Painter
    using to copy attributes, 57, 84
    using to copy attributes to objects, 120
formatting attributes, copying, 84
formatting mini toolbar, displaying, 99

G

Glow and Soft Edges option, using with chart
    elements, 134
gradient backgrounds, creating for slides, 156–157.
    See also backgrounds
graphic attributes, copying, 57
graphics, inserting, 33. *See also* themed
    graphic effects
graphs
    axes in, 130
    copying and pasting from Excel, 128–129
    editing data source attributes for, 129–130
    explained, 115
    Format dialog boxes for, 133, 135
    formatting axes in, 138–140
    formatting data labels in, 137–138
    formatting gridlines in, 141–142
    formatting legends in, 136
    formatting plot area in, 141
    formatting text in, 141
    identifying cells in, 130
    inserting, 126–129
    x-, y-, and z-axes in, 126
gridlines
    formatting in charts, 141–142
    showing and hiding in tables, 110
grids and guides, displaying for objects, 119–120
groups
    Dialog Box Launcher icon for, 6
    including in ribbon, 5
guidelines, moving, 120

H

handout master, changing, 74–76
handout thumbnails, removing borders
    from, 67
handouts
    printing, 62, 65
    using headers and footers on, 66
headers
    inserting on slides, 205, 207
    using on notes and handouts, 66
heading font
    choosing, 53
    using, 51
Help option, using in File view, 8
Help system, accessing, 19–20
hidden slides, hiding and printing, 205
Home & Business version, accessing, 4
Home & Student version, accessing, 4
HTML outlines, inserting, 36
hyperlinks. *See also* action buttons
    changing colors of, 58
    inserting in presentations, 57–58,
        184–185
    inserting on slides, 184–185
    removing, 58

I

identifying information, adding, 17–18
illustrations, types of, 114–115
images
    bitmap versus vector, 118
    types of, 114
indents, increasing and decreasing, 36
Info option, using in File view, 6
insertion point, being aware of, 50

K

keyboard shortcut commands
    arrow pointer, 200
    copying slides, 50
    copying text, 82
    cutting and pasting text, 87
    cycling through windows, 43
    decreasing indents, 36
    deleting text, 86
    ending slide shows, 42
    hiding ribbon, 42
    increasing indents, 36
    inserting slides, 50
    inserting text, 86
    moving down line/slide, 36
    moving to placeholders, 42
    moving pointer in text, 86
    moving up line/slide, 36
    navigating between slides, 42
    removing slides, 50
    reversing actions in Quick Access toolbar, 111
    ribbon, 6
    selecting text, 86
    starting new presentations, 50
    starting slide shows, 12, 42
    toggling size of ribbon, 8
    viewing ribbon, 42

L

laptops
    synchronizing to monitors, 193
    using as control devices, 192
    using monitors with, 192
    using projectors with, 192
    using to control dual monitors, 192–194
layout master
    creating, 71–72
    editing, 69–71

layout templates, availability of, 26.
    See also templates
layouts, selecting, 32–33
leader lines, adding to pie charts, 138
lists
    changing numbering styles, 84
    choosing bullet shapes for, 83
    using SmartArt for, 84–85
logo, adding to notes master, 74
Loop Continuously option, using with slide
    shows, 196
lowercase text, using, 81

M

margins
    setting in tables, 100
    setting in text boxes, 81
markings, hiding and printing, 205
master layout. *See also* layouts
    creating, 71–72
    editing, 69–71
master slides. *See also* slides
    changing font attributes in, 72
    creating, 71–72
    creating templates as, 26
    creating title master, 68
    duplicating, 68
    editing, 69–71
    editing text in, 72
    guidelines for use of, 69
    retaining, 69
media files, compressing, 176
menus, using, 5–6
merging presentations, 59–60
Microsoft Excel
    copying and pasting charts from, 128–129
    editing chart data in, 129

    entering chart data in, 130–131
    using to create tables, 98
    x and y axes in, 130
Microsoft Support view, displaying, 20–21
Microsoft Word
    copying tables from, 97
    inserting outlines from .doc files, 36–37
mini toolbar, displaying, 17
mirror images, creating for shapes, 163
Mobile version, accessing, 4
monitors. *See also* dual monitors
    adjusting resolution of, 193–194
    checking active status of, 194
    checking configuration of, 193
    maximum available for slide shows, 192
    setting display controls for, 192–194
    synchronizing laptops to, 193
    using laptops with, 192
movies
    filling screen with, 178
    looping, 178
    resizing, 178
    rewinding, 178
    setting fade in/fade out transition for, 179
    setting volume for, 179

N

narratives
    recording for presentations, 176–177
    turning timings on and off, 179
New option, using in File view, 7
New Presentation dialog box, opening, 8–9
Normal view
    opening, 10
    returning to, 10, 43
notes
    adding objects to, 62
    changing backgrounds of, 62

creating, 94
creating with Excel, 98
deleting, 100
deleting columns in, 111
deleting rows in, 111
displaying border lines in, 106
drawing, 94–95
entering text into, 98–99
erasing lines in, 95
formatting text in, 99
hiding border lines in, 106
hiding gridlines in, 110
inserting colors in, 95
inserting columns in, 111
inserting from scratch, 94
inserting from templates, 92–93
inserting rows in, 110
irregular column and row sizes in, 96
merging cells in, 112
merging cells to enlarge pictures, 106
as objects, 115
removing border lines from, 107
rotating text in cells, 100
rows and columns in, 94
selecting, 110
selecting cells in, 110
selecting columns in, 110
selecting rows in, 110
setting height and width for cells in, 112
setting margins in, 100
showing gridlines in, 110
splitting cells in, 112
using Borders tool with, 106
using font groups with, 99
using Pen Color dialog box with, 107
using preset styles with, 103–104
tabs
    contextual tabs for, 5
    using, 5–6
taskbar, pinning PowerPoint to, 2

tasks, adding commands for, 15–16
templates. *See also* layout templates
    choosing, 8–9
    creating, 30–31
    creating as master slides, 26
    finding, 30
    saving, 26
    saving presentations as, 23
    saving to folders, 30
text
    adding to slides, 32
    aligning, 83–84
    aligning in cells, 99
    animating, 147
    changing in WordArt objects, 159
    converting to WordArt styles, 72
    cutting and pasting, 87–88
    deleting, 86
    disabling word wrap for, 81
    dragging and dropping, 88
    entering into tables, 98–99
    fitting in AutoShapes, 88
    fitting in text boxes, 88
    formatting in charts, 141
    formatting in tables, 99
    inserting, 86
    moving, 87–88
    moving pointer in, 86
    rotating in cells, 100
    selecting, 17, 86
    typing within shapes, 161
text attributes, copying, 57
text boxes
    anchoring text in, 81
    changing fill color in, 79–80
    choosing paragraph settings for, 80
    choosing tab settings for, 80
    copying, 78
    deleting, 78
    entering text into, 77

    inserting, 77
    layouts for, 76
    moving, 78
    positioning precisely, 79
    rotating, 78–79
    rotating text in, 82
    setting margins in, 81
    setting up columns in, 82
text placeholders. *See also* placeholders
    aligning to slides, 84
    borders of, 77
    manipulating, 77
    resizing, 78
    using, 77
text selections, copying, 85
text-editing commands, availability of, 72
textured backgrounds, creating, 157–158.
    See also backgrounds
theme colors
    changing, 50–52
    changing customizations of, 55
    customizing, 53–56
    restoring, 54
theme customizations, saving, 56
theme fonts
    changing, 51
    creating new set of, 51, 53
theme thumbnails, seeing effects of, 28–29.
    See also thumbnails
themed graphic effects, changing, 53.
    See also graphics
themes. *See also* design themes
    applying to slides, 30–31
    availability of, 26
    choosing, 8
    components of, 26–27
    creating presentations from, 30
    finding, 30
    setting default for, 31
Thesaurus options, using, 20